AMERICAN INSTITUTE FOR ECONOMIC RESEARCH

Richard Ebeling

For a New Liberalism

For a New Liberalism
By Richard Ebeling

ISBN 978-1-63-069178-3

Cover design: Vanessa Mendozzi

Richard Ebeling

For a New Liberalism

AIER | AMERICAN INSTITUTE *for* ECONOMIC RESEARCH

Contents

Acknowledgements   **1**

Introduction   **3**

Chapter 1 - The Classical Liberal History and Heritage of Freedom   15

Chapter 2 - Through Foreign Eyes: American Liberty and
Prosperity in the 19th Century   27

Chapter 3 - Freedom is Why Immigrants Have Come to America   53

Chapter 4 - Free Market Liberalism and the Dignity of Labor   65

Chapter 5 - Liberalism, Rightly and Wrongly Understood   77

Chapter 6 - Competition and the Liberal Economy   93

Chapter 7 - Free Markets and the Misunderstanding of Monopoly   105

Chapter 8 - How Expectations Coordinate Free Markets   119

Chapter 9 - Free Markets and Asymmetric Information   135

Chapter 10 - Public Goods and Free Market Liberalism   145

Chapter 11 - Why Not Private Provision of Many Government
Services?   157

Chapter 12 - Educational Socialism versus Free Market Schooling   165

Chapter 13 - Central Banking is a Form of Central Planning   173

Chapter 14 - Diversity and Inclusiveness in the Liberal Society   187

Chapter 15 - Free Market Liberalism as the Ideology of Freedom
and Moderation   203

Chapter 16 - Society is Not a Family, Government is Not a Parent 217

Chapter 17 - Socialism, Like Dracula, Rises Again from the Grave 227

Chapter 18 - All Socialisms are Antisocial 237

Chapter 19 - The Market Democracy vs. Democratic Socialism 249

Chapter 20 - Tyrants of the Mind and the New Collectivism 261

Chapter 21 - Collectivism's Progress: From Marxism to Race and
 Gender Intersectionality 275

Chapter 22 - "Identity Politics" Threatens the Open and Free
 Society 287

Chapter 23 - The Nightmare Fairyland of the Green New Dealers 299

Chapter 24 - Why Neo-Liberalism is Really Neo-Socialism 313

Chapter 25 - Has Liberal Modernity Made an Indecent Society? 327

Chapter 26 - The Plague of Meddling Political Busybodies 341

Chapter 27 - Reasons for Anti-Capitalism: Ignorance, Arrogance,
 and Envy 353

Chapter 28 - Free Market Liberalism is Needed More Than Ever 367

Chapter 29 - The Case for Liberty, Through Thick and Thin 379

Chapter 30 - Learning Liberty and the Power of Principles 393

Appendix: Suggested Reading List on Liberalism and Freedom 407

Index **421**
About the Author **435**
About AIER **435**

Acknowledgements

I wish to thank Jeffrey A. Tucker, Editorial Director at the American Institute for Economic Research (AIER), for suggesting the idea for this book, and proposing its title, *For a New Liberalism*. I have known Jeff for many years as one of the most tireless and dedicated voices for individual liberty and free market liberalism in the United States. He is, also, an extremely clear and insightful writer in his own right, as well as an outstanding editorial administrator.

I also wish to thank Jeff for the opportunity to regularly contribute essays on political and economic policy issues to the website of AIER in the capacity of a senior fellow with the Institute. Many of these essays have served as the basis for a majority of the chapters in this book.

My thanks on this extends, as well, to Edward P. Stringham, president of the American Institute for Economic Research, who is continuing the important work began by AIER's founder, Col. E. C Harwood, who was dedicated to sound economic thinking and the liberal society; the very principles being followed under Ed's creative leadership.

Ed and I were colleagues for a delightful academic year at Trinity College in Hartford, Connecticut in 2008-2009, when I was also serving during that year as a senior research fellow with AIER, spending part of each week at the Institute's charming grounds and wonderful facilities in Great Barrington, Massachusetts.

A number of the following chapters have, also, developed out of essays contributed to the website of the Future of Freedom Foundation (FFF) or its monthly publication, *The Future of Freedom*. Jacob G. Hornberger, the founder and president of FFF, and I have been long-time collaborators in the intellectual battle for liberty and the free society. And it is a great pleasure to acknowledge my appreciation to him as well.

Finally, and as always, my deepest and most sincere debt is to my wife, Anna, who has been by friend, supporter, and partner in all that I have done over nearly, now, three decades. And without whom very little in my life would or could be possible. Thank you, my darling.

Introduction

This book is entitled, *For a New Liberalism.* This implies that any current liberalism has in some way failed or not met up to expectations, and needs to be changed, reformed, or transformed. It can also mean that the current political environment is non- or illiberal and a new liberalism needs to replace the anti-liberal climate of opinion and policy.

A premise in this book is that both are true. What has been called "liberalism" for a long time in the United States is a far cry from what liberalism used to mean at an earlier time, and has brought about numerous anti-liberal policies. At the same time, a growing number of political figures and policy proponents around the world have declared their belief that "liberalism" is both passé and undesirable.

In the early decades of the 20th century, liberalism began to change its meaning and intent for a growing number of intellectuals and social and economic reformers. In the process, by the 1930s and 1940s, the premise and content of liberalism had a conception of man, society and government very different from its original ones in the 19th century.

This has created a noticeable confusion in thinking about what liberalism means, what type of social system it represents, and what is the role of government in a liberal society. This very ambiguity has raised questions about what it is that critics of liberalism oppose? The liberalism of the 19th century? The liberalism of the 20th century? Or both?

The Meaning of Liberalism and Individual Freedom,

Perhaps it is best if I explain liberalism as I understand it, and consider the basis of a free and prosperous society. Liberalism is founded on the idea of the distinct and unique individual human being. The individual should be considered the slave and property of no other man; he owns and governs himself. He decides on his own ends and selects his own means to pursue his goals, and give meaning, value and purpose to his own life in all its aspects. He respects the equal rights of all others, and therefore accepts and tries to live by the moral principle of mutual respect and peaceful association in all dealings with his fellow man.

The free man, in spirit as well as in action, abjures envy of the achievements and successes of other people. He accepts the fact that while all people should be recognized as possessing equal rights to their respective life, liberty and property before the law, human beings are amazingly diverse in their natural talents and their chosen inclinations. Each chooses his own way, but he is not guaranteed success in all things or protection at other's expense when he experiences disappointments and failures in life.

Since no man is an island, every reflective human being understands that he lives among others and shares a community of everyday life with them. But the liberal outlook is to see the ethical avenues and the most effective practical means to the common concerns and interests among men to be the voluntary associations of civil society. The voluntarist approach is ethical because it recognizes each human being as a self-owning and self-directing person for his own chosen ends, who should not be compelled to accept or participate in any activity or group without his own consent.

Secondly, the liberal understands that human knowledge is imperfect and divided among all the multitudes of people in any society. The answers to common problems needing to be solved is far more likely to be found when people are at liberty to decide how best to apply what they know in conjunction with others, than when all are forced to follow the designs and dictates of a few who arrogantly presume to know enough to solve the joint matters of human concern.

The liberal also believes that the freeing of all the minds of society will produce the creative innovations in the marketplace of supply and demand that will, over time, improve the qualities and standards of living of all, and far better than when confined within the restrictions of government regulations and controls over how best men should apply their talents and on the terms they consider most attractive, all things considered.

Liberal Optimism, Tempered by Political Suspicion

The liberal is both optimistic and cautious about the characteristics of his fellow human beings. He has confidence that man has the ability to plan and direct his own life. He believes that human beings can understand and follow the longer-run rules of social order that permits each to have their liberty, and which also facilitates cooperative collaboration in markets and voluntary associations.

Yet, his reason and the sad experience of human history warn that his fellow creatures are too easily tempted to turn to the use of private or political force to obtain the things desired, when the costs of applied coercion are less than the costs of mutual and peaceful agreement with others. The liberal, therefore, has a healthy skepticism and concern for any and all unrestrained political power, regardless of the authoritarian or democratic form it may take.

Thus, the liberal strongly proposes and, indeed, insists upon clear and explicit constitutional limits on the delegated and enumerated functions assigned to any government, with its duties confined to the protection of the individual rights of the citizenry, with fewest linguistic ambiguities through which power might be extended and expanded beyond the securing of people's freedom.

Collectivism Presumes Groups and Demands Planning

The starting premise of collectivism, in all its proposed and experienced forms invariably begins with the presumption of groups rather than individuals. It may be "social classes" (as was declared by Marxists), or nations (as was heralded by fascists) or races (as was insisted on by Nazis) in the 20th century. But in each one the individual is submerged and disappears within the collective that is made the defining characteristic of each and every human being from which escape is virtually impossible. Individuals are expected to think, value, and act in the context of their classified collective. To think, value or act differently than how your group is asserted to require demonstrates only one of three possibilities: you have been wrongly indoctrinated to not understand where your "true" interests lie; or you are in the paid and traitorous service of an enemy social class, nation or race; or you are a renegade individual who "selfishly" betrays his group for his own personal gains.

Furthermore, collectivism insists, in any of its variations, that the individual must conform to the central plan designed and implemented by those in political power who declare their superior knowledge about what the "purposes" of society should be, and who insist that all must be confined within "the plan," with each person's rightful share of the collective production being decided for him based on some claimed notion of "social justice."

Indoctrination for acceptance and obedience; compulsion to assure fulfillment of the goals of the plan; and de-individualization of all relationships and attitudes in society so everyone's actions conform to the collective idea and ideology imposed on society. These are the presumptions of socialism.

Collectivism can impose one overarching and uniform central plan (as represented in the former Soviet Union, for instance), or it can have a set of interlocking plans based on the politicking of competing pressure groups within the collectivist society deciding the goals and dividing up the group output. This latter is "democratic socialism," when partly or fully implemented.

Liberalism Transformed into Political Paternalism

Modern 20th century American liberalism abandoned much of its individual freedom, free market, limited government roots during the 1930s with the coming of the New Deal during the Franklin D. Roosevelt Administration. This trend had already noticeably begun in the earlier part of the 20th century, especially during the Woodrow Wilson Administration in the heyday of the "Progressive" movement. But after the 1930s, "liberalism" became the outlook and policy tool-kit of Big Government. A government that heavily regulated, more highly taxed, and lavishly spent growing sums of taxpayer's money on redistributive programs that served an expanding circle of special interest groups throughout American society.

And which increasingly had few or no qualms in covering dollars spent on government programs through deficit spending that began to dramatically grow the national debt, especially now in the 21st century when it has been going up exponentially.

For most of the 20th century, this new American "liberalism" insisted that what they wanted was a "mixed economy" of some competitive private enterprise with government regulations to see that "business" was channeled into the socially desirable forms and directions, along with various redistributive programs to compensate for income inequality without killing the private enterprise goose laying all the economic golden eggs from which the government took its tax take. At the same time, it was argued that these economic encroachments on economic freedom could be introduced and implemented with little or few restrictions on personal and civil liberties.

From Market Choice to Government Decision-Making

The private sector has an amazing degree of adaptability even in the face of heavy-handed government intervention and redistribution. But the fact is that every extension of such controls, regulations, restrictions, and prohibitions reduces the extent to which the outcomes of the market reflect and represent what free consumers desire to be produced in the society, and in the forms and types they wish to demand.

Every dollar siphoned off by government transfers buying power (and the purchasable resources those dollars represent) to political decision-makers and reduces those many dollars to be freely spent by the productive income-earners in society. This is the case whether the dollars spent by the government have been taxed or borrowed from financial markets. It reduces private sector spending ability and choice by that full amount.

Control over social decision-making is transferred to that extent from the individuals making up the society to those in political power or their bureaucratic representatives. Therefore, government is then planning the uses of things produced and to be produced rather than the citizens, themselves. That offers one measurement of the extent to which the command economy has replaced a more free market society.

As was said earlier, those in political authority, claiming to know and speak for the social collective, supersede the individuals in that society, who otherwise could be left free to more fully guide and direct and fulfill their own lives as would be reflected with a greater degree of free choice in their roles as private producers and consumers.

From "Social" Liberalism to "Democratic" Socialism

Once the premise is implicitly and them explicitly in place that government could and should have the power of redirecting society into channels different from those that would be followed in a free market liberal society, the political arena becomes a battleground for control among those who want to command all of the people in different ways.

There is now the paradox that the "mixed economy" social liberalism that grew out of the earlier Progressive Era before the First World War and the New Deal Days of the 1930s, and the Great Society programs of the 1960s is now labeled by the more radical "democratic socialist progressives" as "neo-liberalism," which they define as unrestrained capitalism serving the interests of profit-seeking capitalists out to exploit "marginalized" women and "people of color," while destroying the physical planet.

The free market-based, "classical" liberalism of a much earlier era is now blamed under the "neo-liberal" label for all the political corruption, plundering, pandering and special interest privilege bestowing that is a product of contemporary "social" liberalism created during the 20th century by the collectivist predecessors of America's new "progressives" and democratic socialists.

In all of this, the original liberalism, in my opinion, the right and true liberalism has been lost from view. This is not only in the United States, but also in too many other places in the world. Political leaders in other countries hail the end to liberalism and its relevancy. They declare a turn to "illiberal" democracy, to new models of authoritarian paternalism, to restored populist nationalism, and the recovered spirit of 18th century Mercantilism and protectionism under which governments direct the domestic and international economic dealings of their respective citizens in the name of "national greatest."

In the United States, the philosophical, political, social and economic underpinnings of what remains of the older classical liberal spirit is under attack by the new tribalism of "identity politics" that constrains and confines the individual within the concepts and inside the categories of social class, gender and race. The individual, along with his destiny and place in society, is to be tied to the political power plays of different, organized groups pushing and shoving for place and position through the power and privileges in the planned "democratic" socialism to come.

It is in this ideological and political setting that I call "for a new liberalism." By which I mean not merely restoring the reality of 19th century liberalism, but a more consistent and principled classical, or free market, liberalism, that is true to the ideas and ideals of individual liberty, freedom of association, trade and private enterprise, with equal individual rights to life, liberty, and honestly acquired property before an impartial rule of law, in a system of constitutionally limited government. A government that offers favors and privileges to none, and secures unbiased justice to all in their individual rights and freedoms of peaceful, voluntary, and mutually agreed to association both within and beyond market supply and demand.

Outline of the Book

The first five chapters focus on the underlying principles, ideas and some of the historical accomplishments of liberalism, including part of the 19th century American experience, even with its admitted inconsistences, contradictions, and sometime cruelties, along with the degrees of unparalleled personal and economic freedom that made it the magnet for millions of immigrants yearning to breathe free. It is also explained how, perversely, this older classical liberalism was undermined and preempted by "progressive" social liberalism, and why it is that the true liberalism was the system of ideas that liberated labor and gave dignity to the worker.

Chapters 6 through 13 explain the nature and workings of the competitive free market economy in a system of liberty. In the process of this analysis, many of the misunderstandings surrounding the meaning of "competition" and "monopoly" are discussed, as well as how markets coordinate the multitudes of free individuals cooperating in a now globally encompassing system of division of labor. Misconceptions concerning the misuse of asymmetric knowledge in society are dispelled, and it is shown how competitive markets generate the incentives and institutions for fair dealing between seller and buyer.

We also suggest why the arguments for government evolvement due to supposed "public goods" are often misplaced, and how many social and infrastructure activities presumed to be inescapably in the realm of government action, in fact, can be better served by private enterprise. In this context, the case is made for the full privatization of schooling, and the benefits from private competitive free banking are discussed, instead of government central banking.

Chapters 14 through 16 demonstrate that in spite of much of the political rhetorical that is bandied about, is the liberal society that offers the greatest avenues for diversity and inclusion, compared to the rigid and artificial ones of government involvement. In this context, it is also shown that free market liberalism is, in fact, the social system of compromise and moderation, rather than the too frequent exclusionary extremism of government command and control. A false premise in the notion of beneficial political paternalism is the idea that "society" should be viewed as a family with politicians and bureaucrats serving as the "parents" telling us what to do and how to live; this perverts the actual meaning and role of family and freedom in society.

Chapters 17 through 27 turn to a critical analysis of the recent rebirth of "democratic" socialism and the call for "identity politics" based on race and gender. It is detailed that no matter what may be claimed, democratic socialism cannot fully distance itself from the totalitarian and central planning socialisms of the 20th century. Whatever may be the language and claimed intention, the nature of government control and command is to impose political planning increasingly on all facets of everyday life.

The individual is not longer a free agent guiding and planning their own life, but a cog in the tribal network whose place and future in society is determined and dictated for him. Included in identity politics has come a tyranny over mind, words, and actions, that cannot, if fully implement, escape from being totalitarian in its structure and outcome. The totalitarian element in democratic socialism is captured in the proposal for a Green New Deal, which requires all in society to be made subservient to a national and even global central planning in the name of "saving the planet."

At the heart of much of the political paternalism is the psychology of the meddling busybody who cannot overcome an uncontrollable desire to tell other people how they should live. It is, therefore, also useful to understand what motivates the meddler, a good portion of which seems to be arrogance and envy.

Finally, in chapters 28 to 30, I explain why it is that liberalism in its true meaning and application is needed very much in our own time so freedom may be regained in wider areas of each of our lives, and market-based prosperity can continue to offer humanity a growing standard of living that improves the circumstances of all. I then turn to the issue of how the friend of freedom is to defend liberty and the dignity of all in society. I argue that it is not enough to demand the end to as much coercion in society as is possible; it is also necessary to speak for and respect the dignity of all, even when the choices and peaceful actions of others are not the ones we would choose for ourselves.

In this context, I reason that the true liberal must speak out against not only politically imposed racism and sexism in its various forms, but must criticize and oppose it even in the private affairs of people. People in a free society are at liberty to live their lives as they choose, including personal bigotry and prejudice. But the true liberal, who believes in individualism and the sanctity of every human being to be treated accordingly, must not allow such attitudes to go unanswered and unchallenged in their own corners of society.

In the last chapter, I explain the importance of each and every one of us who believe in liberty to bear apart of the burden of defending it. This requires each of us to become informed and educated about the meaning and nature of the free society, as best we can. And to defend liberty in the most uncompromising and principled ways, even when victory seems so far away and "impossible." We should use the examples of liberalism's triumphs in the past as models to inspire and guide us. If we each do this, in our own ways, the cause of liberalism will succeed, and the hope and dream of a truly free society will become a reality.

CHAPTER 1

THE CLASSICAL LIBERAL HISTORY AND HERITAGE OF FREEDOM

There has been a great paradox in the modern world. On the one hand, freedom and prosperity have replaced tyranny and poverty for tens, indeed, for hundreds of millions, and now for billions, of people around the world over the last two centuries. Yet, the political and economic system that historically has made this possible has been criticized and condemned. That political and economic system is classical or free market liberalism.

By liberalism, I do not mean American "progressive" liberalism, which is historically a modified and reduced form of what used to be called "socialism," that is, government planning of all economic affairs. In its modern "progressive" form it has been watered down to mean extensive and intrusive government regulation of private enterprise with wide redistribution of wealth based on a prior conception of "social justice."

Nor do I mean what in many other parts of the world is often referred to as "neo-liberalism." While it is frequently claimed that neo-liberalism is a wild and unrestricted capitalism, in fact, it is institutionally far closer to American progressivism, under which private enterprise and profit-seeking is permitted, but, again, an extensive interventionist-welfare state, combined with government-business "crony" favoritism and corruption, hamper and restrict the functioning of a truly free and competitive market.[1]

What is lost in all the labeling is the original meaning and significance of political and economic "classical liberalism," which has nothing to do with what passes for American "progressive" liberalism or "neo-liberalism" in other countries around the globe.

Classical liberalism, the liberalism that began in the 18th and 19th centuries and which transformed the world in ways that has bettered the material and social circumstances of humankind, has been going down an Orwellian "memory hole." Yet, it was this older, or classical, liberalism that began the liberation of humanity from tyranny and poverty, and wherever residues and remnants of this original form of liberalism still exist or prevail the forces of liberty and prosperity continue to survive and blossom.

The Ancient Dream of Unfulfilled Freedom

Since ancient times, there have been thinkers who dreamed of a world with greater freedom for all men. But for most of human history this remained only dreams. The ancient Greeks spoke of the importance of man's reason and the need for freedom of thought if our minds were to challenge each other's logic and understandings

---

1 See, chapter 5, "Liberalism, Rightly and Wrongly Understood."

as we groped toward a more complete awareness of the objective world around us.

The Romans argued about a higher more universal or general law for men to live under, if only they came together to reason and agree about what could be a just "natural order" in society, given the nature of man. Jews and Christians appealed to a "higher law" concerning "right" and "justice" that was above the power of earthly kings and princes, and to which all men are subservient and responsible since it was given to them by the Creator of all things.

But for all of human history men lived under the earthly powers of conquerors and kings who claimed "divine rights" to rule over them. They were objects to be used and abused for the ends of those who held the whips and swords over their heads. Their lives and their efforts were to serve and be sacrificed for something that was said to be greater than and above them.

Their lives were not their own. They belonged to another. They were slaves, regardless of the names and phrases used to describe and defend what was a master-servant relationship. Human society was a world of the unfree.

Then this began to change, first in men's minds, then in their actions, and finally in the political and economic institutions under which people lived and worked.

Classical Liberalism and Natural Rights

While it is today often ridiculed or discounted by philosophers who frequently find it easier to speak about ethical nihilism and political relativism, the modern world of freedom had its origin in the conception of "natural rights." These are rights that reside in men by their "nature" as human beings, and which logically precede governments and any man-made laws that may or may not respect and enforce these rights.

Political philosophers such as John Locke (1632-1704) articulated the meaning of these rights in the 1600s and 1700s. "Though the earth and all inferior creatures be common to all men, yet every man has a 'property' in his own 'person'," insisted Locke in his *Second Treatise on Government* (1689). "This nobody has any right to but himself. The 'labor' of his body and the 'work' of his hands, we may say, are properly his."

While every man has a natural right to protect his life and his peacefully produced or non-aggressively acquired property, men form political associations among themselves to better protect their respective rights. After all, a man may not be strong enough to protect himself from aggressors; and he cannot always be trusted when, in the passion of the moment, he uses defensive force against another that may not be reasonably proportional to the offense against him.

Here in a nutshell is the origin of the ideas that germinated for nearly another century after John Locke, and then inspired the Founding Fathers in the words of the Declaration of Independence in July 1776, when they spoke of self-evident truths that all men are created equal with certain unalienable rights, among which are life, liberty and the pursuit of happiness, and for the preservation of which men form governments.

While every American schoolboy knows – or should I say, used to know – by heart those stirring words in the Declaration of Independence, what most Americans know less well is the remainder of the text of that document. Here the Founding Fathers enumerated their grievances against the British crown: taxation without representation; restrictions on the development of trade and industry within the British colonies and regulations on foreign commerce; a swarm of government bureaucrats intruding into the personal and daily affairs of the colonists; and violations of basic civil liberties and freedoms.

What aroused their anger and resentment is that a large majority of these American colonists considered themselves to be British by birth or ancestry. And here was the British king and his parliament denying or infringing upon what they considered to be their birthright – the customary and hard won "rights of an Englishman," gained over several centuries of successful opposition against arbitrary monarchical power.

Freedom is the common intellectual inheritance left to us by the great thinkers of the West. But it is nonetheless the case that much that we consider and call individual rights and liberty had it impetuous in Great Britain, in the writings of the political philosophers like John Locke and David Hume, legal scholars like William Blackstone and Edward Coke, and moral philosophers and political economists like Adam Smith.

What their combined writings and that of many others gave the West and the world over the last three or four centuries was the philosophy of political and economic liberalism. What began as the "rights of an Englishman" became by the late 18th and early 19th centuries a universal political philosophy of the individual rights of all human beings everywhere and at all times.

The Classical Liberal Crusade Against Slavery

What was the vision and agenda of 18th and 19th century classical liberalism? They may be understood under five headings:

First, was the freedom of the individual as possessing a right of self-ownership. The great British classical liberal crusade in the second half of the 18th and the early decades of the 19th century was for the abolition of slavery. The words of the British poet William Cowper (1731-1800) in 1785 became the rallying cry of the anti-slavery movement:

> We have no slaves at home – Then why aboard? Slaves cannot breathe in England; if their lungs receive our air, that moment they are free. They touch our country, and their shackles fall.

The British Slave Trade Act of 1807 banned the slave trade, and British warships patrolled the west coast of Africa to interdict slave ships heading for the Americas. This culminated in the Slavery Abolition Act of 1833, which formally abolished slavery throughout the British Empire on August 1, 1834.

Though not overnight, the British example heralded the legal end to slavery by the close of the 19th century through most of the world that was touched by the Western nations. The end to slavery in the United States took the form of a tragic and costly Civil War that left a deep scar on the country. But the unimaginable dream of a handful of people over thousands of years of human history, that no man should be the slave of another, finally became the reality for all under the inspiration and efforts of the 19th century classical liberal advocates of individual freedom.

The Classical Liberal Crusade for Civil Liberties

The second great classical liberal crusade was for the recognition of and legal respect for civil liberties. Since Magna Carta in 1215, Englishmen had fought for monarchical recognition and respect for certain essential rights, including no unwarranted or arbitrary arrest and imprisonment. These came to include freedom of thought and religion, freedom of speech and the press, and freedom of association. Above it all was the wider idea of the Rule of Law, that justice was to be equal and impartial, and that all were answerable and accountable before the law, even those representing and enforcing the law in the name of the king.

In the United States, many of these civil liberties were incorporated into the Constitution in the first ten amendments, which specified that there were some human freedoms so profoundly fundamental and essential to a free and good society – freedom of speech and the press, freedom of religion, a right to armed self-defense, freedom of association, protections against self-incrimination and unwarranted search and seizure of private papers and property, and speedy trials along with impartial justice – that no government should presume to abridge or deny them.

The Classical Liberal Crusade for Economic Freedom

The third great classical liberal crusade was for freedom of enterprise and free trade. Throughout the 17th and 18th centuries governments in Europe controlled, regulated and planned all the economic activities of their subjects and citizens as far as the arms of their political agents could reach.

Adam Smith (1723-1790) and his Scottish and French allies demolished the assumptions and logic of Mercantilism, as the system of government planning was then called. They demonstrated that government planners and regulators have neither the wisdom, nor the knowledge, nor the ability to direct the complex interdependent activities of humanity.

Furthermore, Adam Smith and his economist colleagues argued that social order was possible without political design. Indeed, "as if guided by an invisible hand," when men are left free to direct their own affairs within an institutional setting of individual liberty, private property, voluntary exchange, and unrestricted competition, there spontaneously forms a "system of natural liberty" that generates more wealth and coordinated activity than any governmental guiding hand could ever provide.

The benefits of such economic liberty made Great Britain and then the United States the industrial powerhouses of the world by the end of the 19th century; classical liberal economic policy rapidly did the same, though at different rates, in other parts of Europe, and then, slowly, to other areas of the world, as well. Population sizes in the West grew far above anything known or imaged in the past, yet increased production and rising productivity were giving those hundreds of millions of more people an increasing standard and quality of living. Indeed, if enough economic freedom and open competition continue to prevail, it is possible that by the end of the 21st century, human abject poverty will be a thing of the past everywhere around the world.

The Classical Liberal Crusade for Political Freedom

The fourth classical liberal crusade was for greater political liberty. It was argued that if liberty meant that men were to be self-governing over their own lives, should that not also mean that they participate in the governing of the society in which they live, in the form of an enlarged voting franchise through which the governed selected those who held political office under their behalf?

Liberals condemned the corrupt and manipulated electoral process in Great Britain that gave office in parliament to handpicked voices defending the narrow interests of the landed aristocracy at the expense of many others in society. So as the 19th and early 20th centuries progressed the right to vote moved more and more in the direction of universal suffrage, in a growing number of countries around the world, including the United States.

It was not that these earlier liberals were unconcerned about the potential abuses from democratic majorities. In fact, John Stuart Mill (1806-1873), in his *Considerations on Represent-ative Government* (1861) proposed that all those who received any form of financial subsidy or support from the government should be denied the voting franchise for as long as they were dependent in such a manner upon the taxpayers. There was too much of a possible conflict. As Mill expressed it, "It amounts to allowing them to put their hands into other people's pockets for any purpose which they think fit to call a public one ... He who cannot by his own labor suffice for his own support has no claim to the privilege of helping himself to the money of others." Alas, his wise advice has never been followed.

The Liberal Crusade for International Peace

Finally, the fifth of the classical liberal crusades of the 19th century was for, if not the abolition of war, then at least the reduction in the frequency of international conflicts among nations and the severity of damage that came with military combat.

In fact, during the century that separated the defeat of Napoleon in 1815 and the commencement of the First World War in 1914, wars at least among the European Powers were infrequent, relatively short in duration, and limited in their physical destruction and taking of human life.

It was argued that war was counter-productive to the interests of all nations and peoples. It prevented and disrupted the natural benefits that can and did improve the conditions of all men through peaceful production and trade based on an international division of labor in which all gained from the specializations of others in industry, agriculture, and the arts.

Due to the classical liberal spirit of the time there were some successful attempts to arrange formal "rules of war" among governments under which the lives and property of innocent non-combatants would be respected even by conquering armies. There were treaties detailing how prisoners of war were to be humanely treated and cared for, as well as the banishing of certain forms of warfare deemed immoral and ungentlemanly.

It would, of course, be an exaggeration and an absurdity to claim that 19th century classical liberalism fully triumphed in terms of its ideals or its goals of political and economic reform and change. The counter-revolutionary forces of socialism and nationalism gained momentum and influence before classical liberal policies could be fully followed and implemented in the years leading up to the First World War in 1914.

However, if there is any meaning to the notion of a prevailing "spirit of the age" that sets the tone and direction of a period of history, then it cannot be denied that classical liberalism was the predominate ideal in the early and middle decades of the 19th century. And that it changed the world in a truly transformative way. Whatever (properly understood) political, economic, and personal liberty we still possess today is due to that earlier classical liberal epoch of human history.

America the Beacon of Individual Liberty

In the new nation of the United States of America at the end of the 18th century, there was a written constitution that in principle and a significant degree of practice recognized the rights of individuals to their life, liberty and honestly acquired property. In America, most individuals could say and do virtually anything that they wanted, as long as it was peaceful and not an infringement on other citizens' similar individual rights. In America, trade across this new and growing country was generally free from government regulations and controls or oppressive taxes, so people could live, work and invest wherever they wanted, for any purpose that took their fancy, or offered them attractive gains and profit. The great contradiction and hypocrisy through this period, of course, was the presence of the institution of slavery in the Southern states into the 1860s, and the failure to fully extend the idea of individual rights to women as well.

It may seem to many as a cliché, but in those decades of the 19th and early 20th centuries, when few migration restrictions barred the door for many people, America stood out as a beacon of hope and promise. Here a man could have his "second chance." He could leave behind the political tyranny, religious oppression and economic privileges of the "old country" to have a new start for himself and his family.

Between 1840 and 1914, more than 65 million people left the "old world" to make their new beginnings in other parts of the world, and about 35 million of them came to America. Many of us are the lucky descendants of those earlier generations who came to "breathe free" in the United States.

Today, in America and around much of the world, this classical liberal idea and ideal of individual liberty, unhampered free markets and free enterprise, and constitutionally limited government, the purpose of which is to secure and protect each person's life and property rather than abridge them, is being lost.

It is disappearing from high school and college and university curricula, or when referred to is condemned or ridiculed as outdated or irrelevant or wrong-headed. The self-appointed "social critics" and intellectual trendsetters of ideas have turned to new collectivist versions of race, gender and social group. This can only end badly for the future of freedom.

The ideas and spirit of classical liberalism, the original and true liberalism, needs to be fully reborn, restated and reintroduced as the guiding ideas for an America and a world of liberty, prosperity and peace. And the chapters in the remainder of this book are meant to discussion various facets of the case for a renewed free market liberalism that will finish and fulfill the promises and partial successes of that original classical liberalism.

CHAPTER 2

THROUGH FOREIGN EYES: AMERICAN LIBERTY AND PROSPERITY IN THE 19TH CENTURY

If you look at the results of relatively open and competitive market economies over the years, the decades, and especially the last two centuries, the only conclusion that can reasonably be reached is that free market liberal-oriented societies provide the conditions and opportunities for constant and continuous material and social betterment for the vast majority of those living in such political-economic systems.

If one reflects for a moment on the fact that the historically normal and natural condition of man for all of recorded history up to about three centuries ago was abject and horrendous poverty and compare that with all that has happened during, especially, the last two hundred years, the transformation in the human circumstance has been nothing short of remarkable if not seemingly miraculous.

Prosperity and Life Expectancy 200 Years Ago and Now

Around 1820, the world's population is estimated to have been about one billion people, out of which demographers and economic historians estimate that at least 85 to 90 percent of who lived at or not much above starvation poverty. In 2019, the world's population numbered more than 7.7 billion people, out of which only about 10 percent are calculated to still live in poverty; and that latter number continues to decrease with every passing year.

In the early 1800s average life expectancy in Europe was between 30 and 40 years of age. By the early 1900s, that had increased to a life expectancy, on average, into the 60s for Europeans and North Americans. And today in these two parts of the world, this has gone up to the high 70s and into the low and mid-80s years of age at time of death. Other areas around the globe are not far behind, with life expectancy in general and on average in Africa now in the 60s and 70s, after being less than 30 years of age in the early 1900s. And life expectancy in most of Asia in 2018 was also in the mid- to high 70s.

What kind of a society makes this all possible – the social, economic and technological and scientific advancements? I would argue, that society which allows the widest latitudes of individual liberty and freedom of enterprise. We take much of this for granted in the United States. Maybe we shouldn't. America and Americans are wide open for scathing criticism today, in terms of our past and our present. What might be being left out?

We live at a time when an understanding and an appreciation of what a free society can or should be like is being slowly lost. Calls are constantly being made for government to do more. Remaining areas of personal life are to be invaded by increased government regulation, redistribution, control, command, and constraint. The idea of the independent and self-responsible individual diminishes in the number of its supporters, or so it appears, with every passing day.

Public policy debates concern not whether something should be overseen and managed by government, but merely how far the interventionist-welfare state should it go at the present time, and who is going to pay for it.

Foreign Visitors and the Lost Memory of Freedom Past

The idea that there was a time in American history when many more matters of daily life were considered the domain of personal decision-making and voluntary collaborative community effort has mostly been erased from people's memory to a great extent this is because it is rarely if ever taught anymore, other than in the most negative of images.

Few people know or take an interest in that history of an especially economically freer America and the lives of those who lived during that earlier time. This makes it worthwhile, however briefly, to take a glimpse of that American past. To have a small flavor of it, sometimes the most interesting accounts are by Europeans who came to visit America in the early and middle decades of the 19th century, and who wrote books about their impressions of this great experiment in a free society on the American side of the Atlantic Ocean.

Many of us are familiar with Alexis de Tocqueville's (1805-1859) famous *Democracy in America* (1836; 1840), in which he recounted his observations and interpretations of America and its institutions after an extended journey around the country in the early 1830s. But, in fact, there were dozens of such volumes by a wide variety of visitors to North America. And you learn from them a lot about what everyday life was like in the United States during, say, the

1830s, 1840s, and 1850s, as well as what people at that time meant by and attempted to live in terms of freedom.

Travel across the Atlantic from England to New York by sailing ship took anywhere between four and six weeks, depending on the weather and the currents. Some of the writers reminded their readers that the great new means of land transportation that was rapidly being introduced particularly in Great Britain and the United States in the 1830s was the railway. They counted up the hundreds of miles of railway track laid or in the process of being constructed across the United States east of the Mississippi River.

They marveled at the speed at which a train could now transport a human being through space in the 1830s – between 30 and 40 miles per hour! However, as one British traveler and liberal member of Parliament, James Sterling, explained in his *Letters from the Slave States* (1857), the railway passenger cars in America each had a coal-burning stove at one end of the carriage that often filled the air with a thick fog of smoke and generated suffocating heat that could only be balanced by opening some windows, which made it uncomfortably cold for those sitting next to one of those open windows in the winter months.

Almost two hundred years before the Internet, travellers acquired the latest news about the city to which they were traveling by railway in an interesting manner. German-born Francis Lieber, who became the first professor of political science at Columbia University in New York City, recounted in, *The Stranger in America* (1836), how there might be two trains traveling in opposite directions between, say, Philadelphia and New York. As they passed each other at 40 miles an hour, with the train tracks close together, people moving in opposite directions would hold out of their passenger carriage windows copies of the day's newspaper from the city they had left so it could be grabbed by someone going to that city as a destination. Sometimes people would play tricks on each other, and pass old newspapers from days or weeks before.

Waterways, Steamboats, and Waves of Migrants

The waterways, natural and manmade, were the other major means of longer-distance travel in those mid-19th century decades. Steam-powered riverboats offered comfort, entertainment, food, and sleeping cabins. Less than $10 could get you from St. Louis to New Orleans along the Mississippi River in just a few days. Of course, this mode of transportation had its problems. German writer, Francis J. Grund, pointed out in *The Americans in their Moral, Social and Political Relations* (1837) that the journey from, say, Pittsburgh to New Orleans by steamboat had the peril of the boat's boiler possibly exploding, or the boat sinking due to tree trunks and other underwater hazards, or colliding into other boats in the darkness of night. Dozens or even hundreds of people would be killed in these ways on a regular basis. But passengers just took this in stride; the dead were mourned and buried, and the surviving travellers simply went on their way.

Another German traveler, Frederick von Raumer explained in, *America and the American People* (1846), that by foot, or covered wagon, or riverboat, or train, the waves of immigrants coming from Europe spread out across the land, clearing fields, building towns, creating communities of private enterprises, schools, churches, charities, and neighborliness. Nothing was static or stationary. Everything was growing and new. Civilization could be seen rising out of the wilderness.

Enterprise, Industry, and Education in America

While Americans, settling in this new land, were focused on practical knowledge of building, creating, and profiting from making things for themselves and to market to others in other parts of America and around the world, already they placed a high value on education, reading, and knowing about the events going in the rest of the United States. Even the smallest hamlet soon had its own newspaper or two, and the "little red school house" was quickly constructed to make literate all the children in the local community. Several of these European visitors emphasized the high level of literacy among the American population in the 1830s and 1840s, compared to Europeans in general, and the normally informed and intelligent conversation on political and social matters that even the seemingly isolated farmer or small town craftsman could frequently and easily enter into.

Men were focused on and tied up with business and enterprise. Rarely did they find a laggard, loafer, and lazybones among the male population, those foreign visitors said. The few that there were, were viewed with disregard and disrespect as failing themselves, their families, and their country in not being industrious, self-supporting, and a good citizen in improving the conditions of America through self-interested, productive private enterprise.

There was little time for reflective readings on philosophy or poetry or the arts. Your financial successes of today could turn into bankruptcy tomorrow. You had to be alert to opportunities for profit and avoidance of losses. And if business failures came, you had to be ready to pick yourself up, dust yourself off, and start all over again. After all, there was this whole continent before you waiting for exploration, agricultural and industrial development, and commercial dealings for gainful employment for all those with just a little bit of self-initiative.

The competitive spirit, as a result, was everywhere. This was especially noted by the French economist and classical liberal, Michel Chevalier (1806-1879), who traveled around the United States in the mid-1830s, and on returning home wrote, *Society, Manners and Politics in the United States* (1839). He described a land of energetic, free men and women who enthusiastically took their lives and destinies into their own hands, fearlessly facing the uncertainties to make their way and their fortunes on what seemed to be a boundless continent of opportunity.

They were not afraid of change or adapting to the personal and financial ups and downs of life. Indeed, they often viewed these as challenges to be grasped and turned to their advantage, rather than something to run away from and then beg for government handouts and social safety nets. Everyday market competition was the life-blood of success and a natural part of processes of human improvement.

The Character and Quality of Earlier Americans

Perhaps it's best to allow Michel Chevalier explain a little bit of his impressions of the Americans of that time:

> The American is a model of industry...The manners and customs are altogether those of a working, busy society. At the age of fifteen years, a man is engaged in business; at twenty-one he is

established, he has his farm, his workshop, his counting-room, or his office, in a word his employment, whatever it may be.

He now also takes a wife, and at twenty-two is the father of a family, and consequently has a powerful stimulus to excite him to industry. A man who has no profession, and, which is the same thing, who is not married, enjoys little consideration; he, who is an active and useful member of society, who contributes his share to augment the national wealth and increase the numbers of the population, he only is looked upon with respect and favor.

The American is educated with the idea that he will have some particular occupation, that he is to be a farmer, artisan, manufacturer, merchant, speculator, lawyer, physician, or minister, perhaps all in succession, and that, if he is active and intelligent, he will make his fortune.

He has no conception of living without a profession, even when his family is rich, for he sees nobody about him not engaged in business. The man of leisure is a variety of the human species, of which the Yankee does not suspect the existence, and he knows that if rich today, his father may be ruined tomorrow. Besides, the father himself is engaged in business, according to custom, and does not think of dispossessing himself of his fortune; if the son wishes to have one at present, let him make it himself!

An American's business is always to be on the edge lest his neighbor get there before him. If a hundred Americans were about to go before a firing squad, they would start fighting for the privilege of going first, so used are they to competition!

Women as the Carriers of Culture and Good Works

What about women in this society of freedom? Women may not have had the vote, but they were not simply barefoot, pregnant and cooking away in the kitchen all hours of the day. In fact, in most instances, it was very much the opposite. This, too, was something that nearly all these visitors to America took time to describe and bring out. To begin with, all these European travellers observed the politeness, respect, and gentlemanliness with which women of any social status or family background were treated. A single woman of any age could travel by day or night; she could do so by train, riverboat, or stagecoach, and virtually never fear of being molested in any way. Formally reported or informally known instances of such conduct were very few and far between from all accounts at that time in American history.

If men were occupied with the business of earning a successful living for themselves and their families, women were expected and encouraged to become educated and well read in all those things that fathers, brothers, and husbands did not have the time or interest to attend to. The famous British author and political economist, Harriet Martineau, in *Society in America* (1837), brought this out by mentioning how while traveling in Ohio an ordinary farmer that she started up a conversation with asked what might be the latest books on philosophy and the sciences published in Europe, so he might order them for his daughter, whose education and knowledge he was always on the outlook to broaden.

Even the most "cultured" (and snobbish) of these European male travellers commented on the frequency and degree to which they had stimulating conversations with American women in different social circumstances, though most frequently those in what we now call the "middle class," about music, art, philosophy, literature, and the sciences. These women often demonstrated acquaintance with the latest works on these themes published in both America and in Europe in several languages, and with a nuanced insight and appreciation in these areas.

Indeed, cultivating of "culture" within the family was the domain of wives and mothers. As was the doings of "good works." Husbands and fathers may have provided the monies for private charity and philanthropy – and, again, many of these writers brought out the extent to which the "private sector" funded, organized, and managed community problems of society – but it was the wives and daughters who gave of their time and efforts for assisting the poor, tutoring the illiterate who often were newly arrived on American shores, and who handled the outreach of church activities in neighborhoods. Indeed, women made society "work" outside of the predominantly male arena of market supply and demand. Women were the societal glue that held it all together. And who often had strong and, again, informed views on political issues even if they could not enter the voting booth.

But besides this, women could and did work on their own, away from home, earning, spending and saving their own money. One foreign traveller visited Lowell, Massachusetts in the 1830s and saw the manufacturing mills, many of them employing single young women who came from other parts of New England. The private enterprises encouraged the establishment of boarding houses in which the female employees could live, in safe and pleasant surroundings. These women could sometimes earn anywhere from $3 to $7 a day. If that seems low, keep in mind that room and board in one of these boarding houses, the traveller tells us, could be had for $1 to $3 per week. A goodly sum of money could be saved and set aside by these independent women for whatever future they might decide upon for themselves.

This did not mean that the America of that time was open to equality for women in all economic and social matters. Harriet Martineau, a fiery classical liberal feminist of her time, was scathing in her criticism concerning the status of women in the United States, in her *Society in America*, based on a two-year journey around America in 1834-1836. Deferred to and treated with chivalrous courtesy in virtually all social settings, nonetheless, it was taken for granted that a woman's purpose was to marry, raise and affection-ately care for her family, and accept the lead of her husband. That they should, in general, be considered fit and free to pursue many occupations and professions was socially frowned upon, certainly by most men but even by many women in American society, as well. Martineau admired the freedoms and opportunities that women in America might already have compared to those in Europe, but the United States still awaited a maturity of thought and action to fully extent its principles of liberty to the other half of the population.

American Individualism Seen as Essential to Liberty

If there were a phrase to describe the Americans of this time it most certainly would have been rugged individualism. In fact, Alexis de Toc-queville used the word "individualism" to convey an essential quality in the American character that he wished to emphasize in his classic two-volume political study of a free society, *Democracy in America*.

Tocqueville was not an uncritical devotee of American individualism, but he believed that its healthy aspects allowed the individual to see himself as a distinct human being separate from the mass of humanity. The individual was able to form his own freely chosen circle of human partners and associations through family, friends, and commercial enterprise. Individualism was a bulwark against one of the most serious dangers in free societies with democratically elected governments: the tyranny of majorities, both politically and culturally.

Tocqueville expressed concerns that the American individualism that he observed could make the individual less conscious and attentive to the general society in which he lived. At the same time, he saw that the answer to the various social problems requiring the efforts and energies of combinations of people outside of family and business had been found among the Americans through the voluntary associations of civil society.

The American Spirit of Voluntary Association

In fact, Tocqueville considered this to be one of the most impressive aspects of American community life, which he felt Europeans should be most attentive to as an alternative to the presumption in the "old world" that all such "welfare" matters needed to be left to the State. In Tocqueville's own words:

> The political associations that exist in the United States are only a single feature in the midst of the immense assemblage of associations in that country. Americans of all ages, all conditions, and all dispositions constantly form associations. They have not only commercial and manufacturing companies, in which they take part, but associations of a thousand other

kinds, religious, moral, serious, futile, general or restricted, enormous or diminutive.

The Americans make associations to give entertainments, to found seminaries, to build inns, to construct churches, to diffuse books, to send missionaries to the antipodes; in this manner they found hospitals, prisons, schools ...

As soon as several of the inhabitants of the United States have taken up an opinion or a feeling that they wish to promote in the world, they look out for mutual assistance; and as soon as they have found one another out, they combine. From that moment they are no longer isolated men, but a power seen from afar, whose actions serve for an example and whose language is listened to.

I have often admired the extreme skill with which the inhabitants of the United States succeed in proposing a common object for the exertions of a great many men and inducing them voluntarily to pursue it ... Nothing, in my opinion, is more deserving of our attention than the intellectual and moral associations of America.

From local fire departments, to friendly societies for mutual assurance, to charitable organizations to assist those in a community who had fallen on hard and difficult times, as well as many other purposes, the spirit of individualism, Tocqueville explained, was to shoulder these responsibilities yourself as a free and responsible human being in voluntary collaboration with your fellows in society.

Self-Government as the Key to American Prosperity

What made America "work," almost all these visitors emphasized, was the spirit of self-government. In the face of the history and practice throughout the ages of tyranny and despotism, monarchy and aristocracy, America was this self-declared and self-established system of representative, republican government. Americans of all political views were proud to call themselves "democrats" with a small "d." Here in America the people ruled. The voting franchise was wider and more extensive than in even the most enlightened of the more liberal societies in Europe during those early and middle decades of the 19th century.

But the real self-government in America was the self-governing individual who guided and planned his own life in peaceful and voluntary association with others in society, and independently of the much smaller and much less interventionist government at that time in American history. Yes, state and federal governments handed out favors, tax monies, subsidies, contracts and jobs to those who had assisted and supported the politicians elected to office.

But, in general, they seem almost microscopic compared to the omnipresence of government in people's social and economic lives today, though in that earlier time political spending was already the basis of many of the political scandals and controversies. It may not have been a theoretical laissez-faire, but the state barely touched or interfered with most people's lives on an everyday basis. Yes, there were blue laws prohibiting businesses from operating on Sundays. And, indeed, the city government of Baltimore would fine you $1 if you played ball or flew a kite on "the Lord's day." Plus, there were strong social (though no longer political) pressures to attend church, but what church you might attend did not matter and was respected by virtually all as matters of private conscience.

Jews in America were equally respected in the belief and practice of their faith. There may have been private prejudices, but there was no politically supported or tolerated anti-Semitism for all intents and purposes. If there did arise religious tensions, it was most often between Catholics (especially with the influx of large numbers of Irish immigrants) and Protestants, due to the belief by the latter that the former were "pope-worshipers" who took their political orders from the priesthood. Ignorance and prejudice led to episodes of violence, but in general religious tolerance was both preached and very mostly practiced.

The Importance of the Self-Governing Individual

America for many was a free land of self-governing individuals who were the basis all the improvements and prosperity in this young and growing land. Adam Gurowski (1805-1866) was a Polish nobleman, who immigrated to the United States in 1849, and after spending eight years in America as a new American taken by the spirit of freedom he found here, he wrote his impressions of the differences between, *America and Europe* (1857). He explained the spirit and results of that free and self-governing individual:

> Every thing great, beneficial, useful in America, is accomplished without the action of the so-called government, notwithstanding even its popular, self-governing character. Individual impulses, private enterprise, association, free activity, the initiative pouring everlastingly from within the people, are mostly substituted here for what in European societies and nations forms the task of governments ...

"But by far the larger number of monuments, works and useful establishments, for industry, trade, for facilitating and spreading tuition and mental culture, universities, schools and scientific establishments, are created and endowed by private enterprise, by private association, and by individual munificence ...

"Neither individuals separately, nor the aggregated people look to the government for such creations; private association and enterprise, those corollaries of self-government – untrammelled by governmental action – have covered the land [with progress] ...

"All this could not have been miraculously carried out, if the American people had been accustomed to look to a government for the initiative, instead of taking it themselves. Without the self-governing impulse, America would be materially and socially a wilderness."

Nor was any of this progress by private initiative at an end in America. It was just beginning. Gurowski was certain that private enterprise would not only continue to do all that it was already doing, but many things still taken for granted as duties for government even in the United States would pass into the superior hands of private enterprisers, including aspects of national defense and foreign affairs:

The superiority of private enterprise over any so-called governmental centralizing action is daily evidenced here. In many branches of administration the government remains behind what an individual enterprise fulfills. Thus the carriage of letters and the whole branch of postal administration is successfully rivaled by private expresses. Many other administrative branches seem destined in the course of time, to be superseded by private enterprise.

A time may come, when even armaments and armies may be levied on the account of states, but by private individuals. Armories and navy docks would today be better managed by private than they are by governmental administration. Even external relations are better secured by the numberless threads of private interests, between America and Europe, which extend and cross each other, than by official representatives, or by the stipulations of treaties and conventions.

For all these things to be done, the American "could not wait for the permission or sanction of those urgings by a government, or submit to receive advice, or move in the leading strings of governmental directions," said Gurowski. "All this is wholly incompatible with the nature of the American, with his mental habits, as well as with the combination of circumstances around him."

The spirit and the institutions of America made freedom, opportunity and increasing prosperity possible. All of these travellers commented on that fact that wages, across the board, were higher in America than in Europe; that self-employment and owning your own business was widely available to almost all who had the will, the determination, and, of course, a bit of luck, to try. The Old World's rigid social structures and aristocratic privileges did not exist in America.

Americans were proud to call themselves those "democrats," with that small "d," not only because so many in the male population had the right to vote, but because there was a sense that everyone was just as good as another. If someone's social status in society was higher than another, it was not because of the accident of birth concerning noblemen and commoners, but because someone had earned recognition in the eyes of others due to merit. That earned merit might have been due to success in business and private enterprise, but could have been earned through any of a number of other peaceful and productive and valued ways in the wider community.

Political Plunder Even in that Earlier America

The idea, therefore, of turning to government for the solution to social and economic problems was clearly anathema to much that was in the American character. Yet, government did exist in this earlier America, and it did more than merely secure people's lives, liberty and honestly acquired property. State and local governments subsidized privately built canals and ferries, gave protection to state-level banks that mismanaged their depositors' funds, and gave out government contracts to special interests close to those in the legislatures.

The British traveler, Charles MacKay (1814-1889), is perhaps best known for his 1841 volume, Extraordinary Popular Delusions and the Madness of Crowds, but he journeyed around the United States in the second half of the 1850s, and then published, Life and Liberty in America: Sketches of a Tour (1859). He spent time in Washington, D.C. and was invited to the White House to meet then President James Buchanan.

Glad-Handing for Presidential Power and Patronage

Charles Mackay shared his observations and impressions of his visit to the White House:

> The White House ... is a plain but elegant building, befitting the unpretending dignity of the popular magistrate of a country where government is minimized, and where the trappings and paraphernalia of state and office are unknown or uncongenial.

> Here the President – a man who possesses, during his term of office, a far greater amount of power and patronage than the sovereign of any state in Europe, except the Emperors of France, Russia, and Austria – transacts, without any unnecessary forms, and with no formality or ceremony at all, the business of his great and growing dominion.

> "Here he receives, at stated days and periods, ladies and gentlemen who choose to call upon him, either for business or pleasure, or from mere curiosity ... There is no man in the United States who has such a quantity of hand-shaking to get through as the President.

> Never was there a place in which office-hunters and place-seekers more assiduously congregate. The antechambers of the President are daily thronged with solicitants – with men who think they helped to make the President, and who are constantly of the opinion that the President should help to make them.

I thought, when presented to Mr. Buchanan, that he seemed relieved to find that I was an Englishman, and had nothing to ask him for – no little place for self, no cousin, or friend, or son for which to beg his all-powerful patronage.

Of course, when Chevalier, de Tocqueville, and MacKay traveled around the United States, there was another plague across the land besides the growing special interest plunder, privilege and favoritism that eventually grew into the 20th century's full-blown interventionist-welfare state. That was the institution of slavery.

Slavery as the Sore in the American Soul

We have a tendency to think that the times we are living in is a turning point in history. And so, those European observers recorded the controversies and fears among the Americans of that time: the rich will be an overbearing and despotic aristocracy that will destroy America's free government; the democratic majority will become a mob manipulated by a demagogue who will tear down the institutions of society, creating chaos and despair. Can we successfully integrate into mainstream American society all those drunken, hot-tempered Irish immigrants who worship and obey the Pope in Rome? What about those Germans immigrants who form their own communities and want to speak German rather than learn English? And all the newspapers accused their rivals for readership of spreading what today we call "fake news." In the 1830s, Andrew Jackson seemed to arouse about as much blind loyalty and hysterical opposition as Donald Trump today. Was he the savior of America or its destroyer? Sound familiar?

But the one issue all these foreign visitors inescapably devoted some time to write about based on their journeys around America was slavery. Whatever the other issues and arguments, slavery was the political point of gravity around which everything else in American politics eventually seemed to revolve. It was the sore eating away at the soul of the country.

Harriet Martineau said that in evaluating and judging America in her book, she would not use any of the past or existing institutions of Europe as a benchmark, but, instead, judge Americans by their own stated founding principles, and the extent to which they lived up to and practiced them. Slavery was the clearest inconsistency and contradiction. To gain the South's acceptance of the new Constitution of 1787, the Northern states acquiesced in the practice of slavery in the Southern part of the country. And the free states became accomplices to the crime of slavery in agreeing to return runaway slaves to their Southern masters. Martineau said:

> I know that slavery is only recognized by the constitution as a matter of fact; and that it is only twice mentioned; in connection with representation, and with the restitution to their masters of "persons held to labor escaping into another Slate": but the fact remains that a man who abhors slavery is compellable by the law, which his fathers made, to deliver up to the owner a slave whose act of absconding he approves. It is impossible to estimate the evils which have proceeded from, and which will yet arise out of this guilty but "necessary" compromise.

The Sickness of American Slavery

At every turn the issue of slavery impressed itself in American politics; the national conflict and controversy always kept coming back to the legitimacy of slavery in a free society, and the designs by Southerners to extend their "peculiar institution" into the Western territories and states.

Charles Mackay visited one of the auction sites in New Orleans; he was shocked when on orders of an auctioneer, female black slaves came up asking him to buy them. "I felt a sensation something similar to that of the first qualm of sea-sickness to be so addressed by my fellow creatures – a feeling of nausea, as if I were about to be ill. I entertained at that moment such a hatred of slavery that, had it been in my power to abolish it in one instant off the face of the earth by the mere expression of my will, slavery at that instance would have ceased to exist."

A Russian visitor to America in 1857, Aleksandr Borisovich Lakier (1825-1870), also saw slavery in action in New Orleans. He went to the levee to watch the unloading of the ships that had come down the Mississippi River or up from the Gulf of Mexico. "Most of the work is done by Negroes, who, under the watchful eye of the white overseer, carry bales of cotton and barrels of flour, sugar, and molasses from the steamboats to the shore," Lakier explained. "The overseer, whip in hand, keeps account of the goods brought ashore and zealously drives the slaves to keep working without resting. If they tarry or daydream, the whip is always ready."

Lakier, too, visited one of the slave auction sites in New Orleans. Thinking that Lakier was a potential buyer, the auctioneer took him around the premises. "If we stopped in front of a Negress, he turned her around, displayed her charms and spoke in my ear about her various recommendations. The poor women, forgetting her natural shame, smiled and asked that I buy her."

The only thing that matched "the feeling of revulsion one brings to a place where Negroes are sold" Lakier said, was to read the advertisement flyers offering rewards for the capture and return of runaway slaves. There was included a description of the physical characteristics of the human being to be hunted down that was "precisely how we in our country [Russia] describe distinctive marks when we advertise for a missing dog."

This blight on the politics, economics, culture, and soul of the American people was finally ended a few years after Mackay and Lakier witnessed this shame and insult to the universal principles of individual liberty upon which the country was declared to be founded. Unfortunately, it only came about through a destructive and devastating Civil War, the full effects from which the United States has still not yet completely recovered.

The American Ideal of Freedom Continued to Shine

But out of the shadow of this terrible crime against humanity and morality, America still continued as a hope and a reality of the possibility and potential for liberty and prosperity for tens of millions who came to the United States from many other parts of the world. Here a man did not have bow low to those who claimed to be their aristocratic betters due to military conquests from long ago. Here your past and its mistakes mattered much less than what you could demonstrate as your abilities to freely offer others what they may want in voluntary trade and exchange as the peaceful and productive means to your own betterment compared to anything possible in the "old country."

Here you could say pretty much (if not completely unrestrictedly) what you wanted, write what you wanted, go where you wanted, work at what you wanted, associate freely with others as you wanted, without permission or approval of kings, princes or their government ministers. Also, here in America to be wealthy was neither a sin nor something to be embarrassed by or feel guilty about.

Walter Raleigh Houghton (1845-1929) was a professor of political science at Indiana University in the late 19th century. In 1886, he authored, *Kings of Fortune, or the Triumphs and Achievements of Noble, Self-Made Men*, a series of biographies of people from many walks of life – scientists, inventors, philanthropists, lawyers, artists and actors, and merchants and businessmen – who demonstrated excellence and enterprise in achieving recognition and stature in American society.

The Glory of America: Freedom of Industry and Enterprise

But what is noteworthy is that Professor Houghton especially emphasized the significance and mark left by private enterprisers on American society. Their successes were indicative of what the country was all about. He said:

> The chief glory of America is, that it is the country in which genius and industry find their speediest and surest reward. Fame and fortune are here open to all who are willing to work for them. Neither class distinctions nor social prejudices, neither differences of birth, religion, nor ideas, can prevent the man of true merit from winning the just reward of his labors in this favored land. We are emphatically a nation of self-made men, and it is to the labors of this worthy class that our marvelous national prosperity is due ...
>
> To an American, business is the quintessence of energy, the wellspring of ambition, and the highway to wealth, honor and

fame. On it are based the push and the drive which are daily adding millions to the treasures of this nation, as well as giving us reputation and integrity among the peoples of the world.

What was wanted in any American for there to be a prosperous and ethical country were the qualities of honesty, integrity, industry, politeness, and courtesy. In another of his books, *American Etiquette and Rules of Politeness* (1883) Professor Houghton tutored the young would-be businessmen on the personal qualities to cultivate in all that he did in his interactions with others:

> Form good habits and be polite to all; for politeness is the key to success. Be cheerful and avoid breaking an engagement. If you have to fail in carrying out an engagement you should make the fact known, stating your reasons. Do not deceive a customer. It will ruin your business. 'Honesty is the best policy.'

> Never loose your temper in discussing business matters. Meet notes and drafts promptly. To neglect this is to ruin your reputation. If you cannot pay, write at once to your creditor, stating plainly the reason why you cannot pay him, and say when you will be able. Pay bills when presented. Never allow a creditor to call a second time to collect a bill. Your credit will be injured if you do. When you collect a bill of a man, thank him.

Political Destruction of Private Virtue

The private sector in America still retains many of these characteristics in daily life. To a great extent this is because the market has not been totally destroyed, and voluntary association in this arena means that it still pays to act and see the personal benefit from so acting in a setting in which you can lose business that could have been yours if you do not practice those things about which Professor Houghton was preaching to the possible youthful private enterprisers of the 1880s.

What honesty, truthfulness, politeness, or sincerity exists today in American politics? These qualities were, no doubt, wanting in the politics of that earlier time in the 19th century about which those foreign visitors wrote. But today the political arena in America really is nothing but a cesspool of connivance and corruption.

An understanding and appreciation of those underlying principles of a free society upon which the United States was originally established must be regained. Because even with its many contradictions, inconsistences, and sometimes cruelties during parts of its past, and into the present, the idea and ideal upon which it was founded, that principle of individual freedom, was and still is the only enduring hope for mankind.

CHAPTER 3

FREEDOM IS WHY IMMIGRANTS HAVE COME TO AMERICA

America! The word has meant hope, opportunity and freedom for tens of millions of people over the last two and half centuries. For a good part of those 250 years, the words on the Stature of Liberty in New York harbor have rang true:

"Give me your tired, your poor,
Your huddled masses yearning to breathe free,
The wretched refuse of your teeming shore.
Send these, the homeless, tempest-tost to me,
I lift my lamp beside the golden door!"

Between 1840 and 1914 it is estimated that over 65 million people left tired, tyrannized, and troubled Europe to find new homes, second chances, and better lives for themselves and their children, especially in the "New World." Of that 65 million about 35 million of them made their way to the United States.

Historian, R. R. Palmer, explained this massive movement of people in his *History of the Modern World* (1950):

> Perhaps most basic in the whole European exodus was the underlying [classical] liberalism of the age. Never before (nor since) had people been legally so free to move. Old laws requiring skilled workmen to stay in their own countries were repealed, as in England in 1824. The old semi-communal agricultural villages, with collective rights and obligations, holding the individual to his native group, fell into disuse except in Russia ... Governments permitted their subjects to emigrate, to take with them their savings of shillings, marks, kroner, or lire, and to change nationality by becoming naturalized in their new homes.
>
> The rise of individual liberty in Europe, as well as the hope of enjoying it in America, made possible the great emigration. For so huge a mass movement the most remarkable fact is that it took place by individual initiative and individual expense.

Immigrant Hopes and an Imperfect America

Until the early part of the 1900s, the United States was more or less an open land for all new comers. Especially European immigrants needed neither passport nor visa to enter America for most of that time through the various ports of entry, especially that of New York City. (The first major immigration restrictions came in 1880s with limitations on the arrival of Chinese migrants, followed by similar limitations on Japanese immigrants. These were crudely racial in their rationales.)

The American philosopher, essayist, and poet, Ralph Waldo Emerson (1803-1882), said in relation to immigrants, "the capital advantage of our Republic [was] that by the organic hospitality of its institutions it is drawing the health and strength of all nations into its territory and promises by perpetual intermixture to yield the most vigorous qualities and accomplishments of all."

In "The Fortunes of the Republic" (1878), Emerson said that the true mark of the American Republic that drew immigrants to its shores were,

> "Opportunity of civil rights, of education, of personal power, and not less of wealth; doors wide open ... invitation to every nation, to every race and skin ... hospitality of fair fields and equal laws for all. Let them compete, and success to the strongest, the wisest, and the best. The land is wide enough, the soil has bread for all ... It is the country of the Future ... It is a country of beginnings, of projects, of designs, of expectations ... America is another word for opportunity."

My grandparents were among those who made their way as very small children with their families to the United States from Europe in the early years of the 20th century before the start of the First World War. On my father's side, my grandparents were German and Irish. On my mother's side they were Russian and Lithuanian Jews escaping religious and cultural persecution and anti-Semitic violence in Imperial Russia.

They did not find a perfect paradise or immediate acceptance in the United States, in spite of Emerson's encouraging words. Native-born Americans whose ancestors had arrived in the United States much earlier often looked down upon the Irish, for instance. The Irish were often considered to be drunkards, ignorant louts good only for the most undesirable jobs, and often considered a dangerous alien element by the larger American Protestant majority. The Irish immigrants were predominantly Catholic, and were viewed by many of those Protestants as "Pope-worshipers," who followed the dictates of their parish priests and could never be "real" Americans.

During a good part of the 19th century, German immigrants were often times looked at with suspicion, also. Oh, yes, the Germans had a reputation for hard work and diligence. But they would form their own new communities almost completely of fellow Germans; they supposedly resisted learning English, published German-language newspapers that circulated in their neighborhoods, and dreamed of remaining "Germans" within the United States. How could they ever become "real" Americans? The same anti-immigrant attitudes were experienced, often times, by those who arrived in America from, say, Poland or Italy, as well.

Anti-Semitism in America

Some Americans treated Jews, like my grandparents from Russia, as the "Jesus-killers," who also would kidnap Christian children to use their blood to make Matzo bread, and who, besides, were considered to be all a bunch of subversive communists. Discrimination abounded. My mother's father had hoped to become a medical doctor, and in spite of very good grades, had the door to admission into medical school shut in his face; at that time there were informal and unwritten quotas on how many Jews would be admitted into medical schools and the medical profession in the United States.

Instead, he followed his second best alternative for a professional career: he applied to and graduated from pharmacy school, received his pharmacist's degree, and opened his own drug store in New York City in the mid-1920s. Unfortunately, his business went bust during the Great Depression in the early 1930s, and my grandmother had to find other ways to earn a living to support her family after my grandfather suffered a debilitating stoke that left him half paralyzed for the remaining twenty years of his life. My mother told me that when she was looking for her first job after graduating from high school in the late 1930s, it was still possible to find want ads in New York City newspapers that said, "Jews need not apply."

The way to success for these waves of immigrants was hard work, determination and not allowing the ethnic or religious stupidities of others to prevent them from going as far as they could, and hopefully making the start that would at least lead to a better life for your children.

The path to such success was education. When I was a small boy, my Jewish grandmother on my mother's side drilled into me: "Get an education. Become a professional man. Then you have a skill and maybe you're too valuable for the Gentiles to kill."

My grandmother was not a backward or illiterate woman. As a young girl she had studied for the opera (she even auditioned before Florenz Ziegfeld for a role in the "Ziegfeld Follies"), loved classical music, memorized many of the famous and classic poets and was widely read in literature.

But the memories of the Cossacks coming into her village in the Ukraine, and burning homes and killing people merely because they were Jews had left its mark. You needed to take your own life into your own hands and make a secure place in a freer country than the one she had left as that small child.

And she constantly repeated one phrase to me: "The world does not owe you a living." And this from a woman who voted socialist or liberal Democrat, and cried when FDR died! The spirit of American individualism had become an inseparable part of even my "socialist"-leaning grandmother.

Why am I telling these stories? To prove that America has never been a perfect society? That hypocrisy and discrimination towards different types of minority groups from many different races, religions, and ethnicities have suffered hard times in the United States? And that forms of it continue up to today, only now sometimes against different minority groups than in the past? Or that America has not always lived up to the promises of its own stated principles of political, social, and economic individualism?

All that is not a secret either to the people who experienced it in the past or those who may still sense it today. So what made and still makes America different? Very few people permanently leave America to find better lives in other places, though admittedly a small handful do. For these last 250 years, the massive migration flows have all been the other way: from the rest of the world to the United States.

American Freedom as the Magnet Drawing Immigrants

President Donald Trump wants to build a Wall along the southern border of the United States. Many of us think this is an undesirable and dangerous thing to do. But what is the rationale for wanting it? To keep people from trying to come into the United States; to keep people out of the country. Compare that with the Berlin Wall that the Soviet Union built in August of 1961 physically splitting the city of Berlin in half until that Wall came down in November 1989. What was its purpose? The Soviet Union and its East German puppet rulers made that very plain: it was to keep people in, to prevent East Germans and East Berliners from escaping to West Berlin and West Germany.

So why have people come to America and almost always stayed? Put simply, individual freedom. We say and refer to this so much and so often that it has almost become an empty phrase, like when you repeat the same word quickly over and over and over again in your head or from your mouth until it seems to have lost its meaning in your mind and is just some sound.

But it is, nonetheless, true that it is freedom that has drawn people to America. People usually stay in the region or country where they have been born for a variety of reasons: its where they grew up with family and friends, and it represents "home" in all its various aspects; it's the language and culture that they feel part of and with which they feel comfortable; it may be the physical environment that they have come to love and care about. It is not easy for many people to give these things up, to uproot themselves by moving to a new land that is "foreign" to them in language, culture, customs, attitudes, and institutions. To make such a move is very much a conscious and deliberate choice.

So why have so many come? The reason is that in America, far more than in most other lands in the past and in many cases even now, the political is separated from the economic, the government from the marketplace. It is not that government has not or does not interfere into economic activities, but that throughout most of American history the pattern of political intervention, regulation, control and restriction was noticeably less than that practiced in other countries around the world.

The Liberal Principle of a Free Society

What guided America was a set of classical liberal principles. Or as the German free market economist, Wilhelm Röpke, expressed it in a slightly different context in his book, *International Order and Economic Integration* (1959):

> It is the liberal principle that economic affairs should be free from political direction, the principle of a thorough separation between the spheres of the government and the economy, between sovereignty and the apparatus which provides economic goods, between the Imperium and the Dominium, between the political power and the economic power ...

> [To a significant extent in the 19th century] the economic process was thereby removed from the sphere of officialdom, of public and penal law, in short from the sphere of the "state" to that of the "market," of private law, of property, in short to the sphere of "society," and this did away with the greater part of the causes of conflict [between governments, and among people in society].

This absence of government interference from much of economic and social life stood out as a unique quality to the American experience. It was noticed and commented upon by almost all of the visitors who came to the United States in the early and middle decades of the 19th century, and who then wrote accounts of their journeys upon returning to their home countries in Europe. They highlighted the reality of free men, making and finding their own way, through the voluntary associations of commerce and markets,

charitable and community affairs, with little government involvement and interference.

Private Bigotry in the North, Political Slavery in the South

At the same time, they did not turn a blind eye to the bigotry, bias,
and some time individual or mob acts of violence they observed
against some migrant groups trying to make their new lives in
America. They described them and condemned such conduct as
morally repugnant in themselves and as an insult to the ideals upon
which the United States was founded, and which hypocritically
those same Americans glorified in their rhetoric.

But except in the South before the Civil War, there were far
fewer instances of state-sponsored, state-endorsed or state-enforced
discrimination and persecution of ethnic, racial or religious groups.
There had been in earlier colonial times, but by the mid-decades of
the 19th century, neither the federal government nor few state governments gave their legal sanction to most such actions (though there
were such instances as the infamous Fugitive Slave Act of 1850, or
Illinois's infamous notorious legislation banning free blacks from
entering or living in the state in the decade before the Civil War).

Though women did not possess the voting franchise, the classical
liberal and feminist British author, Harriet Martineau, in her *Society
in America* (1837), based on a two-year visit to the United States,
pointed out that in spite of the social prejudices among men
concerning the role of women in the greater society, women in
America had wide latitude to own and inherit property, manage
and direct commercial enterprises and farm businesses, and take
leadership roles in important issues of that time, especially, though
not only, in the anti-slavery abolitionist movement in the North.

Only in the old South did the problem of a pervasively politicized marketplace exist because of the "peculiar institution" of slavery that separated free and slave-owning whites from black Africans held in perpetual bondage and compulsory servitude. It is notable that as those waves of immigrants poured into America in those decades before or even after the Civil War, few chose to make their new homes and lives in the Southern states. They looked to the Northern and Western free states and territories for their new futures.

Private Prejudice Could Not Prevent Immigrant Opportunity

Why? Because in the North and West, the political was far more greatly separated from the economic, the governmental from the marketplace, so private prejudices and bigoted behavior could not persistently stand in the way of those waves of immigrants. Regardless of their linguistic, religious, and national backgrounds, they could not be permanently hindered from making their way and rising to stations in life far above anything possible if they had remained in their respective countries of origin.

You settled the land and built your farm. You founded a town or opened a business in an existing one, and no one legally could stop you or regulate you out of existence. Some private persons might shun you because of, say, the Christian denomination you declared as your faith, or chose not to trade with you because of your national background. But no one could formally use the power of the state to prevent others not sharing those prejudices from doing business with you or participating in various social and charitable associations with you reflecting common interests and community concerns.

And, besides, many if not most native-born Americans, in spite of weak moments of biases, tended to practice what they preached:

America was a land of freedom and opportunity, where your past in the old country was behind you, and all that mattered was who you were as an individual in terms of your industry, honestly, and character as a person wanting to be a fellow citizen in liberty.

Even if you faced those problems of private prejudice and bigotry, it was worth putting up with it because you were confident and already the young history of America had shown that your children and grandchildren would be fully accepted as and in themselves be "Americans" with all those prejudices behind them, from which they would never have been able to escape in the country from which the immigrant had come.

This is for the most part still true today, in spite of a far more politicized marketplace of government regulation, restriction, and redistribution. It is amazing and amusing how patriotic many immigrants are if you talk with them, compared to native-born Americans. They are thankful and happy to have had their chance to escape from poverty, tyranny, war, and political plunder to now be in a country of general peace, prosperity, and opportunity.

They often work long hours at jobs than many native-born Americans do not want to do, and for pay that those other Americans won't accept. They build our homes, they take care of our gardens, their clean up our offices after hours and in the middle of the night, they watch our children while we are at work, and they labor as owners or employees in many everyday small shops and stores that service our consumer wants.

If we could go back in a time machine fifty years or a hundred years, the same kinds of work had to be done in the various corners of the marketplace, only we'd see different faces from different parts of the world, speaking different languages, and practicing some other faiths. Where are those who did these jobs in those earlier times? They and certainly their children and grandchildren moved up the socio-economic ladder to other professions, occupations and businesses, just like earlier generations of immigrants had done before them. They joined the American melting pot, as simply "Americans."

The danger in American society today is not the arrival of new waves of immigrants from various other parts of the world compared to the past. There are plenty of jobs to fill from engineers to janitors now and in the future. The melting pot has plenty of room for adding new human ingredients to the mix. And there is plenty of space for them to live and work; America is a big country.

The danger comes from the ideological turn away in America from a free marketplace to a mindset wanting more political planning of society based on an identity politics of race and gender, or a presumed social class, and a dislike and disregard for the ideas and ideals of individual liberty, free enterprise, and voluntary association for human dignity, material betterment, and social harmony and peace.

If these collectivist ideas do triumph over the individualist tradition upon which America was founded and flourished, then a day may come when migration flows will move in the other direction away from the United States because the hope, dream, and however imperfect reality of America as the great experiment in liberty will have been turned away from and finally lost. The story of America will have reached its end, and everyone in the world will be the worse for it.

CHAPTER 4

FREE MARKET LIBERALISM AND THE DIGNITY OF LABOR

The free market liberal economic system has transformed the material world in amazing and wondrous ways over the last two hundred years. Poverty, once the natural condition of virtually all of humanity, is being lifted from people's shoulders, not only in the Western world but also increasingly everywhere around the globe. But the complaints and criticisms against free market liberalism continue, among them the idea that "labor" is not treated with dignity, fairness and respect in the capitalist economy. Nothing could be further from the truth.

As we saw in an earlier chapter, in 1820, the total world population numbered around one billion people. Out of that one billion, demographers and economic historians have estimated that about 95 per cent of humanity lived in poverty, with 85 percent of them living in "abject" poverty. Only a small fraction of the human race had any form of material comfort, though we need to keep in mind that what was considered a comfortable existence in 1820 would be viewed as material wretchedness by most in the 21st century.

In 2018, we pointed out, the world population had increased to over 7.7 billion people. In 2015, the World Bank calculated that less than 10 percent of those human beings living on the planet live in serious poverty anymore. In two hundred years, the population has grown by more than 6.5 billion people, while poverty has sensationally fallen to less than 10 percent of that much larger total. If this trend continues, it is not unreasonable to anticipate that before the end of the 21st century poverty, as humankind has known it for all of its time on Earth will be an historical thing of the past.

All may not have the same standard of ease and quality of living in, say, 2075 or 2090. But the differences will likely be reduced to degrees of comfortable and material enjoyment of life, not whether some have it, while others do not. This should be praised to high heaven as one of the great accomplishments in human history.

The Disrespect and Indignity of Labor in the Ancient World

Instead, the majority of intellectuals and academics and political pundits condemn and reject the economic system that has been and is making this improvement in the human condition possible. Free market liberalism, they declare, is based on greed, crass materialism, as well as exploitation or unjust treatment of the "common person" and those in "minority" statuses in the society.

Why did it take so long for humanity to escape from poverty after 200,000 years of human-like creatures being around on this planet? It is really only over the last 200 to 300 years out of that 200,000 years that the mass of mankind has come to no longer wonder whether they shall starve tomorrow or next week or next growing season.

For all those thousands of years people lived in tribes (roving or finally settled down), under kings and conquerors, tyrants and terror, and cruelty and callousness concerning human life. Slavery was the dominant social institution of human association. Those not killed in wars were captured and held in bondage to do the work that the victor could not do or did not want to do.

Everyday labor had neither dignity nor respect. It was beneath the slave master and the free members of such a society. For the ancient Greeks, the slaves were there to do what was needed and necessary so the free citizen of, say, the Athenian city-state could devote himself to the common affairs of the community and have the leisure to pursue the higher callings of philosophy, art, literature, and family life.

To work with your hands, to devote one's time to the production of material wealth for the base needs of human existence were contemptuous ways of spending one's existence. Thus, slaves who were directed to such activities were concerned with the "lower aspects" of life. As the French social philosopher and liberal economist, Louis Rougier (1889-1982), expressed it in, *The Genius of the West* (1971):

> The slave was not considered a human being; he had no legal existence. He could be sold, bequeathed, rented out, or given away. In the hands of his master he was a thing, a 'living tool,' as Aristotle said. His fate depended on the discretion of the owner ... Manual work, because it was performed by slaves, discredited craftsmanship and the mechanical arts. The attention of citizens and scholars was turned away from anything involving the work of the hands ... Manual labor, regarded as destructive of the beauty of the body, came also to be regarded as destructive of the human mind and soul.

Some were Masters and Many were Servants Before Capitalism

As many historians have pointed out, the rise of Christianity began to change these beliefs and attitudes about human labor and work. For his sins, Adam was cast out of the Garden of Eden, and he now had to work with the sweat of his brow to live, and through his work redeem himself in the eyes of God. Work, therefore, when devoted to the glory of God and His purposes for man, had dignity and was deserving of respect.

But this philosophical turn concerning man and labor did not and could not significantly affect societies based on politically sanctioned and enforced hierarchy and status, as existed in the Middle Ages and into the more modern age. It required the emergence of market-based human relationships and the accompanying change in attitudes toward work, innovation, and individual independence, which really only started to take root in the 1500s and 1600s and after, as economic historians like Deirdre McCloskey have emphasized in her works, *The Bourgeois Virtues* (2006) and *Bourgeois Dignity* (2010).

Before the last few centuries, some were masters and many were servants; the few ruled and the multitude obeyed; some considered themselves better than the large number of the rest, while those in the "many" took it for granted that there were those who politically and socially were better than them and to whom they had to defer in almost all things.

The peasant worked on the nobleman's land, the craftsman earning his living by serving the needs of the lord of the manor, and the peddler passed through the nobleman's domain, and had to plead and pay for the privilege of passing through his properties so he could make his meager living with his limited items for trade. None of them received or expected dignity, respect, or any independently recognized "rights" from those who ruled over them. Theirs was a "privilege" to serve those above them in the institutional structure of that social order.

Emerging Markets Gave Opportunity and Independence

The slow rise of liberal capitalism began to change all this. Emerging market relationships widened the horizons for the peasant, the crafts-man and the traveling merchant to have customers for their wares outside of the confines of the nobleman's estate. Loss of the lord of the manor's favor and good graces no longer meant starvation or hardship and loss of earning a living or physical punishment.

Markets began to provide independence and greater autonomy for the ordinary person outside of the political realm. Markets meant freedom to live and choose and associate outside of the dominating eyes of the politically privileged and powerful. Markets came to represent liberty. This did not happen all at once or to the same degree everywhere in Europe. But the ideas and institutional oppor-tunities of it slowly influenced men's minds and their conceptions of themselves, their relationships with others in society, and the purpose of the political order.

In the classical liberal political and economic heritage, as captured in John Locke's philosophy of individual rights and the American Declaration of Independence, the human being is free and self-re-sponsible. He belongs to and is owned by himself. There are no permanent and ruling masters with the authority and legitimized power to make others do (or not do) what they do not wish.

Market Liberalism Brings Respect Through Free Exchange

This means that a cornerstone of the liberal market order is freedom of association and exchange. No one may be forced to participate in any activity or transact with others in any trade without their voluntary consent and mutual agreement. Such is part of the meaning in Adam Smith's famous words in *The Wealth of Nations*, "It is not from the benevolence of the butcher, or the brewer, or the baker, that we expect our dinner, but from their regard to their own interest. We address ourselves, not to their humanity, but to their self-love, and never talk to them of our own necessities but to their advantages"?

The implication is that every person must approach his fellow human beings and make an appeal for their assistance in some way that would be beneficial to them. But he may not threaten physical harm, he may not use force, and he may not practice fraud or deception to gain the other's consent and participation. A person can reason and try to persuade, or offer something in return that would be sufficiently attractive that the other individual shall be willing to do what is asked of him. But violence is banished from the human condition to the greatest degree possible for a free society to still effectively function.

There are few of us who enjoy being ridiculed, treated with contempt and disregard or bullied and intimidated. Such behavior directed toward us may result in our turning down what otherwise might have seemed an attractive offer, because the conduct and behavior of the other person is found to be too distasteful and offensive to be put up with and tolerated. Even when circumstances may result in our putting up with a lot that we find demeaning or rude and impolite, even a "desperate man" will finally have a breaking point beyond which he will not take it any more, and he will walk away.

But in a developed and complex market economy, many alternatives exist and potentially can be available to people, both in our roles as consumers and producers. An impolite or discourteous sales person soon finds that existing and potential customers turn away to buy what they are looking for from someone else, rather than put up with disrespectful conduct on the part of those who are trying to get their business.

While each of us, no doubt, have had frustrating experiences with sellers in the marketplace; such instances usually stand out in our minds precisely due to the fact that they are the exceptions to the rule. We expect and almost always experience the opposite: courtesy, politeness, deference, helpfulness and respectfulness in the conduct and demeanor of those from whom we buy things in the market.

People in their own self-interest find it advantageous to practice and develop respectful good manners in their interactions with others in the marketplace. Success and profitability may depend on it. The nature of markets serves to cultivate "good manners" and "social etiquette" in all who enter the arena of exchange. Thus, free markets foster the emergence and evolution of civil society and its unwritten codes of conduct that are part of the hallmark of a refined and polite civilization.

This was partly articulated by Adam Smith in his *Lectures on Jurisprudence* (1766), in which he highlighted the positive influences that commerce played in developing the traits of honestly, politeness, and deference to those with whom one interacts in trade:

> Whenever commerce is introduced into any country, probity and punctuality always accompany it ... It is far more reducible to self-interest, that general principle which regulates the

actions of every man, and which leads men to act in a certain manner from views of advantage, and is as deeply implanted in an Englishman as a Dutchman.

A dealer is afraid of losing his character, and is scrupulous in observing every engagement. When a person makes perhaps 20 contracts in a day, he cannot gain so much by endeavoring to impose on his neighbors, as the very appearance of a cheat would make him lose.

When people seldom deal with one another, we find that they are somewhat disposed to cheat, because they can gain more by a smart trick than they can lose by the injury that it does to their character ... Wherever dealing are frequent, a man does not expect to gain so much by any one contract as by probity and punctuality in the whole, and a prudent dealer, who is sensible of his real interest, would rather choose to lose what he has a right to than give any ground for suspicion ...When the greater part of people are merchants they always bring probity and punctuality into fashion, and these therefore are the principle virtues of a commercial nation.

Individual Liberty and the Dignity of Labor

Another aspect of the market system of division of labor in the liberal society is that it generates an increasing awareness and recognition of the dignity of all honest and hard working labor, regardless of the task being performed. Why? Because every niche in the market system of specialization represents a role, task or activity that is needed and considered worth performing, otherwise it would not be done and paid for.

It became a bit of a joke and cliché at one point when garbage collectors became "sanitation engineers," or doormen became the "entry way professionals," or dogcatchers became the "animal retrieval specialists." But it highlighted something important, and that was that everyone in the marketplace does something that is important to someone, and if it were not done would leave some minor or major part of everyday life less comfortable and more inconvenient.

Thus, what a person does for a living should not be looked down upon or demeaned, because if the person hired to provide that service or supply that good did not, you'd have to perform the task yourself or do without it. There is dignity in every activity in the division of labor, if performed well and with equal respect for the person having it done. In American colloquial expression, it has long been captured in the phrase, "What makes him think that he is any better than the rest of us?" In the American political and economic tradition, certainly as understood in the heyday of classical liberal cultural attitudes and beliefs, no man has rights before the law any different than everyone else.

He may put on "airs" and presume to look down upon others, but has he demonstrated any special gift or ability that has been recognized by others in society as reflected in the higher income he has earned for work done or for social recognition received for community service performed? And even if so, before God and the law, he remains a man no different from the other members of society. In a country like America, a land of immigrants with usually humble beginnings for either yourself or your parents, the phrase was, "Don't forget where you're from," no matter how high you or your family may have socially climbed from more modest circumstances.

Competition Assures Workers Receive the Full Value of Their Hire

Equally, the worker whose labor is for hire in a developed market economy almost always finds him or herself with more than one option for employment. The competition among employers means that workers must be wooed with wages equal to or greater than what is the next closest attractive alternative, including fringe benefits, and other related perks that may come to be seen as part of many hiring packages.

There are always two sides to competitive markets, the demand and the supply side. It is certainly true that anyone selling their labor services is competing against those looking for similar employment. But this is matched by the competition from the private enterprisers needing workers to assist in the production and manufacturing of what they ultimately wish to offer to the consumers in society.

The upshot is that the long-run tendency on a free, open and competitive market is for all those looking for employment to be offered and receive what the hiring employers best estimate the value of the (marginal) contributions those workers can bring to the production processes of the market.

Finally, we must always keep in mind that in all of this we are talking about human beings, a creature that is less than a perfect life form! When there is a low or minimal cost to being rude, crude and offensive to others in your dealings with them, some of us may be more prone in exercising such behavior with less of a market check on their conduct.

Few of us have fond and happy memories of dealing with employees at government offices such as the department of motor vehicles, where you often wait on long lines to renew your driver's license or pay for the sticker attached to your license plate. It's the only game in town – the government has a monopoly on supplying and selling such things – so if you do not like the waiting or the demeanor of the State employees, well, there is not much you can really do. What you don't want to do is to get one of them mad at you, because they can, in principle, make your life a living hell.

The Respectful, Courteous and Fair Dealing of Market Liberalism

Politeness, courtesy, respectfulness and treating others with dignity grows out of an institutional setting in which failure to do so carries with it undesired costs and negative feedback. Free market liberalism fosters and cultivates just such institutional rules, both formal and unwritten.

By insisting that each and every individual has rights to their life, liberty, and honestly acquired property, they are declared to be free and independent human beings who may not be violated and abused through private or political use of force or its threat.

By requiring that all human association is to be voluntary, anyone desiring the assistance and participation of their fellow human beings in some undertaking must make it attractive and desirable for them to do so. And, at the end of the day, cultivating such cooperative collaboration in the arena of free exchange means treating others in those deferential and respectful ways, so as to not drive them into different relationships with others who are practicing better and more sincere good behavior, besides the purely monetary terms being offered.

Everyone performs tasks useful and valuable to others to one degree or another in the interdependent social system of division of labor, otherwise there would be no value placed upon it and thus making it someone's worthwhile to see that it is taken care of. Thus, no job in the market economy does not have its worth and dignity in its performance, especially when done with professionalism and pride in the work done, however modest and mundane the task.

Finally, competition fosters a tendency to see that everyone hired receives the market's best estimate of the value of what he contributes to the production processes in society. It is not from the benevolence of the employer, per se, but from the inevitable rivalry of competing employers in needing different types of human hands to perform the tasks to be done to bring a potentially profitable product to market.

This is why free market liberalism has brought about not only growing prosperity for more of humanity, but has cultivated a polite and more respectful society to accompany the material betterment of the human condition.

CHAPTER 5

LIBERALISM, RIGHTLY AND WRONGLY UNDERSTOOD

Over time words sometimes change their meanings or connotations. Think of the words "naughty" and "nice." Apparently, naughty originally meant to have or be nothing (naught or zero), but then it took on the extra sense of something being worth nothing; until finally a person who was considered worth nothing then became a bad or immoral individual, or at least someone who is mischievous, such as, what a "naughty boy," with an accompanying wink.

On the other hand, "nice," it seems, early on meant someone who was ignorant, but then took on the added meanings of being a silly or foolish person. By the 1700s, it had its more current meanings of an agreeable or pleasant person. Though it can be used sarcastically, for instance, with the phrase, oh, yah, that's "real nice"; meaning something said or done that is rude, disrespectful or nasty towards another.

The same thing has happened with the word, liberalism. Friends and foes have changed its meaning several times over the last couple of centuries, and in the eyes of some it has been transformed beyond any recognition with its original content or connotation.

American Liberalism as Meaning Big Government

Since at least the 1930s, during Franklin D. Roosevelt's New Deal, liberalism in America has carried the meaning and content of public policy perspectives that insist that government should and must take on a wide and extensive paternalist role in society. Such political paternalism is presumed to encompass the need for government regulation of business and industry in a wide variety of forms. Indeed, its reached the point where there is little that goes on in the production, the buying and selling, and the consumption of virtually every good and service offered on the market that does not entail the oversight, approval, dictate, prohibition and control of some branch and level of government in modern society.

Matching this has emerged a vast network of redistributive programs and activities through which government transfers income and wealth from one segment of the society to another. Taxes are garnered from certain segments of the society and redirected by government to other segments through either cash or in-kind benefits.

But as some critics of this modern liberalism have pointed out, it is not so much a taxing of income and wealth from Peter to give to Paul; instead, it is transfer of authority and decision-making from private individuals in the society about how best to spend their own honestly earned money to those in political power to then decide how the wealth that others have produced is to be redirected for other purposes and peoples that those in government consider to be more deserving.

Conservative Criticisms of Liberalism

For those labeled as conservatives in the United States, modern American liberalism connotes disrespect for traditional beliefs and values, including certain religious faiths; it carries the notion of licentiousness and luridness of "anything goes" that threatens to undermine the cultural foundations of the country; and it entails a dangerous Big Government intruding everywhere and micro-managing everything.

Conservatives do not, necessarily, disapprove of government having a long arm that involves a certain degree of "bigness." They would just like a government of a different size and reach to restrict and impose other and different types of restraints and commands than America's "leftie liberals" want to see in place. They do not completely disapprove of government regulations or prohibitions in the marketplace when it concerns those forms of personal activities and social interactions of which they disapprove.

Progressivism's Opposition to "Neo-Liberalism"

Liberalism has a different connotation for those farther along what is called the political or ideological left in the United States. In this permutation, liberalism is relabeled "neo-liberalism," the supposed dominant form of liberalism around the world today. It is asserted that neo-liberalism ideologically rationalizes and politically runs the world for an elite of global capitalists wishing to pursue international profits at the expense of the needs and wants of the local peoples living in different countries on the planet.

American progressives and democratic socialists increasingly reject any and all forms of liberalism, insisting that both modern neo-liberals and conservatives in the United States have been apologists for and facilitators of racism, sexism, oppression of social and ethnic minorities, and supporters of income inequality that benefits a wealthy few at the expense of far too many in society. They desire to see more of a consciously planned society with less tolerance or legal protections for words and actions that they consider hurtful and harmful to the establishment of a more socially just humankind.

What is clear is that for both conservatives and "progressive" democratic socialists, liberalism, in many ways, epitomizes what they both commonly dislike and of which they strongly disapprove. Liberalism, therefore, seems to be the common enemy of both many conservatives and a growing number of progressives and democratic socialists, though how they see the nature of the liberalism that each criticizes has noticeable points of difference.

An interesting ingredient in these interpretations of "liberalism" by conservatives, on the one side, and progressives and self-proclaimed socialists, on the other, is that what they label as or assert to liberalism has little to do with its original meaning and the policy views of many of its early and later adherents. Just like the words naughty and nice, the meaning of liberalism has changed significantly from where it began, with completely different connotations.

Liberalism as a Defense of Individual Liberty Against Tyranny

Through most of the 19th century, liberalism was strongly identified with the belief in and the defense of individual liberty in various spheres of life. Generally, a "liberal" was one who was open-minded, tolerant, and respectful for different ideas, faiths, and values that may be held by others in society. Such openness, tolerance and respect did not necessarily mean an agreement with or sympathy for a particular idea, faith or value on the part of such a liberal person; but it did mean that others holding them should not be legally persecuted, or politically oppressed and discriminated against for holding them.

This liberal attitude and outlook on the ideas, faiths and values of others, perhaps, was most persuasively defended in the 19th century by John Stuart Mill (1806-1873) in his famous essay "On Liberty" (1859). Mill reminded his readers that no one of us can claim intellectual infallibility, and that it is only through discourse, discussion and debate that it may be found out if the truth of some matter is on one side or the other, or somewhere in between. The eccentric, strange, or socially unacceptable idea, attitude or belief of the past has sometimes become the accepted ones of the present. And the same applies between the customs, traditions, values and ideas of the present and new ones that may become the common-place of tomorrow.

This led Mill to warn, therefore, of the danger of the tyrannies of both minorities and majorities. In the past, he said, tyrannies of the minority often took the form of kings, princes and their aristo-cratic circles that imposed their political rule as well as their social, religious, and other ideas on a majority of others over whom they had governmental control or ecclesiastical authority.

The tyranny of majorities, Mill said, could be both cultural and political. Mill was a strong defender of those some might consider to be the eccentric and the nonconformist; thus, he warned against the oppression of custom and tradition. The imagery may be of the small, closely knit village or town in which he who does not follow the widely accepted social customs and traditions is ridiculed, shunned, or otherwise psychologically tormented and abused by his neighbors due to his going and living his own way.

The other tyranny of the majority, Mill warned, was from the new political ideal and institution of democracy. If before, it was the few ruling and controlling the many through absolutist monarchy, in the new age of democratically elected government, now what threatened was a political majority using its power through those they elected to impose their coercing will on social, economic, and cultural minorities within the nation.

Indeed, as one indication of this concern, in his later, *Considerations on Representative Government* (1861), Mill suggested that all those who receive employment or redistributions from the government should be denied the right to vote for the time they are in that status; otherwise, the pickpocket is getting to vote on how much will be taken from his victim's wallet. Surely, Mill said, this is a serious conflict of interest!

Eliminating denials of civil liberties and restrictions on equal treatment before the law were, therefore, leading rallying cries of 19th century liberals, and was identified with the reforming impulse of liberalism as a political movement. While those ruled by a government should have a much wider voting participation in the process of electing those who hold political office, liberals were also conscious of the dangers from democracy unrestrained. The American Bill of Rights reflected this concern by placing certain freedoms of the individual outside of and protected from even the largest of majorities that might wish to compel, plunder, and persecute a person due to his beliefs and ideas, his peaceful actions in pursuit of his own purposes, his honestly earned financial status, or his voluntary associations with others in the society.

Private Property as the Base of Freedom and Prosperity

Matching these personal and political liberties, 19th century liberalism championed economic liberty as well. And, indeed, the liberals of that time considered it foundational to and inseparable from any defense and protection of these other types of human liberty. The corner stone to the recognition and securing of economic liberty was the right to private property and wide latitude of its peaceful and voluntary use.

Property also serves as the stimulus in industry and innovation, and creates a setting of potential mutual gains from trade where each knows that what he owns is his and may only be separated from him through a voluntary transaction in which he finds something more desirable than what he trades away to get it. The British liberal and political economist, John R. McCulloch (1789-1864) explained this most clearly and concisely in his *Principles of Political Economy* (1825, 6th ed., 1864):

> Let us not, therefore, deceive ourselves by supposing that it is possible for any people to emerge from barbarism, or to become wealthy, prosperous, and civilized without the security of property ... The protection afforded to property by all civilized societies, though it has not made all men rich, has done more to increase their wealth than all their other institutions put together ...

> The establishment of a right to property enables exertion, invention, and enterprise, forethought and economy to reap their due reward. But it does this without inflicting the smallest imaginable injury upon anything else ...

Its [property's] effects are altogether beneficial. It is a rampart raised by society against its common enemies – against rapine, and violence, plunder and oppression. Without its protection, the rich would become poor, and the poor would be totally unable to become rich – all would sink to the same bottomless abyss of barbarism and poverty.

Natural Liberty and Market Order Without Central Planning

The most important insight and analysis from the liberal economists of that time was and, in my view, remains that there exists the potential for social order and betterment without planned political and economic design. Liberal economists such as Adam Smith called it a "system of natural liberty," under which government would be limited to the provision of police, courts of law, national defense, and a small number of what today is usually called public goods.

But for the rest, each individual would be free and at liberty to follow any profession, undertake any production, and peacefully compete with any rivals for the voluntary and mutually agreed upon business of others in the marketplace as the means of earning his living.

For most of human history, it was taken for granted that a material and social gain for one human being often times resulted in the worsening of another's personal wellbeing. Conquest, plunder and murder were primary means by which some in the world obtained and increased what they had through the use of violence and coercion. Human interactions and institutionalized associations were very frequently zero or even negative sum gains.

The great discovery of the second half of the 18th century, especially in the writings of the Scottish Moral Philosophers and the French Physiocrats, was that when each individual was left to follow their own personal judgments about how to best apply their own efforts and industry to better their own life, the cumulative outcome was far superior to the vain attempts of those in governmental positions to determine and direct the economic affairs of humanity.

Non-Interference Removes Privileges and Frees Enterprise

This was summarized by another British liberal economist of the early 19th century, Nassau W. Senior (1790-1864):

> For centuries, the government has labored to fetter and misdirect the industry of people. Instead of confining itself to its true task of defending its subjects from foreign and domestic violence and fraud, it has taken on itself the task of rendering them, or of rendering certain classes of them, rich. It has dictated to them what they shall produce, and to whom they shall sell, and what they shall purchase, and to what markets they shall resort.

> It has considered the whole body of consumers as a prey to be sacrificed to any class, or to any section of a class, that choose to ask for a monopoly. And when one class has complained of the privileges granted to another, it has bribed it into acquiescence by allowing it to inflict a further injustice on the public ...

> The advocate of freedom dwells on the benefit of making full use of our own peculiar advantages of situation, wealth, skill, and availing ourselves to the utmost of those possessed by our neighbors ... He observes, in the words of Adam Smith,

that it is the maxim of every prudent master of a family, never to make at home, what it will cost him more to make than to buy. The tailor does not make his own shoes, but buys them of the shoemaker. The shoemaker does not make his own cloths, but buys them of the tailor. The farmer attempts to make neither the one nor the other, but employs their whole industry in a way in which they have some advantage over their neighbors, and to purchase, with a part of its produce, whatever else they have occasion for.

The principle of free trade is non-interference: it is to suffer every man to employ his industry in the manner which he thinks more advantageous, without pretense on the part of the legislator to control or direct his operations ...

The liberals of that time did not consider that people never made mistakes or errors of judgment. This was as obvious to them as it surely is to us. But they did believe that each individual, all things considered and looking over the society as a whole, knows his own circumstances better than any other can, and most certainly better than some politician or bureaucrat situated far away with little or no knowledge of that particular person's actual existence and his surrounding opportunities.

Intervention Misdirects Production and Fosters Corruption

It was all too easy for those in political power to feign interest, concern, or knowledge of various people's conditions and concerns as rationales for the pursuit of their own personal purposes in government, and to serve various special interests that furthers their own political ambitions. It is through government intervention, the 19th century liberals argued, that political power is used to benefit some at the expense of others in society. As was explained by the French liberal economist, Jean-Baptiste Say (1767-1832), in his *Principles of Political Economy* (1821):

> Strictly speaking, there is no act of government but what has some influence on production ... When authority throws itself in the way of the natural course of things, and says, the product you are about to create, that which yields the greatest profit, and is consequently the most in request, is by no means the most suitable to your circumstances, you must undertake some other, it evidently directs a portion of the productive energies of the nation towards an object of less desire, at the expense of another more urgent desire ...

> If one individual, or one class, can call in the aid of authority to ward off the effects of competition, it acquires a privilege to the prejudice and at the cost of the whole community; it can then make sure of profits not altogether due to the productive services rendered, but composed in part of an actual tax upon consumers for its private profit; which tax it commonly shares with the authority that thus unjustly lends its support.

> The legislative body has great difficulty in resisting these importunate demands for this kind of privileges ... Moreover, arbitrary regulations are extremely flattering to the vanity of men in power, as giving them an air of wisdom and fore-sight, and confirming their authority, which seems to derive

additional importance from the frequency of its exercise.

It would be a gross exaggeration to suggest that all the liberals of that earlier era were strict and unreserved proponents of laissez-faire. But, in general, the presumption was that all forms of government regulations and interventions not concerned with the clear and present threat of violence or fraud among private parties were undesirable, and always carried the potential for numerous secondary negative effects. For instance, Jean-Baptiste Say, after discussing what he considered possible limited exceptions to totally free market liberalism, emphasized to his readers:

> I wish to empress upon my readers, that the mere interference [by government] is itself an evil, even where it is of use: first, because it harasses and distresses individuals; and, secondly, because it costs money, either to the nation, if it be defrayed by government, that is to say, upon the public purse, or to the consumer, if it be charged upon the specific article; in the latter case, the charge must of course enhance the price, thereby laying an additional tax upon the home consumer ...

Classical Liberalism's Successes and Social Ideal

This 19th century liberalism, or classical liberalism, as it has more widely come to be called, therefore, was grounded in the idea and ideal of the individual and his right to personal, economic and political liberty. The efforts made by the liberals of that earlier era were momentous in their impact, in that many of the freedoms that people have and continue to take for granted were the result of the liberal crusades of that time: ending slavery, widening civil liberties and impartial rule of law, increased political participation, freeing industry and trade from the heavy hand of government regulation and control, and attempting to reduce the frequency and destructiveness of war among nations.

One of the other leading British liberals of that earlier time, Thomas Babington Macaulay (1800-1859) summarized the core ideas and ideals of 19th century liberalism as reflected in the Great Britain in which he then lived:

> It is not by the intermeddling of ... the omniscient and omnipotent State, but by the prudence and energy of the people, that England has hitherto been carried forward in civilization; and it is to the same prudence and the same energy that we now look with comfort and good hope. Our rulers will best promote the improvement of the nation by strictly confining themselves to their own legitimate duties, by leaving capital to find its most lucrative course, commodities their fair price, industry and intelligence their natural reward, idleness and folly their natural punishment, by maintaining peace, by defending property, by diminishing the price of law, and by observing strict economy in every department of the state. Let the Government do this: the People will assuredly do the rest.

Classical Liberalism's Ideal of Free Minds and Open Debate

This earlier classical liberalism has nothing to do with the changed and distorted meanings assigned to "liberalism" by both many conservatives and progressive, democratic socialists. John Stuart Mill's defense of open debate and discourse on the customs, traditions and other values and ideas upon which a social order rests is not a call for their abolition or destruction.

As Mill insisted, they are likely to have a sounder hold over people's minds if they have been more consciously reflected upon and appreciated in terms of their origins and purposes for social stability and prosperity; if errors and weaknesses are found in them, then surely it is better to be aware of them than for society to find itself in some undesirable and possibly harmful institutional cul de sac.

Nor is the ideal of open and free deliberation a subterfuge or rationale to justify "hurtful" or "oppressing" ideas and institutions, as those on the political left increasingly insist. The opposite is closer to the truth. When ideas are suppressed, and when their expression or discussion are forbidden, they are more likely to fester in the darker corners of society. They remain unchallenged, unrefuted, and possibly perversely attractive as intellectually "forbidden fruit," as well as left lingering in the hearts of some people.

If racist ideas are indeed harmful, how do concerned citizens ever know what exactly they are, why and how they came about, and what are the better or best responses to demonstrate the logical and factual errors in their rationales and justifications, if they cannot be publicly, dispassionately, and opening understood, discussed and analyzed? Closed mouths and banned ideas can only lead to atrophied minds and arrested societies.

Free Market Liberalism as the Liberator of Humanity

Likewise, the liberal defense of private enterprise and free markets is the opposite of how their critics portray them. Changed meanings often can bring about blurred ideas. The 19th century liberals defended economic liberty precisely because they opposed favoritism, privilege, and plunder in society. That was the social order that preceded the victories of political and economic liberalism in the 1800s.

Selected groups and individuals in society received special statuses from the government that hindered innovative and cost-reducing competitive enterprises wishing nothing more than the opportunity to produce and market better and less expensive goods to a widening circle of the consuming public. Freedom of enterprise and free trade meant more, better and lower priced goods for the mass market of the "common man," the "working man" whose condition was improving through more employment positions due to the greater rivalry of employers looking for hands to hire, and the growing quantity and variety of goods placed within the reach of those increasing numbers of people employed by those private enterprises.

Free market liberalism was the great liberator of humanity from material poverty, social stagnation, and political oppression. The original liberals and their intellectual heirs today see nothing in what they advocate or want in what is often times nowadays referred to as "crony capitalism." It has been the abandonment over the last hundred years of that freer market liberalism that has returned government policy to a system of privilege and plunder that benefits special interest groups at the expense of market rivals and consumers.

One of the perversities in the changed meaning and understanding of political and economic liberalism is that it is now labeled and burdened with responsibility for the very type of government favoritism and corruption that it arose to oppose and repeal. In the eyes of too many, it is identified with the very interventionist and regulatory system that it fought against and partly succeeded in doing away with in the 19th century.

The ills in society will not be solved or cured by the politically compromised conservatism that still doubts and opposes a wide variety of civil liberties, but has now also has turned its back on its earlier defenses of free trade and free enterprise. And society's problems will most certainly not be overcome by the more radical turn by America's progressives and new democratic socialists who would straightjacket all of the country's economic activities under the type of tried and failed government central planning approaches that they hail as the policy path to a bright and beautiful future. If these socialists have their way America will have neither freedom nor prosperity.

What is needed, therefore, is a return to the original meanings of the clearly articulated principles of political, economic and social liberalism, properly understood. The classical liberalism of the 19th century needs to be the reborn, new liberalism of the 21st century, to once more offer an ideal of individual freedom, free enterprise, impartial rule of equality before the law, and limited constitutional government. These are the keys to freedom and prosperity.

CHAPTER 6

COMPETITION AND THE LIBERAL ECONOMY

Rivalrous competition is at the heart of the free market liberal system. It serves as the driving force for creative innovation, the mechanism by which market supplies and demands are brought into coordinated balance for multitudes of goods, and an institutional setting for individuals to freely find their own place to best earn a living in society.

Yet, listening to the critics of free markets, competition is made out to be a cruel and dehumanizing process that feeds unnecessary wants and desires, or has a tendency to evolve into anti-competitive market-based monopolies contrary to the "public interest." Competition fosters a "selfish" disregard for the "common good" and misdirects resources from their most important "socially valuable" uses.

Competition Through Political Means

As long as resources are scarce and social positions are too limited to satisfy everyone's desire to have a certain status in society, competition will exist. The crucial questions concern: how will it be decided what gets produced and for whom, and how shall social positions in society be determined and filled? For almost all of human history these questions were determined by conquest and coercion. Those with greater physical strength or manipulative guile used these superior abilities and skills to gain the goods they wanted and the status they desired over others.

In a competition between the physically "strong" and the "weak," it was often the case that "might made right." Pillage and plunder enabled some to seize the goods they wanted that others possessed and to then subjugate and enslave those they conquered to work for them and accept their conquerors as their legitimate masters.

Most, if not all, forms of competition were battles for political power and position. Closeness to the throne and having favor with the king or prince gave one control over land and people, and therefore possession of material wealth in the forms in which they existed in those earlier times. The mythologies of the aristocratic nobility – the lords of the manor –asserted that they were the repository of grace, charm and culture, the carriers of civilized manners and the benefactors of civilization. This hid from view that their appearance of leisure time for and attention to the "higher things" of life were only made possible – to the extent that any of them were actually concerned with anything other they their personal pleasures and pastimes –due to their success in having the legitimized authority to live off the productions of others.

Commerce and trade is as old as recorded history. Anyone who peruses, for instance, Marco Polo's (1254-1324) famous account of his journeys and experiences traveling to China from Europe and back in the late 1200s finds descriptions of merchants and traders, businessmen and manufactures, and exporters and importers everywhere that he went around the Mediterranean, the Middle East, Central Asia, and Eastern and Southern Asia. But all these market activities operated under various forms of government regulations, controls, restrictions and prohibitions, given the reach of and the methods of control by the political rulers of the time in different parts of the world.

Entry into professions, occupations and crafts, for example, were all controlled by trade guilds in the Europe of the Middle Ages. The guilds limited competitive entry into various lines of employments and they restricted the methods of production that sellers could use in manufacturing goods to those approved by the, respective, town and city guild associations. In the countryside, the peasants were tied to the land owned by the nobility, and bound within the tradition-based techniques of farming and craftsmanship to meet the needs of those living on the properties of the lords of the manor.

Market Competition Liberated People and Provided Opportunities

The slow liberation of men and production from these restraints and the opening of both labor and manufacturing to greater market-based competition freed a growing number of people from a life of oppression and wretched poverty. Competition meant that a man could leave behind the legal tethers that had tied him to the land and obligatory work for the aristocracy; an individual could now more freely find work more to his own liking where it might be offered in towns and cities far away from where he had been born, and earn a far greater income than he ever had in the rural areas, however modest those incomes may seem by today's standards.

Competition meant that a resourceful individual with a willingness to bear risk and self-employed responsibility could found his own business, make a product of his own choice, and market it to those with whom he increasingly freely negotiated and contracted. He could experiment with new manufacturing methods and techniques, he could hire whom he wanted on mutually agreed upon terms of work and wages, and he could retain the profits he may have earned to not only live better himself, but to plow a good part of those profits back into his business to expand production in new and better ways.

Production no longer was focused on meeting the wants and whims of the privileged few around the king and the landed aristocracy. Market-based competition now was directed to serving the growing wants of the wider and general population who were increasingly participating in the manufacturing processes of the emerging and intensifying industrial revolution. The "revolutionary" character of the new industrial era of the late 18th and then 19th centuries was due to the fact that men were freer in mind and body to try, to experiment, to do, and to voluntarily associate with others in ways radically different than had been the case for ages before.

Free Markets and Philosophy of Individual Rights

Liberal "capitalism," as this new economic arrangement of society came to be called, had as its hallmark the new philosophy of human liberty based on the revolutionary idea that individuals have inherent and inviolable rights to their respective life, liberty and honestly acquired property. Individuals own themselves; they are not and may not be the owned property of another. They have liberty to live for themselves guided by their own conception of the good, meaningful and valued life; they may not be coerced into the role of sacrificed servant to the wants and desires of others.

The ethical principle behind free market liberalism is the moral and legal prohibition on coercion in all of human relationships. If you want what others have, if you would like to have the material means to achieve the ends and goals that will offer you happiness (as you define it), if you desire the association and companionship of others to advance purposes that you consider worthwhile, your only means to them are mutual agreement and voluntary consent with your fellow human beings.

Free Markets as a System of Cooperative Competition

In Ludwig on Mises's (1881-1973) famous treatise on economics, *Human Action* (1966), he explains:

> Competing in cooperation and cooperating in competition all people are instrumental in bringing about the result, viz., the price structure of the market [for consumer goods and the factors of production], the allocation of the factors of production into the various lines of want-satisfaction [consumer demand], and the determination of the share of each individual [the relative incomes earned in the market].

If we step back and look at competition as a wider social process at work, Mises's words help to explain the logic and the humanity of the market economy. Peaceful and voluntary cooperation is the hallmark of the free market system. Sellers compete in offering their goods to the potentially buying public, and buyers' existing or possible demands attract sellers to produce and market what they decide to manufacture. All cooperate in this competitive process by following the "rules" of the market game that excludes violence and fraud. Everyone must attempt to get what they want by focusing their mental and physical efforts on devising ways to offer to others what they want and are willingly to take in agreed upon trade.

Each must apply his abilities, talents and skills to offer better products, new products, and less expensive products to their possible trading associates, since each knows that every one of those potential exchange partners is at liberty to accept the offer of some rival who is also keen on getting their business. The interaction of these competing buyers and sellers brings about the resulting structure of relative prices for all the goods and services offered on the market, and determines how much of each one is bought and sold in a way that tends to bring about a coordinated balance between what is demanded and what is supplied.

At the same time, virtually all that is bought and sold first must be produced. This means the existing resources in society must be directed and applied to produce those goods that all of us as demanders desire to purchase and use for various purposes. Those in the social system of division of labor who undertake the role and task of entrepreneur – the designer, coordinator, and director of the activities of a private enterprise – must marshal the land, labor and capital judged to be most economically effective and efficient in bringing a final, finished good to market.

These enterprising entrepreneurs must compete amongst each other for the hire of the requisite workers, resources and raw materials, and the capital goods (machinery, tools, and equipment), through the coordinated use of which over time the potentially consumer-demanded good might be placed on the market. Entrepreneurial competition determines the appraised estimate of what each of those various factors of production is judged to be worth in assisting in one line of production as opposed to some other.

In turn, the owners of those factors of production – the workers looking for employment, the owners of rentable or saleable land and resources, and lenders of savings who are looking for interested borrowers – offer their services or products to those competing entrepreneurs. The cooperative outcome, again, of this two-sided competition determines the allocation of those scarce means of production based upon the appraisements and judgments of their most highly valued use in producing alternative goods and services. This, also, determines the earned remuneration of each of those factors of production, including the wages of different types of labor, upon which each of those factor owners may, then, reenter the market as income-earning consumers to demand the very products that, combined and cumulatively, their productive activities have assisted in bringing to market.

Entrepreneurs as the "Driving Force" of the Market

As Ludwig von Mises summarized the nature of the competitive process:

> The market economy is the social system of the division of labor under private ownership of the means of production. Everybody acts on his own behalf; but everybody's actions aim at the satisfaction of other people's needs as well as the satisfaction of his own. Everybody in acting serves his fellow men ...

> This system is steered by the market. The market directs the individual's activities into those channels in which he best

serves the wants of his fellow men. There is in the operation of the market no compulsion or coercion. The state ... protects the individual's life, health and property against the violent or fraudulent aggression on the part of domestic gangsters and external foes ...

Each man is free; nobody is subject to a despot. Of his own accord the individual integrates himself into the cooperative system. The market directs him and reveals to him in what way he can best promote his own welfare as well as that of other people. The market is supreme. The market alone puts the whole social system in order and provides it with sense and meaning.

The market is not a place, a thing, or a collective entity. The market is a process, actuated by the interplay of the actions of the various individuals cooperating under the division of labor.

The entrepreneurs who imagine, coordinate and direct those production activities through time are what Ludwig von Mises referred to as the "driving force" of the entire market process. While it is consumer demand that ultimately directs all the activities of the market, it is the entrepreneurs – the decision-making enterprisers and businessmen – who decide what shall be produced, how, where, and by whom. All production takes time, whether this is a day, a week, a month or even years. Thus, decisions must be made "today" concerning production processes to be set in motion looking to the days and months ahead so a finished product can be offered on the market at some more distant "tomorrow."

Thus, entrepreneurs have the task in the system of division of labor to anticipate the future consumer demands of others in society, to decide at what prices those desired products might sell for in that future, and which ways of producing them would minimize their production costs so as to (hopefully) earn a profit – that is, revenues greater than incurred expenditures. While all others participating the processes of production normally do so for contractually agreed upon remuneration – wages, input prices, rent, interest – the entrepreneur bears the uncertainty of whether or not he will, in fact, gain a profit from the enterprise that he directs and oversees. This means that he also runs the possibility of suffering losses rather than earning profits, and that burden of uncertainty resides with him alone.

Profit and Loss and the Spirit of Entrepreneurship

Entrepreneurial competition, therefore, is ultimately a rivalry over alternative visions of the shape of market things to come in the minds of these decision-makers, which they competitively put into play but with the determination of the final outcome in the hands of the consumers who may or may not buy their products, and who may or may not pay prices for the quantities they purchase such that revenues earned cover or exceed the expenditures incurred.

Unsuccessful entrepreneurs who suffer losses and who are unable to repair their faulty pre-visions of what's ahead in the market finally go out of business, with their properties and assets passing into the hands of other existing or new enterprising entrepreneurs who are confident that they can more effectively manage their use to serve the consuming public. Successful entrepreneurs are able to use all or a part of the profits they have earned to expand their businesses to better fulfill the demands of consumers, looking to the future once more.

Thus, the competitive processes of the market through the profit and loss mechanism is always tending to put business decision-making and allocational discretion over the scarce means of production into the hands of those who more successfully demonstrate their competency in this chosen entrepreneurial role in the social system of division of labor within the free market economy. But as Mises also emphasized in his essay on "Profit and Loss" (1952), entrepreneurial success is ultimately based on the creative imaginings of the human mind, the capacity of seeing the possibilities and potentials of the future better than others and bringing production to fruition, which is, then, tested by the choices of consumers in the market:

> In the capitalist system of society's economic organization the entrepreneurs determine the course of production. In the performance of this function they are unconditionally and totally subject to the sovereignty of the buying public, the consumers.

> If they fail to produce in the cheapest and best possible way those commodities which the consumers are asking for most urgently, they suffer losses and are finally eliminated from their entrepreneurial position. Other men who know better how to serve the consumers replace them ...

> It is the entrepreneurial decision that creates profit or loss. It is mental acts, the mind of the entrepreneur, from which profits ultimately originate. Profit is a product of the mind, of success in anticipating the future state of the market. It is a spiritual and intellectual phenomenon.

Competition as a Discovery Procedure

To this may be added Friedrich A. Hayek's (1899-1992) focus on "Competition as a Discovery Procedure" (1969). Competition is useful and, indeed, essential to the creative processes of the market. As Hayek pointed out, if in, say, a foot race we already knew ahead of time who would come in first, second, third, etc., along with each runner's relative times, what would be to point of running the race? It is only through competition that we can find out how a race will end. Only through the competitive process can we discover the abilities of each individual relative to the others. It is also true that each individual cannot know for sure what he or she are, themselves, capable of in a particular setting unless they try to find out what they can accomplish by challenging and pushing themselves.

What is it that consumers may want in the future in terms of existing or new goods and services; who can effectively devise the most cost-efficient way of bringing a good or service to market; which competitor can do so better than his supply-side rivals; what applications of factors of production will reflect their most highly valued uses among the alternatives? There is no way of really knowing the answers to any and all such questions independent of a open competitive market in which the opportunities and incentives for earning profits and incomes exist and individuals have the motives to try.

All of these characteristics and qualities to a competitive market economy are only possible and available due to the institutional prerequisites of a free market liberal system that were mentioned closer to the beginning of this chapter. It is the liberating of individuals from political restrictions and restraints, the freeing of market interaction and exchange from governmental regulations and prohibitions, and the recognition that every market participant must be presumed to possess and have protected his rights to his life, liberty and honestly acquired property that enables competition to fully come into play. And from which liberty and prosperity are made possible for mankind.

But what about the critic's criticisms that left to itself, competition may degenerate into socially harmful and detrimental monopoly, or that competition serves misdirected and wasteful consumer demands? We will turn to these issues in the following chapters.

CHAPTER 7

FREE MARKETS AND THE MISUNDERSTANDING OF MONOPOLY

Numerous misunderstandings and mythologies surround the meaning of free markets and competition, but few match the confusions over the meaning and relevance of "monopoly" in the workings of the liberal economic system. When looked at dispassionately, factually, and historically, monopoly has almost always represented a problem in society only when created, protected, or imposed by government intervention.

Critics of free market liberalism have proposed to nationalize "monopolistic" industries, to break them up into smaller "competitive" firms, or to regulate their pricing policies and influence the output they produce. A noticeable amount of the criticism of the existence of or supposed "threats" from monopoly is connected with the particular and peculiar way economists have come to think about "competition" and "monopoly," especially as found in the textbook presentations that practically every student learns who takes an economics class.

The Fantasy World of "Perfect Competition"

The student is told that the benchmark of market analysis is the theory of "perfect competition," a conception in which there are so many competitors on the supply-side of the market that each is too small to influence the prevailing market price for the good they are offering to buyers. Each seller, therefore, takes the market price as "given" and to which they respond in terms of the most optimal output to produce and offer on the market, given their (marginal) costs of manufacturing.

In addition, it is presumed that each of the sellers in their specific markets offers a product that in terms of their qualities, features and characteristics is exactly like the ones being offered by their competitors in that same market. In other words, in the world of "perfect competition" there is no competitive product differentiation in the sense of the individual seller trying to devise new, better and improved versions of his product to get an edge on his rivals in the market in which he operates.

It is assumed that entry and exit from any market is effortless and costless, so any discovered profits to be earned or losses to be avoided due to, say, a change in market demand, is appropriately adjusted to virtually instantaneously, so those profits or losses are eliminated in seemingly non-existent time.

And what assures all of the above is the additional assumption that all buyers and all sellers in each and every market have a "perfect" or "sufficient" knowledge of all relevant circumstances and conditions that no errors or mistakes can or will be made by buyers paying too much or sellers accepting to little for what they are, respectively, demanding and supplying.

The Logical Absurdity of Perfect Knowledge in Perfect Competition

University of Chicago economist, Frank H. Knight, is often credited with formalizing this, now, textbook conception of "perfection competition" in *Risk, Uncertainty, and Profit* (1921). But five years earlier, in 1916, Knight emphasized the fictitious and logical absurdities in:

> ... the impossible conditions of ideally perfect competition, where time and space were annihilated and universal omniscience prevailed ...

> It is the fact of omniscience [perfect knowledge], however, which is the prerequisite to perfect competition, and if this were realized in any other manner, no amount or kind of change would disturb the operation of ideal economic law [the optimal equilibrium of the 'perfect competition' market].

Once it is postulated that individuals in the marketplace possess "perfect knowledge," then it is assured that the market will always be in a state of perfect long-run equilibrium, because no other state of affairs can exist.

Nothing can ever be in the wrong place at the wrong time, and no good or service can ever be priced at the wrong price. Total "costs" always and everywhere equal total revenue. Profits can never be earned, and losses can never be suffered.

Since each individual wishes to "maximize" their subjective satisfaction ("utility") or their profit, then having a perfect knowledge of all current and future circumstances and conditions, each can act in no other way than the "objectively" most "optimal," one, because to act otherwise would be to act contrary to the purpose of maximizing utility or profit.

The absurdity of the perfect knowledge assumption in the theory of perfect competition was, especially highlighted by the Austrian economist, Oskar Morgenstern in, "Perfect Foresight and Economic Equilibrium" (1935):

> Full foresight ... must mean a foresight up to the end of the world ...

> In consequence of the interdependence of all economic processes and given conditions on one another, and this with all other facts, no instance could be given of a sector, however small, of the event, the foresight of which would not mean, at the same time, the foresight of all the rest ...

> The individual exercising foresight must thus not only know exactly the influence of his own transactions on prices but the influence of every other individual, and of his own future behavior on that of others, especially of those relevant for him personally ...

> The individuals would have to have a complete insight into theoretical economics, for how else would they be able to foresee action at a distance?

As Austrian economist, Friedrich A. Hayek, explained in his famous articles, "The Use of Knowledge in Society " (945) and "The Meaning of Competition" (1946), such a theory assumes away all the reality of what we normally think of as competition: an active rivalry among sellers each of whom has limited and imperfect knowledge, and is attempting to discover ways and means to make new, better and less expensive goods to offer to the consuming public, precisely as the method by which profits may be made and losses avoided. It is this active and dynamic real competitive market process operating with prices not already in equilibrium that tends to move markets into a coordinated balance between supply and demand, and in which, over time, profits may be competed away and losses eliminated.

The notion of "perfect competition" assumes the already existence of the hypothetical "perfect" market equilibrium that it is the task of real world dynamic competition to tend to bring about. Actual market conditions are then evaluated and judged by a standard or benchmark, Hayek said, that almost by necessity condemns any real competitive situation at most moments in time as being "anti-competitive" and therefore potentially "monopolistic."

The Textbook Portrayal of Monopoly

But what makes a market supplier's actions "monopolistic" in the theoretical world of "perfect competition"? In essence, that he is able to influence the market price at which he sells his product, and make his product different from that offered by any other seller in a given market. In the textbook expositions, the "monopoly seller" is able to select that higher price and lower quantity combination that maximizes his profit, but which does not reflect the lower price and total larger quantity that would be offered on the market if there were a multitude of sellers rather than only one.

The textbooks portray the monopolist's situation and his ability to pick and choose the price-quantity combination of his choice in a supply and demand diagram. However, this monopoly situation as shown in the textbook diagram has neither a past nor a future. It is the "frozen picture" of a market situation that is "out of time." The diagram, by itself, does not answer the following questions:

What market or other forces in the "past" brought about this current situation? Given this situation at a moment in time, are there any market forces at work looking to "tomorrow" that would change the circumstances from its present "monopolistic" state? Are there any non-market, that is, any government, barriers or prohibitions that would prevent such a change over time?

In other words, the monopoly situation pictured in the diagram is presented without a context to reasonably analyze and interpret what conclusions might be made in terms of whether the "social" significance of this monopoly situation suggests the need for an economic policy to "correct" some "problem" with it.

Or whether, instead, when looked at and analyzed from a perspective of a market process in time and through time, there may be no "monopoly problem" at all, but just one of the "transition" stages through which markets are passing all the time.

Reasons Why There May be a "Single Seller" in a Market

The word "monopoly" originates from the ancient Greek: "mono," meaning single, and "poly," meaning seller. But there are a variety of reasons why there may be only one seller in a market at or over a given period of time. First of all, it may be because an entrepreneur has creatively developed a new or significantly different product, and as a result he is the first and only supplier of this good on the market. After all, every new idea must begin in some individual's mind, and that person's willingness to undertake the entrepreneurial task of bringing it to market.

To the extent that he has correctly anticipated future consumer demand for this new or different product, the very profits that he may earn will attract the competitors who will enter his market and, over time, compete away the profits he as been earning by their devising ways to make similar versions of his new idea with more attractive features and offered at lower prices than the "monopolist" initially was charging.

If, on the other hand, this single seller has misjudged future market demand for his product and suffers losses, it would not be socially desirable for rivals to enter his market and waste more time and resources producing a loss-making product – unless, of course, if they see a way to make profitable that which the initial "monopolist" could not.

Second, there may be a single seller in a market because the consumer demand is too limited to make it profitable for more than one seller to operate in that market. Imagine the small, rural town with one general store. The owner may be making a profitable go of it, but if a rival entered the area and opened a competing general store, the sales and revenues now divided between the two of them may not be enough to cover their respective costs of operations; the end result being that both might face losses. The market is too limited to sustain more than one seller.

Third, there may be a single seller in a market due to their ownership or control of a vital resource or raw material without which a product cannot be successfully produced and marketed. This was a hypothetical possibility pointed out by Austrian economists, Ludwig von Mises and Israel M. Kirzner.

The Dynamic Workings of Free Market Competition

However, if we allow time to pass, that is, if we look beyond the situation at a moment in time, we can see countervailing market forces that likely will be set in motion if there are potential profits to be made from selling this resource-specific product.

First, this situation would create incentives to prospect for and extract any possible alternative supplies of this resource or raw material outside the control of the "monopolist," so competitors could enter his market at some point in the future.

Second, and more immediately as well as over time, if this is a profitable product, there would be incentives for competitors to market substitutes to his product out of alternative types of resources or raw materials outside of the monopolist's control, and offer their substitute products at lower prices than the monopolist's price. Thus, over time, competitive market forces would either eliminate or weaken even a "monopoly" position of this type.

The Austrian-born economist, Joseph A. Schumpeter, argued that the essence of the dynamic market economy is the innovative entre-preneurs who introduce the new, better, and improved products as well as new methods of production. To understand what Schumpeter called the competitive process of "creative destruction," it is necessary to look beyond any seemingly "monopoly" situation at a moment in time, and take the longer historical perspective of the market as a dynamic process through time.

Textbook conceptions of "perfect competition" and "monopoly" are of little relevance or help, therefore, for understanding how markets actually work. As Schumpeter explained it in *Capitalism, Socialism and Democracy* (1942):

> In dealing with capitalism we are dealing with an evolutionary process ... that incessantly revolutionizes the economic structure from within, incessantly destroying the old one, incessantly creating a new one. This process of Creative Destruction is the essential fact about capitalism.

> The fundamental impulse that sets and keeps the capitalist engine in motion comes from the new consumers' goods, the new methods of production or transportation, the new markets, the new forms of industrial organization that capitalist enterprise creates.

> In capitalist reality as distinguished from its textbook picture ... The kind of competition which counts ... [is] the competition from the new commodity, the new technology, the new source of supply, the new type of organization ... The competition that commands a decisive cost or quality advantage ...

> It is hardly necessary to point out that competition of the kind we now have in mind acts not only when in being but also when it is merely an ever-present threat. It disciplines before it attacks. The businessman feels himself to be in a competitive situation even if he is alone in his field.

Market Competition Best Understood as a Process Through Time

The market economy, to the extent that it has as a noticeable degree of competitive freedom, is an arena of change, transformation, and creativity. But looking at the textbook diagram of a supposed monopoly situation easily misses all this, by ignoring what preceded it or what may follow it.

Suppose you are shown a single frame of a motion picture, one that contains the image of a person hanging in midair just off the edge of a cliff. What conclusions are we to draw from this image? It all depends upon what preceded that frame, and what follows it. Suppose that the person was cornered by an attacker who has thrown this unfortunate fellow off the cliff with the intention of killing him on the rocks far below. But what if he saw his attacker coming, and this person chose to jump off the cliff to escape this aggressor, hoping to survive the fall by successfully landing in a river below and swimming to safety.

We do not know how to evaluate and judge the situation captured on that single frame taken out of the motion picture. It all depends. And in the same way, we do not know how to evaluate a market situation of a single seller in the market unless we know the market processes before and after that diagram-depicted moment in time.

To show the relevance of taking this longer view of competitive and monopoly situations than merely the frozen moment in time of the economics textbook, economist, Mark Perry, on the website of the website of the American Enterprise Institute (October 20, 2017), compares the lists of Fortune 500 firms in 1955 with those six decades later in 2017.

Only 59 enterprises were on the list in both these years, or less than 15 percent. Many of the companies on the 1955 Fortune 500 list were not only not on the 2017 list, but they no longer existed. Many of the companies on the list both of those years held different relative positions, with some higher and others lower in 2017 than in 1955. And a good number of companies on the 2017 list had not even existed sixty years earlier and therefore could not be on the 1955 list.

Government Intervention as the Cause of Monopoly Problems

What, then, may be the cause behind a single seller situation, a "monopoly," that may be considered as "anti-competitive" and "socially harmful"? This requires us to appreciate the role of the state in creating and perpetuating such a situation.

There may be a single seller in a market (or a small number of sellers) because of a legal privilege given by the government to be the only producer and/or seller of a good or service within a part or the whole of the geographical area over which the government has political authority. This is one of the oldest meanings or definitions of monopoly frequently used by economists since Adam Smith published *The Wealth of Nations* (1776).

In this case, the privileged monopolist may be in the position to limit supply and raise his price to generate higher profits because he is protected and sheltered from any direct market competition, since the government has made it illegal for all others to compete in this market. This is the one case in which the "frozen picture" of the textbook monopoly diagram is most appropriate because market competition cannot change the "picture." The government prevents any market process from working over time from generating the competition that would likely emerge in a more open market.

However, it would be expected that potential competitors might still try to develop and offer various substitutes for the government-protected monopoly product; to the extent they could do so without breaking the law. Also, it might still occur that illegal, "black markets," might emerge if profits were sufficiently high to make it attractive to run the risk of being caught and imprisoned by the government.

In modern American history, it was the government that legally provided a monopoly position to AT&T in the provision of telephone services around the United States through most of the 20th century. It was government regulation that limited market entry and controlled pricing and routes to a handful of passenger airline carriers from the mid-1930s to the end of the 1970s. It was government control of the airwaves that restricted radio and television broadcasting to a limited number of companies, again, until the late 1970s.

But once these government-created and protect monopoly or near-monopoly situations were abolished through legislative repeal, the markets for communication, travel, and information and entertainment exploded into the vibrant and diverse array of far more competitive providers and suppliers and offerings that we now happily take for granted, than under the system of government privilege and restriction.

Taking the market process long-view, the appearance of single sellers and seemingly "monopoly" or near-monopoly situations is easily shown to be limited moments in the wider horizon of dynamic and creative competition over and through time. As long as government secures and protects private property rights, enforces all contracts entered into voluntarily and through mutual agreement, and assures law and order under an impartial rule of law, "monopoly" as an economic or social problem is virtually non-existent. But introduce government intervention into the market system, and monopoly invariably becomes a social harm and an economic problem.

CHAPTER 8

HOW EXPECTATIONS COORDINATE FREE MARKETS

Open, competitive markets have a resilient capacity to successfully coordinate the actions of, now, billions of people around the world. With an amazing adaptability to changing circumstances, the actions and reactions of multitudes of suppliers and demanders are brought into balance with each other. Yet, none of this requires government planning, regulation or directing control. But how does this all come about?

The key to this coordinating process is often assigned to the pricing system of the free market economy. All the minimal information that anyone needs to bring his own actions as supplier or demander into balance with multitudes of others with whom he is interdependent is provided by the changing pattern of relative prices for finished consumer goods and the factors of production (labor, land, raw materials and capital).

Types and Uses of Knowledge in Society

Austrian economist, Friedrich A. Hayek, explained how this came about 75 years ago in his famous article, "The Use of Knowledge in Society," first published in the *American Economic Review* in September 1945. He emphasized that matching the division of labor is an inescapable division of knowledge. Specialization necessarily means that each of us knows things that others do not.

Each of us possesses different types of knowledge in different complementary combinations. For instance, all of us, to one degree or another, have acquired what Hayek referred to as scientific or "textbook" knowledge. This is the type of knowledge we learned in school, and while we all learned many of the same things in our classroom experiences, especially in college or university, we each focused on and acquired far more specific and detailed knowledge about some subject in which we majored than many others who selected different majors at the same and different institutions of higher learning. The medical doctor knows many things that the criminal lawyer does not, just as the lawyer has a detailed knowledge of his area of the law that the biologist or the architect do not possess based on their classroom and assigned textbook learning, and so on.

Localized Knowledge of Time and Place

But Hayek pointed out that there is also another type of knowledge that we each possess in different ways, what he called "the localized knowledge of time and place." This is the particular knowledge that is only learned, appreciated, and useable based on an individual working and interacting with others in a specific corner of the society and the marketplace.

The recently graduated entry-level young employee shows up for his first day of work in the enterprise that has hired him. There is a period of getting oriented: Meeting the other employees and finding out what, exactly, they do; the nature of the way "things are done" within the firm in terms of rules and procedures; learning who are the individuals and groups of buyers and sellers that company sells to or buys from that may be relevant to that new employee doing his own job properly; finding out how the production processes or service activities undertaken and performed may be distinctly different from how things are done in competing firms in the same industry or from those in other markets.

Little or none of this knowledge could be learned in the classroom or read about in any readings assigned to pass and master a high school or college course taken. Yet, such "intimate" knowledge in all these "mundane" matters are crucial for everything in each corner of the market system of division of labor to run smoothly and effectively.

The entrepreneur, in particular, needs to know all of these and many other details about his specialized area of the market in which he operates if profits are to be earned and losses avoided. And, in addition, all of these localized circumstances and situations are subject to continual change in a dynamic market setting in which things today may be different from yesterday, just as tomorrow may vary from the situation today.

Inarticulate Knowledge of Knowing How, What and When

Hayek later highlighted a third type of knowledge, what the chemist and philosopher of science, Michael Polanyi, called "tacit" or "inarticulate" knowledge. This is knowledge that each of us possesses in various forms and ways that concern how to do something, when and what to do, but which we often find it difficult or "impossible" to easily put into a written or spoken form to convey or share with others.

Think of the auto mechanic who can "just tell" from listening to and looking at an engine that is not functioning properly what is wrong with it, based on years of experience, but which he cannot easily put into words to the car owner. Or the master sculptor who knows just the right amount of hand pressure to place upon the watered piece of clay on the wheel whose speed he is controlling with a foot pedal, but which he could never precisely put down on paper so others could readily copy the technique that he uses to produce a pleasing piece of art. Or the successful businessman who has never taken an economics class or a marketing course, but has a tacit knack for "reading the market signals" about when consumer demands might be likely to change or a new advertising message might just do the trick to attract more customers.

Using All the Knowledge No Planner Can Master

These diverse and varying types of knowledge, which are possessed in different combinations and forms in the individual minds of all the interconnected and interdependent people in a modern complex market system and social order can never be known or mastered, Hayek argued, by any one mind or group of minds, no matter how wise and determined they may seem or try to be.

Hayek's point was that if we are all to benefit from what others know that we, personally, do not, but which when brought to bear in different ways for different things can improve our own circumstances in ways we cannot fully imagine ahead of time, then the individuals possessing all this decentralized and diffused knowledge must have the liberty and market-based latitude to utilize it in ways that they understand and see best. Otherwise, much that is known and potentially used by many others that could improve our own circumstances will not be taken advantage of or never even discovered.

But if not under the commanding instructions of a central planner or government regulator, how shall people know how, when and for what to apply their unique and distinct bits of knowledge, which cumulatively adds up to all "the knowledge in the world," but resides in no one mind or group of minds?

Worldwide Knowledge and the Price System

Hayek's answer was the competitive pricing system of a free market. It is not necessary for everyone to know what all the others in society possess as their unique knowledge. It is sufficient if there is an institutional mechanism through which people can convey a minimum required amount of information to others, so producers and suppliers may know what products consumers want and how intensely they desire them, and that consumers can find out what are the terms under which suppliers may find it profitably advantageous to apply what they know to satisfy the market demands of others.

And, likewise, it is not necessary for every private enterpriser thinking about undertaking a production process to know all the other businessmen who have a competing use and demand for all the different types of means of production (land, labor, raw materials, and capital), to make up their minds about how best to manufacture a product that minimizes the cost outlays to hopefully maximize the profits that might be earnable.

Consumers and producers "speak" to each other through the prices that are bid and offered on the market. This tells multitudes of suppliers what products are wanted by consumers and what price might be paid for them, just as the prices offered by rival enterprisers and accepted by labor and resource owners looking for employment tell each businessman the relative costs to be paid to hire or purchase various combinations of inputs relative to the anticipated selling price to be earned by producing and marketing a particular output to potentially willing buyers.

Thus, businessmen and workers and resource owners thousands of miles away from each other on other sides of the world can make reasonable and informed decisions about how to apply their own specialized and local forms and types of knowledge in ways that they hope profitably improves their own circumstances by satisfying the wants and desires of many others; others who they will never meet or personally know and who may live far away or around the corner; nor do they need to fully understand why and for what purposes that which they produced was wanted by any particular consumer following his own goals, purposes and plans in his buying choices in the part of the world in which he lives.

Knowledge Needed for Forming Expectations

But there is, in fact, a fourth type of knowledge that is equally essential for social and market participants to successfully coordinate all they do that is interdependent with the actions of many others. Hayek insightfully explained the central role of market-based prices for bringing together the dispersed and decentralized knowledge of the world to help bring into balance all that is done by those buying and selling in the social system of division of labor.

But when prices change, that is, when a price or group of prices rise or fall, or even stay the same "today" as they were "yesterday," what are they telling the various and relevant market participants about what it suggests will be the situation "tomorrow"?

In other words, prices need to be interpreted to successfully form expectations about the actions and reactions of others in the marketplace in deciding how best to use one's own specialized knowledge in effective and profitable ways for the achievement of one's own ends.

An understanding of how people actually form many of the expectations that guide and direct their interactions with others was developed in the writings of the famous German sociologist, Max Weber (1864-1920), in his monumental work, *Economy and Society* (1921), in the works of the Austrian sociologist, Alfred Schutz (1899-1959), especially in *The Phenomenology of the Social World* (1932) and in a variety of his essays written in the 1950s, and in the works of the Austrian economist, Ludwig von Mises, most particularly in *Human Action: A Treatise on Economics* (1949, 3rd revised ed., 1966) and *Theory and History* (1957).

Max Weber on Meaningful Action and Ideal Types

Weber argued that what makes "human action" distinct is that it is conscious conduct to which an individual assigns a "subjective" (a personal) meaning or purpose, and that the meaning or purpose defines what kind of action the individual is undertaking and with what end in mind. But no man is an island; he interacts and associates with others. As a result, Weber said, "social action" is conscious human conduct in which individuals "orient" their actions intentionally toward one another.

For instance, Weber argued that what makes the physical transfer of two objects between two individuals an act of "free exchange," as opposed to being, say, some compulsory transfer, is how the transactors conceive of and view their own intentions and that of the other with whom they are interacting. Weber's primary focus was developing various interpretive tools of analysis for the study of history.

Thus, he argued that a central tool of history and sociology is the "ideal type." This was meant to be a composite image of a "type" of an historical person or activity. Thus, one might construct an image, or "mental picture," of the "typical" characteristics of a Latin American military dictator, or the qualities and characteristics of the "typical" Medieval "lord of the manor." Or it might reflect the "typical" aspects and forms of development of the "typical" Western European city in the modern era.

Alfred Schutz and the World of Intersubjective Meanings

But it was the Austrian sociologist, Alfred Schutz, who had studied at the University and Vienna and who was part of Ludwig von Mises's circle of scholars in the Vienna of the 1920s and early 1930s, who took Weber's ideas and combined them with aspects of Austrian Economics to develop a theory of how expectations are formed and used by human actors in society.

While we may reasonably speak about the general qualities and characteristics discoverable in any and all human conduct – what Mises named, "praxeology," the logic of human action – Schutz emphasized that filling in the actual "content" of that general logic of action comes from the social setting into which people are born and within which they interact with others.

We are born into an existing social world, and we learn a language, customs, traditions, rules of conduct of "good" and "bad" behavior, etc., by growing up in a family, around friends, within a society of other human actors from whom we absorb the intersubjective (interpersonal) structures of meaning that define and "objectify" the meaning of actions and objects.

For instance, this object is a "book" and this other object is a "Halloween mask." This object is a "knife" for carving meat, while another sharp object is a "surgeon's scalpel" for performing a "medical operation." This person's "kneeling" before a woman is a "proposal of marriage," while this other person's "kneeling" before a "royal queen" is being "knighted" for acts of "valor" or "heroism."

The division of labor brings about not only a specialization of tasks, but particular forms of standardized conduct in performing them in various social and market settings, Schutz explained. Thus, we come to "expect" that anyone understood as performing a certain task in a certain way, and, perhaps, dressed in a specific manner is a "policeman," or "fireman," or airplane "steward," or "bank manager," or "server" at a restaurant, or "mailman" on their delivery rounds, or ...

Regardless of which concrete, specific, individual is "playing this role" in society we anticipate each will act toward any others with whom they interact in a generally prescribed way. And, likewise, that a person expects anyone interacting with them to act and interact in expected ways. The "mailman" does not expect any of us to ask him what may be the cause of a heart palpitation. Nor will the "fireman" expect that a person whose house is on fire is going to ask him what is on the menu for lunch in "business class" on a plane flight they are scheduled to be on later in the week. These "ideal typifications" of tasks and routinized conduct in various specialized roles in the division of labor provide essential everyday points of interpersonal orientation and expectations for planning one's own actions.

Thus, if I go into a bank I know that if I sit down with a "bank manager" he will be able (and is expecting to) to offer information to me for applying for a home or car loan, or opening a new account. If I make an appointment with a "dermatologist," I know he will be able (and he expects) to do an examination and offer a diagnosis of a skin problem I may have.

Our Personal "Ideal Types" of Each Other

Alfred Schutz also highlighted that such "ideal types" of people are along a spectrum. At one extreme are those most general and wide characteristics of any and all human action, which is the basis for Ludwig von Mises's formulation of a general logic of choice and action, "praxeology." In the middle of this spectrum of ideal types are those just explained of "typical" roles and specialized activities often routinized in the division of labor.

And at the other end of this spectrum is what Schutz called the "personal ideal type." This is not the general characteristics discoverable in any and all human action or the specialized "types" of actions expected from any individual performing a particular role in the division of labor. Instead, these are the qualities or characteristics "typifying" a particular, distinct individual. This is our "mental image" not of all men, or some men performing specialized tasks, but of this specific human being.

I explain to my students that when they entered one of my classrooms for the first time, what could they anticipate about me? Certainly, that I am a human being and they could expect that I would demonstrate those qualities known to be true about any other person. But they also had an image in their mind, an "ideal type," of a "college professor," and a college professor who (hopefully!) knows what he is talking about in an introductory economics class.

But as they sit in the class and watch, listen, and interact with me they come to formulate in their minds an image, an "ideal type," not of all men, or some men in the division of labor, but of this particular person with his specific mannerism, behavioral characteristics, ways of expressing himself and moving about.

We all develop and use these "personal ideal types" of others, and on the basis of which we form expectations of what to expect when we interact with these specific individuals. If you laugh at Joe's jokes, his is likely to buy you a round of drinks. If you mention sex to Bob, he usually acts embarrassed and becomes quiet. If you mention to Sally that "a woman's place is in the kitchen," you're going to get a "lecture" on the place of women in modern society. If you criticize socialized medicine in Europe, George is likely to go into a rant on the "evils" of the profit motive.

It should be evident that many if not most of the ideal types discussed by Alfred Schutz also overlap with that category of tacit or inarticulate knowledge. In our interactions with others, we all form these types of mental images of those with whom we associate in various settings. But it is something we do "tacitly," that is, without consciously thinking about it very much, if at all. And while we often know "how to interact" around someone based on our "ideal type" of them in our mind, it is not always easy to express in written or spoken words to someone else how and why we see these characteristics in that other person, or how and why we "just know" most of the time that if we do or say "X" around that person we are fairly confident that it will being about response "Y" from that individual.

Ludwig von Mises and the "Thymology" of Market Expectations

Ludwig von Mises came to call this method of understanding and interpreting others through ideal types of various sorts as the subject matter of "thymology," the study of how individuals form images of others in their minds to generate expectations for purposes of interpersonal understanding, planning and the coordination of one's own actions with those of others.

In the conception of the dynamic free market process discussed in earlier chapters, a central actor is the entrepreneur, the individual who anticipates possible future consumer demands, conceives of production plans of action to bring forth a product or service to satisfy that prospective demand, and who organizes the activities of the enterprise that he directs to bring that product to market for purposes of earning a profit.

The entrepreneur must make informed judgments in doing all this, and in doing so, Mises said, he must form expectations of individuals and groups on both the demand- and supply-sides of the market. The knowledge on the basis of which he does so, is built up from the experiences he has personally had, or heard about, or learned from others in some manner concerning the likely actions and reactions of those with whom he interacts in the marketplace, and whose future actions he must anticipate the best he can to design his own plans of action.

How might potential buyers respond to a price reduction for the product, or to a new marketing campaign advertising "new and improved" qualities to the product, or why it is better than the one's offered by rival sellers in the marketplace? He must also, from past experience and other sources of information form expectations about his supply-side competitors. How will they respond to what he is planning, as well as anticipating what they are possibly planning to do to which he must respond effectively in the pursuit of profits and market share?

Ideal types, Mises argued, enable acting man to be what he called "the historian of the future." Forming composite pictures or images of individuals from their past actions in terms of characteristics, qualities, motives and meanings, these "ideal types" enable an individual decision-maker to project himself into the future, imagine that another individual or groups of individuals are confronted or faced with a particular event or change in their circumstance, and then ask the question, "What responses and courses of action would these individuals manifest in this situation?" It enables the formation of expectations concerning patterns or regularity or "types" of response for prediction of a wide variety of circumstances. No matter how imperfect, it introduces an additional source of knowledge for coordination of plans in the complex social setting of the market.

Indeed, it is the "ideal types" of these various forms within the wider social structure of intersubjective meanings (explained earlier), that allows entrepreneurs and other market participants to evaluate and judge the meaning behind competitive prices and changes in them so as to form expectations of what those prices are "saying" in terms of anticipating the actions of other suppliers and demanders when undertaking the economic calculations of potential profits or possible losses.

Mises pointed out that many might consider this a rather unsatisfactory method of anticipating possible social actions in comparison to the claims of more detailed and determinate predictive power in the natural sciences. But he argued that given the uniquely distinct qualities and characteristics of human action in the social world, this in fact might be the best that can be hoped for, given the intentional and choice-based reality of human conduct.

Ideal Types, Expectations and the Free Society

One other aspect of this social institution of "ideal types" for interpersonal plan coordination is that it is part of the wider "spontaneous
order" of the social system. That is, the social structures of intersubjective meaning, the "ideal types" of actors and actions in various
face-to-face and "role playing" tasks in the division of labor, and
the formation of expectations by people in their respective locations of specific time and place within the market order emerge out
of the actions and interactions of multitudes of people in various
societal settings at a moment in time and over shorter or much
longer periods of time.

They are part of the societal "glue" for coherence, cooperation
and coordination, with degrees of complexity and adaptability that
defies the very notion of intentional planning by political actors
asserting the need for and their ability to impose "order" on communities of human beings.

The type of "personal ideal types" of individuals or groups of
individuals that entrepreneurs and private enterprisers form in
their minds from experience and interactions with others in the
actual on-going circumstances of changing and changeable markets
can never be known, understood or shared with those who would
assert the authority to centrally plan or regulate the interactions of
multitudes of people for purposes of coordination of all that goes
on in the marketplace.

Each of us as sellers of labor services as the means of earning the
incomes that enable us to reenter the market as consumers of desired
goods, use the intimate and intricate ideal types that each of us have
formed in our minds to navigate the workplace and employment
opportunities that may be available to us. Likewise, we each have

formed ideal type judgments and estimates of those from whom we regularly buy the goods and services for which we use the incomes we have earned in the production processes of the market.

We each know many things about the character, trustworthiness, and reliability of those with whom we interact in our social and neighborhood surroundings through the use of these ideal types that enable us to decide who to trust and who to avoid; who to confidently associate with for various purposes; and who to not do certain things with if we want or need for some things to get done.

For government planners and regulators to preempt the use of our own knowledge under the presumption that they can know and appreciate what only each of us can fully understand and know from our own built up experiences in our own separate corners of the society with those overlapping ideal types that exist in our individual minds, is to short-circuit the ability for each of us to effectively pursue and achieve many of the everyday and important purposes in our own lives.

Appreciation for the nature, workings and importance of expectations formation processes in the marketplace of the free society demonstrates once more the superiority of the liberal system of individual liberty free markets and limited government, and the absurdity of the pretense of knowledge claimed by political paternalists and social engineers.

CHAPTER 9

FREE MARKETS AND ASYMMETRIC INFORMATION

Free market liberalism is a wondrous human institution for the mutual betterment for all in society. Yet, critics often insist that market systems enable sellers to take advantage of buyers, because those on the demand-side often lack the specialized knowledge that suppliers possess, thus, enabling a possible exaggerated misrepresentation of what is being offered for sale. What is missed is that market competition generates the incentives and opportunities to earn profits precisely by not misinforming or cheating the buyer.

A number of economists, among the most notable being the 2001 co-recipient of the Nobel Prize, Joseph Stiglitz, a professor of economics at Columbia University, have argued that market economies suffer from an inherent inefficiency and potential injustice due to the existence of "asymmetric information." A core element in his theory is that individuals in the marketplace do not all possess the same type or degree of knowledge concerning the goods and services being bought and sold.

Some people know things that others do not. This "privileged" information can enable some to "exploit" others. For instance, the producer and marketer is likely to know far more about a product's qualities, features and characteristics that he is offering on the market than most of the buyers possibly interested in purchasing it.

Perfect Competition and Perfect Knowledge

By withholding or not fully informing the potential buyer about all of the qualities, features and characteristics of his good, he may succeed in creating a false impression that makes the consumer have a greater demand for it and a willingness to pay a higher price for it than would be the case if that consumer knew as much about the good as the seller knows.

This argument is a partially reasonable response to the unrealistic assumptions of the "perfect competition" model of the typical mainstream economics textbook. One assumption is that each seller is, respectively, considered too small a contributor to the supply of a good offered on a particular market to be able to influence the price at which he sells, and, thus takes that market's price as "given," with merely adjusting his output to that point at which his (marginal) costs are equal to his (marginal) revenues.

Another assumption, as we have seen, is that every market participant in each market possesses a "perfect" or "sufficient" knowledge to never pay more as a demander or accept less as a supplier that the "objective" market conditions dictate and require. This also assures that all markets, all the time, are in or rapidly converging to a perfect long-run equilibrium with neither profits earned nor losses suffered.

Markets Integrate and Coordinate Decentralized Knowledge

There is no doubt that in a system of division of labor there is an accompanying division of knowledge and, therefore, an asymmetry of information about things bought and sold by those on the demand- and supply-sides of the market. This is a theme in theories of the market process long ago explained by economists in the "Austrian" tradition, most especially by Friedrich A. Hayek (1899-1992), who also received a Nobel Prize in Economics in 1974.

The Austrians have long emphasized that competition is a "discovery procedure" through which individuals find out things never known or imagined before. The peaceful rivalry of the market-place creates the incentives for entrepreneurs to be unceasingly alert to profit opportunities and to see possibilities that others either have missed or not thought of before. The unknown or barely perceived become seen and understood, and then taken advantage of in the form of new, better, and less expensive products offered to the consuming public.

The purpose of competitive markets and price systems is precisely to provide a way to integrate and coordinate the dispersed and decen-tralized knowledge in any society possessing a degree of complexity. This same competitive market has also found ways to reduce and overcome the asymmetry of consumer versus seller knowledge concerning the qualities, features and characteristics of goods, and thereby to reduce the potential and possibility of "exploiting" what the seller may know at the expense of the market buyers.

Search Goods and Judging Product Quality

In explaining how markets do this, economists sometimes distin-guish between two types of goods offered and sold on the market:

search goods and experience goods. Search goods are those that can be examined and judged by the potential buyer before a purchase is made. For instance, suppose that a supermarket advertises that perfectly ripened bananas are available and on sale in their store. A consumer can enter the supermarket and fairly reasonably judge whether the quality of the good matches what has been promised in the advertising before buying it.

If examination shows that the bananas are either non-eatable green or over-ripened brown, the consumer can walk away without spending a penny on a product that has not met what was promised. By falsely or incorrectly advertising, or even unreasonably exaggerating in its advertising, the business runs the risk of not only losing that sale but the loss of its brand name reputation, with that consumer never returning to that establishment again. Plus, that person can tell others what his "search" of the good came up with, potentially leading to those others not trusting that businesses advertising without inspecting the good themselves.

This creates a self-interested incentive on the part of such sellers to practice "truth in advertising," or suffer the loss of some their regular customers upon whose repeat business their long-term profitability is dependent.

Experience Goods and Market Safeguards

Experience goods are those goods whose qualities, features and characteristics cannot be really fully known and appreciated without using the product in question for a period of time. Think of an automobile; you can go for a test drive, but your own best judgment of its safety, reliability and handling cannot be really known without driving the car in various weather and traffic conditions over a period of time. Or think of a bed mattress; you sit down and bounce on it, or stretch out and lay down on it in the furniture showroom, but you cannot really know if it will give you a comfortable and restful sleep every night until you've gone to bed on it for a period of time. The same applies to many goods, such as household appliances, for instance.

The competitive market's response to this uncertain and imperfect knowledge on the part of potential buyers has been the seller and manufacture's system of product warranties that enable the buyer to return the product over a period of time for his or her money back, or a replacement at no extra cost to the buyer.

It is, again, in the seller's own self-interest to make sure that the product is what has been promised and is reliable in its working order and performance, otherwise, once more, the seller and manufacturer run the risk of losing their brand name reputation concerning quality and trustworthiness. Plus, if a warranty has to be fulfilled it is the manufacturer or seller who is forced to eat the cost of replacing the unit returned due to malfunction or failure to match buyer expectation, thus cutting into their own profit margin.

Market Uncertainty and Franchise Businesses

But what about those situations in which concern about repeat business or brand name reputation do not seem to be as relevant? For instance, suppose you are traveling on business or vacation and are passing through some town you are highly unlikely ever to see again.

You're hungry for a meal or a place to stay for the night. How can you know about the quality of the meal in the local "Joe's Greasy Spoon," or the promised bedbug-free mattress in any of the rooms in the local "Bates Motel"?

The market has provided consumer information about the qualities, features and characteristics of such products and services to overcome this inescapable imperfect knowledge in the form of chain stores and franchises. You may never eat or sleep again in that particular town, but you will likely eat and sleep away from home somewhere at sometime again in the future.

The sight of the MacDonald's "Golden Arches" or the sign for an IHOP (International House of Pancakes) anytime, any place, tells you the quality and variety of foods that you can have in any of their establishments, regardless of where its location in the United States or even around the world. The same applies to seeing the sign for a Motel 6, or a Holiday Inn Express or an Embassy Suites, or a Hilton-family hotel. You may never again go to that particular MacDonald's or Holiday Inn, but if you travel you may very well eat or spend the night at some other chain franchise of that company.

Another instance of this is, for instance, Midas Mufflers. An automobile driver can stop in any Midas store in the country, and know that if there is a problem with a new muffler or its installation, he can return it to any other Midas outlet to have it replaced or reinstalled for free under the warranty. (And each Midas retail store has an incentive to get the installation "right," because if another store has to correct their mistakes, the second store sends the bill to the first store for the costs of doing so, under the terms of the franchise.)

Getting it right the first time and making sure that every franchise member meets the franchise requirements in doing so is important to the "mother company" to assure the repeat business and brand name reputation upon which its own revenues are dependent. Thus, each chain store and franchise is required to meet standards of quality and variety that enables the consumer to have a high degree of confidence and reduced knowledge uncertainty of what he or she is getting when they enter any of these establishments regardless of where it may be located.

What makes this practice in the market consistently happen and successfully relied upon? Market competition and the self-interested profit motive.

Con Men Are Always with Us, Free Markets Constrain Them

Are there con men, hucksters and cheats? Of course there are. They existed in ancient Athens just as they exist today. There are always people who will try to dishonestly get what others have, when doing it that way seems easier and less costly than through honest production and trade.

The question is not whether human nature can be transformed to eliminate this aspect of human conduct. The question is, are there market institutions and incentives that can systemically reduce this type of behavior and, instead, generate more honest and properly informed human interactions?

And the answer is, yes. In fact, most of these positive incentive mechanisms have emerged and evolved out of the competitive market process, itself. These "market solutions" to the "social problem" of asymmetric information were discovered by market participants to be profitable ways of gaining consumer trust and confidence and business, without any government command or imposition. Plus, their discovery and their practiced institutional forms could never have been fully anticipated or imagined in their full detail before and separate from the competitive market processes that have generated them.

Government Failure and Asymmetric Information

Of course, what is rarely pointed out or emphasized by those who worry about the problem of asymmetric information in society is its far more likely a danger and abuse in the arena of government action and intervention.

In the marketplace, the disappointed or disgruntled consumer who considers that a seller has been less than truthful or trustworthy concerning the product the buyer has bought can immediately or in relative short-order stop doing business with the supplier with whom he is disappointed. This is not so in the political arena.

If a voter considers that a politician or the bureaucrats answerable to him have failed to meet up to their promises or have seemingly deceived him in the face of the actual policies those in the government have undertaken after an election, he must continue to fund their activities in the form of the taxes that that voter is forced to pay, as well as to obey the rules and regulations they have imposed on him or others with whom he may desire to do business.

In the marketplace, the consumer may turn to other possible competing providers of the good or service he wishes to buy and use, if a particular seller has appeared to deceive him with false or incomplete or exaggerated information about the good or service in question. He does not have this option in the political arena.

The government often monopolizes or narrows the availability of alternative providers through interventions that limit or prohibit competition in some corner of the market. The frustrated voter cannot supply the type of "negative feedback" concerning his disappointment with the promised product the same way he can by withdrawing his business and shifting to another supplier in a more freely competitive market. Indeed, he may have to continue to use the misrepresented or faulty government-supplied or regulated product rather than face doing without it.

In the marketplace, it is usually fairly clear who is the seller who has marketed and misrepresented the product that has aroused the ire of the buyer. The consumer can more or less easily pinpoint the seller who is responsible for the deceit or inappropriate exaggeration of the product bought and used. But with the government, layers of bureaucracy and indirect chains of responsibility in the labyrinth of the political structure of decision-making, enables those in political power or authority to more easily hide from view those upon whom the charge of lies and fraud should fully fall.

And, finally, in the marketplace, the individual disappointed with presumed misrepresentation or less than sufficient information from a seller can inform others about his experience, but he does not need the approval or agreement of others to change his own pattern of buying things and from whom. He just stops doing business with the seller with whom he is dissatisfied, and finds a more attractive trading partner.

In the political arena, however, to change those holding political office and determining the government policies considered by that individual to be deceitful and undesirable requires him to persuade enough other voters in the society so that a change may be made in who holds political office and what policies may be implemented when, and only when, the next election cycle comes around.

It is the free market competitive process that generates solutions to the knowledge problems of the society, including the "informational asymmetry" that naturally follows from any developed social system of division of labor. All that is basically required, as has been known since the time of Adam Smith in the 1770s, is recognized and respected individual rights to life, liberty and honestly acquired property, enforcement of all voluntary contractual agreements, impartial and biased rule of law, and constitutionally limited government.

CHAPTER 10

PUBLIC GOODS AND FREE MARKET LIBERALISM

The competitive market economy is a powerful institutional mechanism for bringing human ingenuity, energy, and creativity to bear, to improve both the material and cultural circumstances of multitudes of people around the world. Wherever relatively free market liberalism is operating, it succeeds in ending human poverty and brings about rising standards of living for hundreds of millions, indeed now billions, of people. Yet, it is argued that there are some things – "public goods" – that only government can effectively supply to everyone in society.

Private property has long been understood to be a great incentivizing force to motivate individual self-interest in the form of peaceful and productive work, savings, and investment. Under the social system of division of labor, each participant sees the chance for personal gain and profit by directing his efforts to produce those goods and services that others may want so as to obtain through exchange what they can reciprocally provide.

Indeed, many of the classical economists of the 19th century considered private property to be the fundamental and most essential institution for a peaceful and prosperous society. For instance, John R. McCulloch (1789-1864) explained in his widely read *Principles of Political Economy* (1864):

> Let us not, therefore, deceive ourselves by supposing that it is possible for any people to emerge from barbarism, or to become wealthy, prosperous, and civilized without the security of property ... The protection afforded to property by all civilized societies, though it has not made all men rich, has done more to increase their wealth than all their other institutions put together ...

> The establishment of a right to property enables exertion, invention, and enterprise, forethought and economy to reap their due reward. But it does this without inflicting the smallest imaginable injury upon anything else. ...Its [property's] effects are altogether beneficial. It is a rampart raised by society against its common enemies—against rapine, and violence, plunder and oppression. Without its protection, the rich would become poor, and the poor would be totally unable to become rich—all would sink to the same bottomless abyss of barbarism and poverty.

The market order is a social arrangement for "positive sum" outcomes in which every participant in the market network of voluntary exchange betters his own circumstances in the transactions into which he enters as both producer and consumer. As a producer, the individual participates in the manufacturing and marketing of various goods that earns him the financial wherewithal to reenter the market as a consumer.

But since the time of Adam Smith in his *The Wealth of Nations*, it has often been argued that there may be some goods for "which it can never be for the interest of any individual, or small number of individuals, to erect and maintain; because the profit could never repay the expense to any individual or small number of individuals, though it may frequently do much more than repay it to a great society."

This has been the basis for what has become known in the jargon of the economist as "public goods." They have usually been defined as goods that have especially two distinctive qualities: Non-excludable access and non-rivalrous consumption or use. What do these terms mean?

Public Goods: Non-Excludability and Non-Rivalrous Use

A *non-excludable* good is one that someone does not pay for, or can avoid paying for, to use or consume. It is said to be highly difficult or costly to exclude such an individual from having access to it even though he's not paying for it. Thus, such an individual can benefit from its supply without having paid anything to cover some portion of its production costs in making it available on the market or to society in general.

The standard example given is national defense. A "defense shield" of military aircraft, missiles, and naval ships protect large portions of the United States from foreign attack. Such a military shield provides protection not only to the citizens who may have contributed to pay for it but all others who may not have contributed to cover its costs, but who live under its protection.

If Pierre is visiting from France, for the time he is in the U.S. that defense shield protects him from any potential foreign military attack, even though the American taxpayers have paid the costs of providing it to themselves as well as Pierre. There is no way to exclude Pierre from that protection in case of foreign attack. A hole cannot be left in the defense umbrella in the sky into which an incoming missile can vaporize poor Pierre but no one else who has helped pay for the system.

Non-rivalrous consumption refers to the idea that the number of those who benefit from the use or enjoyment of such a public good does not necessarily affect the cost of providing it. For instance, an increase in, say, an extra 10,000 people living in the United States does not impact the marginal cost of providing that defense shield to that addition to the country's population.

If people are watching a fireworks display in a large open field on the fourth of July, an extra person standing in the field enjoying the display does not impact the cost of supplying the fireworks or the launcher equipment, given the planned size of the display. Assuming a relatively large field with unimpeded vision of the sky, whether twenty people are watching the illuminations or two hundred does not influence the cost of providing the holiday entertainment to the viewers.

The Problem of the "Free Rider"

Limited government classical liberals since the time of Adam Smith have taken for granted that such things as "national defense," "police," and the "justice system" are examples of public goods for which government funding by compulsory taxation is essential.

A primary reason, it is argued, is that, otherwise, there is created a "free rider" problem, the result of which is an "undersupplying" or less-than-optimal production of defense, police, or justice. Suppose that there are 100 million people in a country, but payment for national defense is a matter of voluntary contribution by the citizens. Since a resident of the country is not forced to pay for being militarily protected from a foreign attack, he might conclude that he won't send in a voluntary contribution and, yet, enjoy whatever degree of funded national defense ends up being supplied; after all, he can't be excluded from its protection though he will not have contributed to its provision.

Furthermore, suppose that each citizen is asked to pay a voluntary contribution of $100, and 75 million of them actually send in that sum, resulting in the government having $7.5 billion to spend on national defense. If the remaining 25 million citizens had not decided to free ride on the contributions of the others and had also sent in respective $100 contributions, the government would have had an additional $2.5 billion for defense spending for a total of $10 billion. It is argued that this shortfall reflects and measures the degree to which there has been an undersupply of national defense in that country.

No Way to Know a Free Rider's Valuation of a Public Good

The theory of the free rider assumes an ability to estimate or calculate the amount of undersupply there is of a particular public good. However, there is no accurate way of knowing by how much such a public good may be undersupplied since there is no way of knowing what value the free rider would have placed on this good if he had to actually pay for access and/or use of it.

Of course, it would be possible to ask such free riding individuals what value they might attach to this good if they had to pay for it. But the problem is: talk is cheap. That is, a person could say anything in the abstract about by how much he values this good, and some hypothetical price he might be willing to pay for it if he had to, to gain access to it. How you imagine or publicly state you might spend a million dollars if you won it in a lottery and how you would end up actually spending that million dollars if you did win a lottery could be two very different things.

An individual only demonstrates his actual valuation for a good when he is confronted with the need to make a choice and shows whether he really wants to buy this good and the price he would be willing to pay for access and use of a particular quantity. Contrary to how some economists think about such things, people do not formulate and walk around with a clear and formalized "preference map" of their wants and desires in their head that traces out all the possible exchange opportunities and situations that might confront them.

Unless there is an actual market from which interested buyers, some of who may have been free riders, can be excluded if they do not pay some price for access and/or use of this good, there is no way of knowing whether or not this good is, currently, undersupplied or oversupplied or is just right.

Informed observers and economic policy analysts can have very different and inconclusive interpretive judgments about any such claims. For instance, is there too much or too little spent on national defense and homeland security? And what would be the real market-determined value of them as expressed in a competitively generated price system? There is no way of determining this because there is no market for the direct buying and selling between citizen-consumers and supply-side producers of defense services or security against terrorist threats.

Central Planning Qualities of Government-Supplied Public Goods

As a result, government-provided national defense and homeland security suffer from an aspect of the famous "Austrian" critique of socialist central planning as made by Ludwig von Mises, Friedrich A. Hayek, and others. It is true that in a "mixed" or interventionist economy, government still has to purchase on a market the goods and services it wishes to employ in its activities, including national defense. Thus, the government may be able to make reasonable estimates of the monetary costs required to undertake a certain level and type of national defense or homeland security.

But is any government-chosen amount and type of national defense and homeland security worth it? We don't know. In a free-market economy, there is two-sided competition. Demanders must decide how much they are willing to pay to purchase desired goods in competition with other buyers also interested in purchasing them. Suppliers judge what monetary costs they might be willing to incur to bring certain types and amounts of goods to market in competition with other supply-side rivals also interested in purchasing or hiring some of the scarce resources, capital, and labor services.

But with a public good such as national defense or homeland security, it is a group of politicians, bureaucrats, and private-sector special interest groups interested in benefiting from such government spending who interactively decide how much and what type of national defense and homeland security will be provided at taxpayers' expense. They are the joint central planners deciding on the quantity and forms of such public goods.

It is not the actual citizens of the society demonstrating their preferences about the amount and types of these public goods they think are needed by choosing how much they want to spend. There is no way, therefore, to be certain how much defense and security are reflective of the citizenry's preferences since they do not vote for them in the same way that they do as everyday market participants. In the marketplace, we vote with our voluntarily spent dollars, with each of us choosing the types and combinations of the goods and services that serve our purposes, even when this differs noticeably from the market choices of many others in society.

That is what makes the market an arena of real and actual diversity and inclusiveness. In a functioning free-market economy, minority and majority choices can be and are satisfied, all the way down to niche desires. As long as those wanting some marketable good are willing and able to offer some minimally sufficient price to make it profitable for some producers to specialize in its provision, then it usually gets produced and supplied. Multitudes of diverse demands are satisfied, and each of these is included in the production mix of goods produced out of the available scarce resources in the society.

The Politics and Economic Irrationality of National Defense

Now, it may be the case that only government can provide national defense (setting aside in this discussion the argument of those advocating non-governmental provision of such "public" goods and services). But if this is true, then there is an inherent and inescapable economic irrationality in the provision of national defense compared to the producing and buying of normal market-supplied goods and services.

In the case of a country such as the United States, defense spending becomes a matter of government central planning, albeit one in which the politician planners have been democratically elected. And it is one-size-fits-all for the nation as a whole. To the extent that voters have given attention to the foreign policy portions of the platforms politicians have run on, those who disagree with the foreign policies initiated by the winning presidential and Congressional candidates are forced to both pay for them and bear the risk of their implementation.

The citizen-voter may consider that he is being taxed too much or too little, given the global defense threats he thinks are facing the country. He may disagree with sending troops abroad for foreign interventions, and he may want to end the stationing of any American armed forces in other countries. Or he may think there needs to be on-going foreign interventions in the name of national security or "building democracy" in other lands but disagree with the types of such interventions undertaken by the administration in power in Washington. Other than his individual vote in the next election—and its minuscule impact on any outcome as a single voter—he has no way to try to bring about any other "supply" of national defense other than the one in place.

Instead, it is the "experts" in foreign affairs and national security who advise presidents and congressmen. But which of these is "right" about threats to America and the appropriate stance and response? In effect, defense and foreign policies, and the accompanying tax-funded spending, become the outgrowth of the ideas of ideological and "strategic" central-planners who claim they know how to manage America's place in the world. Whether they are "hawks" or "doves," or proponents of "realpolitik" or global "idealism," they all claim to know how to plan America's global presence.

At the same time, these "experts" interact with or are part of the defense, national security, and foreign policy bureaucracies in the government. At the end of the day, those in these bureaucracies may view themselves as trying to do good as they see it, but underlying this is a self-interest in the maintenance and growth of the bureaucratic structures upon which their incomes, positions, and chances for promotion and influence are based.

You do not demonstrate the importance of your place in the bureaucracy, and why you should be promoted up the civil service chain, by being non-interventionist. That stance easily could lead to no promotions and reassignment to dead-end tasks. You are not showing that you've gotten "on board with the program," without which that bureaucratic department or agency has no rationale for existence or funding.

And, finally, there are the private sector corporate and business interest groups whose profit margins and market shares are often heavily dependent upon government contracts for military and national security equipment and tasks. Their "consumers" are not the citizen-taxpayers, but the politicians and bureaucratic procurement departments that determine how much will be spent on defense and national security, and on which particular goods and services those tax-based dollars will be spent.

Foreign policy and national security threats are their bread and butter in the form of tens of billions of dollars of revenues from the federal government. Non-intervention or demonstrations of a "threat-free" world are not the ways to maximize the potentials from doing business with the defense and national security parts of the government.

Costs of Public Goods Like National Defense

Many free market or classical liberals and conservatives strongly believe, as did the Founding Fathers and Adam Smith, that there are some goods or services, such as national defense, that must be supplied by government through compulsory taxation due to their claimed "public goods" qualities. And this may be correct, as most others in society also believe.

But, nonetheless, if the buying and selling of any goods or services are taken out of the arena of competitive free markets, then the decision-making passes into the central-planning hands of those in and around political power.

Inevitably, like all other forms of central planning, the results from public goods such as national defense are reduced individual freedom of choice, persistent inefficiency and waste, and the arrogance and corruption of politicians, bureaucrats, and the interest groups living off government spending as their interactions determine the direction of the country. Nor should it be forgotten that in the case of national defense and homeland security, this also includes a threat to the lives, property, and privacy of the entire population of the country.

CHAPTER 11

WHY NOT PRIVATE PROVISION OF MANY GOVERNMENT SERVICES?

One of the great controversies in modern society concerns the necessary and required functions of government. There are few who disagree that if government is to exist then it certainly has the duty and responsibility to secure and protect essential rights of every individual, including the right to life, liberty and honestly acquired property. But there are a wide variety of tasks that the private sector could better provide that many think must be supplied by the government.

Many of these activities have been subsumed under the general notion of "public goods" that are subject to "free rider" problems. Public goods, as we saw in the previous chapter, are often defined as a good or service from the use or coverage of which an individual may receive a benefit, but from which he is not easily excluded even though he does not pay a price or fee to help cover some portion of the cost of making it available.

Free Riders and Public Goods

This creates the problem, we also saw, of an individual choosing to take a "free ride," that is, not voluntarily contributing to cover the cost of the good or service from which he benefits. The upshot of the argument being that less of this good or service may be supplied than might otherwise be the case if all beneficiaries were required to pay for some part of its costs of production.

The standard example, we explained, that is almost always given is national defense. How can any individual be successfully excluded from an anti-missile defense system that provides umbrella coverage to everyone within the territory of a country, whether or not any particular person has voluntarily contributed to pay for it? Hence, the case is made for compulsory payment in the form of taxation.

But whatever may or may not be the merits of the case for national defense as a "public good," as so defined, there are many other goods that are argued to be in the same category, and thus also requiring government provision through taxation. This is often said to be the case with infrastructure and community conveniences and amenities such as roads, bridges, parks, street lighting, and neigh-borhood recreational areas, as well as town or city planning in general.

Yet, the fact is that very few, if any, of these need be thought of in this way. Indeed, virtually all of them can be marketed with little or no free rider problems, or would be in the self-interest of some market participants to supply free of charge.

Misguided and Undesirable Urban Planning

Let us start with the widest of these presumptions, which takes for granted the need for and necessity of town or city planning. A well-ordered and designed community, it is said, serves the interest of all who are or who may come to live within its environs. Yet, there is no certainty of individual or group interest to voluntarily layout and follow a prior plan before the development of an urban area.

Street grids need to be laid out, zoning ordnances must delimit where residential housing will be built, industrial or manufacturing facilities will be constructed, shopping and entertainment services are to be located, and recreational or "green" areas are to be set aside and preserved.

The question is, why? This presumes that the urban designers, planners and implementers know way ahead of time where the current or future residents in these communities would find it most attractive and useful to live, work and enjoy life. To use the phrase with which F. A. Hayek entitled his Nobel lecture in 1974, this involves a great "pretense of knowledge" on the part of the urban and rural planners.

How can these planners know years or even sometimes decades ahead, what types of neighborhoods and communities people, themselves, may find more useful, convenient and serviceable for their needs, values, and circumstances? Instead, infrastructure and the outlay of communities should reflect and follow where and how people wish to live, work and travel. It should not confine and straightjacket people to the planner's arrogant conception of how he thinks people should live their lives in multiple layers and interconnections with others.

Communities as Spontaneous Orders

Some notable authors on this theme, especially Jane Jacobs (1916-2006) in her various studies of city life, highlighted again and again that localized neighborhood communities within towns and cities historically reflected the circumstances of the people, themselves.

The seeming "chaos" and disorder of people working, living, and shopping all in the same place with apartments above retailing and small manufacturing business enterprises on the ground floors of buildings, and children playing on the streets under the watchful eye of parents or grandparents looking out their apartment windows, in fact made life easier, less costly and more safe. It created degrees of neighborhood cohesion that often is not seen in the planned communities of the urban designers' dreams.

Also, communities change their membership as individuals and groups move up the income ladder or are able to take advantage of employment opportunities in other places. This, too, means that communities within towns and cities need the flexibility over time to reflect the values, needs and circumstances of their new residents. The rigidity of urban planning and zoning laws restrict the capacity for this adaptability to changing times and people.

The apparent disorder and chaos of urban and other areas not created according to central or regional plans may create discomfort and confusion for the city planners, but it represents the patterns, structures and arrangements of the spontaneous order of a free society. This is just another form and instance of the same "invisible hand" process that various economists highlight when they emphasize emerging market order without central intentional design.

Private Thoroughfares vs. Road Socialism

The same applies to thoroughfares. Roads, streets, and highways should be built and shifted and "modernized" over time to reflect where people want to go. But how could markets provide roads, streets or highways? Are these not "public goods" requiring the guiding, planning, and taxing hand of government?

To begin with, toll roads by both government and the private sector have long histories in both Europe and the United States. The fact that so many of us have become used to and take for granted "road socialism" (to use the phrase of the American 19th century economist, Francis A. Walker) does not mean that the private sector and the profit motive could not work here as elsewhere in society. Nor need there be the presumed inconvenient of frequent stops and slowdowns to go through tollbooths.

Many of us have driven on highways that are toll roads in certain states around the country. Sensors on these highways read the electronic "passes" attached to the front windshield of automobiles, and simply automatically deduct the charges similar to a bank debt card. For instance, through the northeast corridor of some mid-Atlantic and New England states is recognized a shared "EasyPass" that the different state's highway sensors mutually respect and recognize.

This "smart" technology helps demonstrate that roads and highways are easily able to charge those using the common thoroughfares. As one observer has pointed out:

> The private roads that exist now have fewer accidents than public roads, probably in part because they're better maintained: If private road builders let potholes remain, get reputations for high accident rates, or do repairs during rush hour, they have to deal with complaints and with people choosing other roads.
>
> Pollution and pollution controls on automobiles would also be handled by road privatization. If auto pollution were to

grow too thick, people living near the offending roads would sue the biggest, most obvious target: the road owners. Road owners would therefore charge higher fees for cars without up-to-date inspection stickers.

Roads and Parking Areas Intentionally Made for Free Riders

In addition, there would be many instances in which land developers would see the profitable gain from supplying and maintain roads at no charge to the users. Go to any enclosed or open shopping mall. There is often a large parking lot surrounding it, with one or more access roads leading to the main, nearby, thoroughfares.

These are usually provided with no parking fees precisely because the company or corporation owning and operating the shopping mall want customers to come on to their property and have easy access to the mall facilities. The more people finding it easy and safe to come do their shopping on their property the more attractive are the rental units inside the mall and, therefore, the willingly paid occupancy fees by the retail businesses who want their stores in that mall.

Many of these malls are entertainment centers all their own. They are well maintained, designed to be aesthetically attractive, and offer holiday festivities to customers at no charge. "Free riders" who enter the mall at no cost, who may simply walk around, or sit on one of the mall walkway benches, and spend the time listening to music, reading a book, or text messaging to friends, and not buy a thing, does not inhibit the mall owners from making it "open to the public" and free of charge.

For every free rider there are many others who actually shop and generate revenues for the retail outlets and the mall owners. The free rider cost is more than worth the revenue generating benefit.

Downtowns, Condos and Housing Associations

Similarly, "downtown" areas with hotels, restaurants, and shops and apartment units could, and no doubt, would form their own owner and renter associations for the providing of related infrastructure, including streets, lighting, parking, and cleaning services in their mutual self-interests, if government no longer was considered to have tax-based responsibility for the provision of many of them.

We see this is in condominiums or gated communities. The developers and maintainers of the facilities have profit-making incentives for supplying common area amenities and conveniences precisely because it makes residence in these areas more attractive and higher valued for owners and rental residents.

Homeowner associations that are not "gated" are the complement to this, with residents paying fees in the areas and communities in which they live as part of the contractual agreement in purchasing a house in that neighborhood. Everything from streetlights, parks, recreational facilities, walking and biking paths, doggy poop bag disposing bins, to tree and shrubbery care in the "public" areas are widely provided, and even when visiting free riders are able to enjoy many of these amenities, and all at the expense of others.

Much Smaller Government in the Society of the Future

My purpose in this chapter has been to briefly bring attention to a few of the non-governmental possibilities in areas of everyday life in which it is presumed that it is necessary for government to provide these services or goods at taxpayers' expense, because it is assumed that they fit some form of the "public goods" category, when in fact they need not or do not.

Some things presumed to be "non-excludable" for many users in fact can be privatized and offered for a fee or a price. At the same time, the world abounds with "free riders," from the person who attends a church service but puts nothing into the collection plate when it is passed around to defray the expenses of maintaining that house of worship, to the individual who sits in a shopping mall to get out of the summer heat and whiles away some free time without buying a thing in any of the stores.

Normally, churches want to attract free riders as part of their outreach to non-believers at the expense of the parishioners who have voluntarily contributed to the religious organization's activities. And many in the private sector offer access to and use of "free" goods as part of the operating costs of attracting customers from whom they hope to directly or indirectly earn profits.

Whatever may or may not be the functions of government, the market and the associations of civil society could easily and, no doubt, far more cost effectively and efficiently would provide a large number of these "public goods" and common area conveniences, rather than being dependent upon any tax-funded government to have them supplied. In a truly free society, the scope of government easily can be reduced to a much smaller domain than even many friends of freedom often think.

CHAPTER 12

EDUCATIONAL SOCIALISM VERSUS FREE MARKET SCHOOLING

Academia has long been thought of as the "marketplace of ideas," the arena where truth may be pursued through dispassionate discourse and openness to competing views. Yet higher education in America has moved a great distance from this ideal and its practice and into arenas of collectivist indoctrination.

Too many of our colleges and universities have become cloistered "hothouses" of bias and intolerance—schools of closed-mindedness. Everywhere we look these institutions are dominated by "political correctness," the common theme of which is disdain and disapproval of the American traditions of individualism, free enterprise, and constitutionally limited government.

The Closed Mind of Modern Academia

No amount of criticism or doubt from outside those hallowed halls seems to affect either the professors or the administrators, who claim to be the stewards of the younger generation placed in their intellectual and moral care. Indeed, more often than not, they demonstrate contempt for those who challenge their entitlement to mentor and mold our sons and daughters as they think fit. Their conduct shows that they consider themselves answerable to no one but themselves.

This should not be surprising considering the special, indeed, unique environment in which they operate. The vast majority of America's colleges and universities have become insular islands of "academic socialism." They are either directly owned or operated by government, or if they are "private," they have become so dependent on government loans, scholarships, and research grants that they have little real interaction with the wider remaining private-sector society.

Regardless of the lack of intellectual merit or usefulness of what is often taught in fields such as history, political science, economics, sociology, and literature, the faculties at these schools are protected from any negative feedback. Their salaries at state institutions are paid through tax dollars; their jobs are secured through lifetime tenure; and the content of their courses are judged as good or bad only by themselves. Any doubts about or dissent against how and what they teach is responded to with shouts of "academic freedom." That phrase has become a mantra to ward off the demons: those of us who may not agree with the "wisdom" they wish to "share" with our children.

Government funding, of course, comes from tax dollars expropriated from the hard-earned income of the American citizenry. Parents are therefore left with fewer financial resources with which to send their children to educational institutions outside the net of state sponsorship and control. Furthermore, the lure of less-expensive state-funded and state-subsidized colleges and universities creates a perverse incentive for parents to send their young to these politically funded schools.

Monopolizing the Minds of Young People

The damage from all this goes far beyond wasting the taxpayers' dollars in guaranteeing these academics their annual incomes. It means that the future of America is predominantly placed in their hands. The vast majority of young men and women pass through their educational processing. They mold how our sons and daughters see and think about politics, economics, history, moral philosophy, and social institutions.

To put it bluntly, they push our children through an intellectual sieve of collectivism; as a result, these young people leave college with no proper and vital understanding of freedom, self-respon-sibility, and the character and value of a free society. They enter adulthood unaware of the noble and courageous struggle that was carried on over the centuries in the Western world to establish the legacy of liberty and prosperity that too many of us take for granted.

What applies to government spending on higher education of course applies no less to government spending on K–12 schooling, as well. Indeed, it can be argued that government's influence at this level is even more disturbing, since these are the most impression-able years, when young minds are shaped by core ideas about their world. Whether it is sex education or conceptions about the environ-ment or even the basic capacity to read and write, the grammar- and high-school years can leave a mark on young men and women for the rest of their lives.

Freeing Minds from "K" Through High School

It is not surprising, therefore, that public-school teachers and admin-istrators are opposed to private competitive education during these formative years. Not only would it wrest from them near-monopoly control over the minds of America's youth, but a free market in education would also show the disastrous job the state system has done in preparing the next generation for earning a living in the global economy.

Compare that with the marketplace of everyday commerce, where the sellers of ideas and the products that embody them must demonstrate their value to the buying public. Sellers must prove that what is being offered is worth the price being asked. If they fail to do so, their clientele drifts away; their market share declines; and their incomes decrease. If a seller does not mend his ways, those who more effectively serve consumers will finally drive him out of business.

In a truly free market, the private seller cannot shout "producer freedom" and claim the right to be protected from the disapproval of his customers. In the free economy there is neither tenure nor government-guaranteed income. Every producer and seller is ultimately answerable to those he serves.

This is what makes competition a mechanism for fostering innovation and excellence. Every day, in every way, sellers must constantly try to stay ahead of their rivals in the marketplace. And they cannot forget that new entrants could come into their corner of the market, apply their creative abilities to better serve the consuming public, and earn some of the potential profits from doing so.

It is clear why so many teachers, professors, and administrators show such hostility to business and market competition. And it is no wonder that they despise the profit-and-loss system. To advocate a real marketplace of ideas would threaten their protected government-subsidized utopian, ivory-tower existence. Defeating "educational socialism," therefore, will require effort to escape the government's control of schooling. A growing number of parents in the United States are undertaking that effort, as demonstrated by the expanding attendance at private schools around the country and the increasing numbers of parents who incur the personal and family sacrifices to home-school their sons and daughters. Having lost all confidence in the government schooling system, they have taken more direct responsibility for their children's education.

Privatizing Public Schools for Better Education

What is needed is a radical change, and in my opinion, this means the denationalization, the full and complete privatization of schooling from kindergarten through graduate education.

Grammar and junior and high schools could be privatized any number of ways. One method might be to offer a school to the existing teaching and related staff, for them, in other words, to have the school transferred to them as shareholders of the school in which they have been working.

Another is to put schools up for auction, either as stand-alone schools, or as possible establishments in a chain of schools bought up by a particular company. They could run them directly or offer, to then resell them as franchises under the logo of the mother company.

This would immediately start to bring in the signals and incentives of any other types of business enterprises concerning current and prospective profitability in offering education that retains or attracts students and their parents.

Matching Selling Schools Would be Tax Cuts

Simultaneous with the any of these privatization methods, once schools are out of government hands, the property and related taxes that had been collected to financially support them as "public schools" immediately should be repealed.

This would help provide the financial wherewithal for parents and families to more easily have the financial means to pay directly for the tuition costs of sending their child or children to school.

At the same time, as these schools, one after the other, now passed into the private sector, forces of competition would be set loose and in motion that over time would work to bring about innovations in the curricula, the facilities, and the cost structure that would result in better learning environments with efficiencies that would make schooling increasingly more affordable.

Would all schools offer the same exact quality of education and comparable facilities? Most likely that would not be the case. But that is the situation now, but at least with privatized schools in a market-based environment all the supply-side incentives would be in the direction of improvements in the types and qualities of the schooling and education offered. This is certainly not the case in too many school districts around the country under our current system of socialized, government schooling.

Greater excellence in teaching at these schools will be dramatically enhanced, again, over time, if there is also the abolition of the current education degree certification to be allowed to teach at the high school and under levels. Allow the market to find and select the qualified teachers for the young people of the nation, and not the teachers' unions and state bureaucracies that have their own financial and political agendas as work.

Make Colleges and Universities Really Market-Based

Colleges and universities should be taken off the federal and state financial gravy trains at taxpayers' expense, as well. Parents and students would soon know the real cost and value of an education at various institutions of higher learning, rather than the current illusions created through government subsidies and grants of one type or another.

State owned and operated colleges and universities could be privatized along the same lines as suggested for kindergarten through high school. And existing "private" colleges and universities would no longer receive federal and state monies, either.

As government colleges and universities were sold off and grants and subsidies were ended for existing private institutions, the relevant taxes should be repealed, putting that money back in the pockets of those who earned it, so they might have better financial means to cover the actual costs of their sons and daughters going on for higher education, if they so chose.

Privatizing Schooling Would End Political Correctness

I would suggest that if schools were privatized in this manner and had to provide education reflecting what parents and students actually wanted and thought worth paying a price for, a large amount of the "political correctness" and ideologically driven courses would soon be replaced with classes and subjects reflecting things much closer to a far more traditional education.

When parents and students have to pay more directly and fully for the credit hours for each class taken, I personally doubt that as many leftist, collectivist, "touchy-feely," courses will have the enrollments that tax-funding enables to be offered and faculty salaries to be paid to those doing the teaching of them.

Education will be more consumer driven in terms of useful and desired content and delivery of knowledge than being "producer driven" in terms of what ideologically motivated faculty and administrators want to indoctrinate young minds with taxpayers' compulsorily collected monies to fund it.

Will the world of education change over night? Of course not, but the institutional incentives and competitive forces will have been set loose that we take for granted as the engines of innovative improvements in so many other areas of life.

This will, at the end of the day, be most important and valuable to those harmed and abused the most by our current system of educational socialism. Free market liberalism will "deliver the goods" here and in more and better qualities and varieties over time, just in every other walk of life in which the competitive forces of supply and demand are allowed to work.

CHAPTER 13

CENTRAL BANKING IS A FORM OF CENTRAL PLANNING

At a time when the appeal of and demands for a new "democratic" socialism seem to have caught the imagination of many among the young and is reflected in the promises of a good number of political candidates running for high office, there is one already existing socialist institution in America with few opponents: the Federal Reserve System.

The fact is, central banking is a form of central planning. The Federal Reserve has a legal monopoly over the monetary system of the United States. It plans the quantity of money in circulation and its availability for lending purposes; and it sets a target for the annual rate of price inflation (currently around 2 percent), while also intentionally influencing interest rates, investment spending, and supporting full employment. Almost all discussions and debates concerning the Federal Reserve revolve around how it should undertake its monetary central planning: which policy tools should be used, what target goals should be aimed for, and who should be in charge of directing America's central bank.

Federal Reserve Independence in the Trump Era

A complementary issue that has received renewed attention concerns the question of how much " independence" the Federal Reserve and other central banks should have to determine and implement monetary and interest rate policy. This has risen to the fore due to comments made by President Donald Trump concerning Federal Reserve interest rate policy and the individuals he has appointed or proposed for positions on the Federal Reserve Board of Governors.

Several times during 2018 and 2019, President Trump expressed irritation and frustration with increases in market rates of interest under the Federal Reserve Board leadership of Jerome Powell, who Trump nominated for Fed chairman, and who has held that position since February 2018. Trump has publicly pouted and whined that Barack Obama while he was president had a central bank that gave him rock bottom low interest rates. Fed Chairman Powell, on the other hand, has raised interest rates several times, preventing America from being as "great" as Trump thinks it can be because of the higher costs of borrowing for both the private sector and the federal government.

Being informed that he really cannot just fire Chairman Powell because he doesn't like Federal Reserve policies, Trump wants to get around the Powell problem by nominating for open positions on the Fed Board those he thinks will more likely direct Federal Reserve policies in the way he wants.

Trump Critics on the Left, the Right and at "The Economist"

Trump has been attacked from both the left and the right for seeming to want to pack the Federal Reserve Board of Governors with "political" types reflecting Trump's desire for loser monetary policy and lower interest rates. Some on the political left oppose his nominees simply because, well, they are Trump's choices.

Others more to the political right don't want them on the Board because they would prefer a more "hawkish" Fed policy. Desmond Lachman, a resident scholar at the conservative American Enterprise Institute, has argued that the Federal Reserve should raise interest rates so the central bank will have the room for future successful monetary stimulus policies when the next economy-wide downturn comes along. In other words, he just wants monetary central planning in a different direction than President Trump.

The Economist magazine had as its cover topic for the April 13, 2019 issue the threat to central bank " independence" from Trump and others like him in charge of governments around the world. What is needed and has to be preserved, *The Economist* argues, are professional monetary planning "technocrats" who rise above and are free from interference by politicians, so those at the central banking helm can focus on long-run price level stability and non-ideological banking and interest rate policies.

The magazine admits that central bankers have not always gotten it right — even the most well-intentioned central planner is only human, let's not forget — but in their wise hands the world has been saved from destabilizing price inflations and short run policy manipulations that might have been harmful to full employment and steady growth.

The "Austrian" Critique of Central Planning vs. Markets

Rarely heard or suggested in all these commentaries on the Federal Reserve is whether the United States needs or should have a central bank. I would like to suggest that the answer is "No," and for many of the same reasons that can be made against socialist central planning in general.

One hundred years, the Austrian economist, Ludwig von Mises, first published his famous critique of socialist central planning in his article, "Economic Calculation in the Socialist Commonwealth" (1920) and then extended the challenge to all facets of collectivism in his 1922 book, *Socialism: An Economic and Sociological Analysis*. The gist of his argument was that a centrally planned economy did away with the essential institutions necessary for rational economic calculation: private property in the means of production, market competition, and a functioning price system.

In a complex and ever-changing social system of division of labor all the multitudes of participants are interdependent for all the things needed for everyday life. It is necessary to have some means of knowing what it is that people want to buy in their role as consumers and the value they place on those things; and it is also essential to know what resources are available out of which desired consumer goods might be produced, and what their values might be in the alternative uses for which they could be applied.

In other words, do consumers desire hats, or shoes, or bananas, or breakfast cereal, or classical music, or serious books on economics, or anything else; and what are the relative values they may place on possibly purchasing them? At the same time, what are the available types and quantities of labor, land, resources and raw materials, and capital goods (machinery, tools, equipment) that may be used in various combinations to produce those consumer items, and what might be their appraised values in being employed in different and competing lines of production?

Market Prices and Economic Calculation

The market solves that problem, Mises explained, through the emergence of a competitive price system for both finished goods and the factors of production. With exchangeable private property there are opportunities to buy and sell; with the ability to buy and sell, people have motives and incentives to make bids and offers to each other; out of those bids and offers may arise agreed-upon terms of trade; and those agreed-upon terms of trade create the complex structure of relatives prices for both those finished goods and the factors of production.

In a complex market system there also historically emerged a medium of exchange to overcome the hurdles of direct barter transactions to better facilitate the buying and selling of virtually everything. As the most widely used and generally accepted medium of exchange, the commodity that becomes the money-good comes to be on one side of every exchange.

People trade their goods for money, and then trade away that money for other goods they desire to buy. Almost every good and service on the market, therefore, comes to have a money price that then enables an ease of economic calculation through which all the physically heterogeneous goods offered on the market may be expressed in a single valuational common denominator – the money prices for everything.

Thus, all traders on the market can readily do their "comparison shopping." What would this bundle of consumer items cost me to buy and what are the relative costs if I substitute one good for another to buy, instead? If I buy one hat for $10, then I have to forgo the equivalent of two pairs of gloves that cost $5 a piece.

The same applies on the supply-side of market production decisions. The entrepreneur can try to make an informed judgment concerning what a consumer good sells for in the present and might possibly sell for in the future if he were to bring some quantity of it to market. Likewise, he can determine what it would cost to rent, hire or purchase alternative combinations of inputs (labor, land, capital) to manufacture some such consumer item, on the basis of which he can decide whether he thinks that doing so it would be a profit-making or a loss-making endeavor; and if seeming to be profitable, which combination of those inputs would minimize his costs of production to potentially maximize the anticipated and hoped for profits?

Central Planning Leads to Planned Chaos

A system of socialist central planning does away with all of this. With government nationalization of the means of production there is nothing to (legally) buy and sell on the production side of the economy. With nothing to buy and sell, there are, obviously, no bids or offers for the factors of production. With no bids and offers for labor, land, resources, and capital, there are no market-based prices for appraising profitable from unprofitable lines of production, and deciding which alternative ways of making finished goods would minimize the costs of production.

It is not surprising that a bit more than a quarter of a century after Mises first offered his criticisms of socialist central planning he titled a short monograph on the same theme, "Planned Chaos" (1947). Without market-based and competitively-generated prices to assist the on-going process of rational economic calculation in a changing world, the central planners would be "flying blind" in trying to decide what to produce and how to produce it to get the most out of the scarce factors of production in value terms in supplying the goods and services consumers actually might want to buy and for which would have been willing to pay.

Most economists around today would find the gist of this argument fairly obvious if asked to agree with it or not, even if many mainstream economists would no doubt insist that there were supposed problems of monopoly, claimed undersupplied public goods, and the asserted need for various redistributive welfare programs outside of the arena of market exchange due to income inequalities. But the notion that market-based, competitive prices enable effective and cost-efficient economic calculation for much that goes on in a complex society would be accepted, in this general formulation, without too much disagreement.

Central Banking Denies Freedom of Choice in Money

On this basis, I would argue that monetary central planning in the form of central banking creates many of the same problems for economic calculation and effective and efficient use of resources as traditional socialist economic planning. First of all, what commodity (or commodities) should be used as a medium (or media) of exchange? Under our current monetary system, anyone who attempts to offer and market alternative monies for use in domestic transactions is subject to legal penalty including arrest and imprisonment.

For instance, back in the late 1990s, Bernard von NotHaus decided to mint and market an alternative "private voluntary currency" for business and related transactions. In 2009, Mr. NotHous was arrested for circulating millions of his gold coins called the Liberty Dollar in over 80 cities on counterfeiting charges and for undertaking a "conspiracy" against the United States government's monetary monopoly. He was found guilty in 2011 and in 2014 he was given six months house arrest and three years probation. In 2018, Mr. NotHous was back, this time saying that he was starting up a cryptocurrency that was to be 100 percent backed by silver. How the government responds this time to his attempt to undermine America's socialist monetary system remains to be seen.

But the fact is, how can any government and even the wisest and most PhD'ed of their Federal Reserve experts know what people in the marketplace would find it attractive, advantageous, and profitable to use as a medium of exchange in market transactions, or whether there might not be a demand for different types of money for different forms of market activities?

The answer is that there is no way of fully knowing this other than allowing private enterprisers and entrepreneurs in the financial and other everyday markets to competitively discover and offer what we the buying and selling public might want for this purpose. It is now more than 40 years since Austrian economist, F. A. Hayek, published his "Choice in Currency" (1976) in which he called for the simple monetary reform of ending legal tender laws and allowing people to choose and use in domestic and foreign transactions any medium of exchange they desire. He considered this a necessary freedom to break the history of abuse under government monopoly money and to allow people to use whatever the money they want.

Only Markets Can Discover the Optimal Amount of Money

Second, how can the monetary central planners know how much money should be in circulation and in the banking system? This is no more possible than the old Soviet central planners knowing how much toilet paper to produce or the quantities and varieties of any other everyday household necessity. What the Soviet planners produced invariably turned out to be in the wrong amounts and in the wrong types. A visit to a "people's" lingerie store (and I use this term very loosely) in Moscow before the collapse of the Soviet Union found one-size-fits-all in women's underpants. Any needed adjustment of the waistband, well, comrade, that is what safety pins are for. No unnecessary quantities or wasteful duplication under bright and beautiful socialist planning. The central planners were, no doubt, Soviet socialism's best and brightest – and with PhD's!

Under a commodity money such as gold in a fully free enterprise system, the amount of money in the market is a reflection of supply and demand. People have uses for gold for either commercial or monetary purposes. Gold has its price in the marketplace. Based on this those on the supply-side could estimate the profitability of prospecting, mining, minting and marketing greater quantities of produced gold for sale for monetary and other commercial uses.

An increased demand for gold as money sees a shift of the commodity from commercial uses to monetary ones, and with the resulting rise in the value of gold in general, a greater profitability from gold prospecting, mining and minting. As the supply increases, the rise in the market value of gold is tempered, with the increasing supply tending to satisfy the greater demand. Yes, there have been noticeable gold-based fluctuations due to newly discovered gold sources in various parts of the world. But in general these incidents have been few and far between, with gold annually being extracted from known pockets based on current and trend demand.

The crucial element in this is that the "optimal" quantity of money is the interactive outcome of the market participants themselves. The gold market provides the price system that reflects the demand for gold in its various uses, of which money is one. And the related markets for the needed means of production to mine, mint, and supply gold provide the cost prices that facilitates the rational economic calculations for an ever adapting and adjusting "optimal" market-guided quantity of money.

The Central Bankers Determine How Much Money

Today we are dependent on the decisions of a handful of central planning executives in the Board of Governors of the Federal Reserve. What is their guide? The personal judgments of what they think the economy needs, based upon the prevailing macroeconomic theories used in the central bank about how the economy works and therefore how much money should be pumped into the banking system.

Our monetary fate is dependent upon whether the central bank experts, this year, are old-style Keynesians, New Keynesians, Monetarists, New Classical Economists, Taylor Rule followers, Supply-Siders, New Modern Monetary Theorists, or any number of other possibilities. In the old Soviet Union, it all depended upon whether Stalinists or Trotskyites were to be in charge in determining "the Party line," and therefore the purpose and direction of economic planning.

Just as it is said that central banking needs to be independent so the "objective" and scientific monetary "experts" can guide the economy based on the latest and "correct" macroeconomic models, it was insisted under Soviet and all other socialisms-in-practice that it was all objective and scientific, being based on Marxian dialectical materialism, given what that meant in any particular situation. It's all a politics and ideology of planning. A few say they know what is right for the many, and will use government to give it to them.

The False Target of 2 Percent Price Inflation

Also important to keep in mind is that there is no optimal rate of price inflation. To begin with, any benchmark meant to determine whether prices in general are rising or falling is based upon some statistical averaging of selected and weighted individual prices tracked through time to determine whether or not a constructed and imaginary basket of goods has become more expensive or less expensive, and if so by what percentage amount from an earlier point in time.

Changes in the cost of living affect each of us differently based on the reality of what we as individuals and separate households choose to buy and in what relative amounts. Also, our individual baskets are not invariant points of comparison even for ourselves, since changes in our tastes and preferences, in the relative prices among the goods we buy, and the market's offering of new and better quality goods on a frequent basis all brings about changes in what goods are in our respective baskets and their relative quantities.

Such statistical creations as the Consumer Price Index are at most very rough and ready general pieces of information for the consumer or citizen concerning what the central bank may doing to the overall value of the money we use. The fact is, its importance is not for you or me, but as one of the signals used by the central bankers to decide the rate of monetary expansion and for influencing interest rates.

It's all based on a macroeconomic conception that in general a falling price level is "bad," and that growth and employment are "stimulated" by modestly rising prices. It has fallen mostly (though not exclusively) to the Austrian School over the last one hundred years to demonstrate that falling prices due to greater outputs and supply-side cost efficiencies are not only not harmful to the wealth and health of modern society, but are an indication of increasing prosperity and rising real standards of living.

Likewise, whether it is the attempt to maintain a relatively stable general level of prices (as partly guided Federal Reserve policy in the 1920s) or the contemporary central bank target of 2 percent price inflation, the primary institutional tool at Federal Reserve's deposal is to buy U.S. government securities (and now a variety of other market assets including mortgaged-backed securities during the financial crisis of 2008-2009 and after) and to increase loanable reserves in the banking system.

This becomes the means for influencing interest rates for investment and all other types of borrowing to try to "stimulate" spending and employment in the economy as a whole. Even the Fed's latest policy trick since the financial crisis to pay banks not to lend the very trillions of dollars of excess reserves the central bank pumped into the banking system is a way for the Federal Reserve to try to influence interest rates and aggregate spending in the economy.

The fact is, interest rates should be left free and competitive to do their job as the network of intertemporal prices connecting and coordinating the savings decisions of lenders with the investment choices of borrowers. In other words, interest rates are the prices that are supposed to bring markets and the use of the factors of production into balance with each other across time.

Instead, by viewing and using interest rates as a policy tool to be manipulated, the Federal Reserve's monetary central planners only succeed in distorting and preventing interest rates from telling the truth: how much savings is in the economy to sustain and maintain a structure of gross and net investments with varying time horizons.

Just as Soviet central planners may have believed that they could coordinate it all for better and more successful outcomes than market economies, our central bankers never fail in their enthusiasm and arrogant confidence that this time they will get it right, that they "now" have the right macroeconomic model of how it all works; they, finally, have bigger and better statistical data and computer capacity to successfully read and measure the entrails of the economic goose.

What they, in fact, bring about are the inflations and recessions, the booms and busts that they insist they are in the central banking business to moderate, if not to prevent. By their fruits you will know them: the post-World War I inflation and depression; the 1920s false promise of prosperity and stability, followed by the Great Depression; the booms and busts of inflations and recessions in the 1950s; the monetary inflation of the 1960s and especially the high price inflation of the late 1970s and early 1980s. Then a relative calm in the 1990s, but followed by the monetary expansion between 2003-2008 that set the stage for the great financial and housing crisis of 2008-2010; and now the great experiment with "quantitative easing" and the ballooning Federal Reserve asset portfolio filled with private sector mortgages.

The long history of central banking, and especially over the last one hundred years of paper monies and out-of-control government deficit spending partly funded by "monetization" of the debt, has more than clearly demonstrated that the epoch of modern central banking needs to come to an end. And in its place, the opening and freeing of financial markets to private competitive free banking, with markets – meaning all of us – deciding what we want to use as money.

CHAPTER 14

DIVERSITY AND INCLUSIVENESS IN THE LIBERAL SOCIETY

Freedom and the free society are once again under direct attack by those who espouse far greater degrees of government control over people's lives. Wrapping themselves in the cloak of progressivism, "social justice," and liberation from oppression and discrimination, they use a lexicon of words that are designed to reflect their view of and desires for the world: diversity, inclusiveness, participatory democracy, pluralism, and peace. But in reality, the only social system able to deliver on these goals is free market liberalism.

To understand this, it is necessary to begin with first principles about human beings and the nature and workings of the social world. Our social justice warriors have as their starting premise the idea that society is composed of elementary groups or collectives, with these defining and determining the facts and fate of everyone in society.

Human Beings Defined as "Social Classes" at War

During the last hundred years, collectivists have differed over the characteristics of these elementary groups. Marxists and other socialists traditionally defined human beings on the basis of their relationship to and ownership of the means of production. Thus, there were, on the one side, the capitalist owners of the means of production and, on the other side, those who sell their labor to those owners as the means of earning a living.

In the Marxian story of human history, the private owners of the means of production extract a portion of what the workers have produced through their productive labors, and take that portion as ill-gotten gains simply because they own the tools and machines with which production is undertaken and without access to which the workers and their families would starve. Hence, the story of capitalism is a tale of exploitation and abuse by the few who own the means of production against the many who do the actual toiling.

Through his clairvoyant reading of the inescapable trajectory of the stages of history, Karl Marx promised that the workers would finally rise up and throw off their economic chains, collectively seize and jointly use the means of production for their common purposes, and the world would be transformed into a paradise on earth of equality and prosperity for all in the communism of the future.

In the Marxian worldview, your place in society, the identification of who and what you are, and your relationship to others are all predetermined by your "objective" status vis-a-vis the private ownership and control over the physical means of production (factories, machines, land, resources and raw materials). How you may think about these things is irrelevant to the reality of the class conflict between the haves and the have-nots. You are your social class. Your future and place in society is tied to the fate of that social class to which you belong.

Escape is impossible. If you do not see yourself and act as a member of the exploited working class there are only two general explanations: either you have been duped and brainwashed by the capitalist class with a "false consciousness" from which you need to be re-educated; or you are a "traitor to your class," that is, a paid hireling who has betrayed his own abused social class for a privileged position or special pay provided by the oppressing private owners of those means of production.

Individuals Submerged Within Nations and Races

The other two dominant collectivisms of the last one hundred years have been nationalism and racialism, with their extreme forms represented by Italian fascism and German National Socialism (Nazism). Fascism declared that the nation was the building block of society, represented by shared culture, heritage, language and history. There was nothing above or outside of the nation-state, Benito Mussolini insisted; the individual owed all his strength and obedience, including sacrifice of his life and all that he considered to be his own, because what anyone considers his own is really the property of the nation-state to which be belongs. After all, the individual passes away, but "the nation" continues indefinitely.

Nazism's twist on this was that who and what you are is defined by "the blood," that is the biological inheritance given to you based on the racial group into which you have been born. The racial characteristics and qualities identified as belonging to various races determines your place and position in the competitions among racial groups for dominance and power in the world.

Those forethoughtful enough to pick pureblooded Germans as their parents wisely assured that they were members of the "master race." Those in whose veins flowed "Jewish blood" were condemned as inferiors and socially dangerous parasites needing to be eliminated for the good of the superior racial group. Here, too, there was no escape from the genetic tribe into which one had been born. You are your race, with the individual a prisoner of his biological background.

The life and death struggles making up the course of human events were conflicts and combats between these groups – social, national or racial. The individual human being was just along for the ride based on the good fortune or bad luck of the collective into which birth and circumstances had placed him. The individual is made nothing more than a passing droplet in the great stream of history, a history and reality of social classes, nation-states and biological races.

Classical Liberalism's Foundation in Individuals and Ideas

Against these collectivisms has stood the social and political philosophy of classical or free market liberalism. Groups of any type do not exist separate from or independently of the individuals of which they are composed. Individual human beings are ultimately the building blocks of society, not collective combinations of them.

Yes, we are born into families, we inherit biological characteristics of our parents and those that preceded them, and we grow up in the social, political and economic institutional orders in which birth and our family circumstances have placed us. All this is no doubt true without deterministically dictating our fate as a distinct human being.

The classical liberals of the 18th and 19th centuries argued that all of these things do not change the fact that each and every one of us is a thinking, reasoning, valuing and acting individual. And it is our thinking, reasoning and acting that ultimately determines how we view ourselves, others around us, and the social orders in which we wish to live.

For instance, are the Germans of the 21st century the same as the Germans of the 1930s? The large majority of them are the descendants of those who lived in the geographical area defined as Germany in that earlier time. And these later Germans are the inheritors of the social and institutional order into which they were born and that had preceded them.

But are they the same "Germans" in certain essential and meaningful senses? Specifically, in the realm of ideas and the actions that follow from beliefs and understandings, the answer is surely, "No." Eighty years ago in 1939, a sizable number of Germans believed in, accepted, or acquiesced and went along with Nazi ideology and Hitler's domestic and foreign policies. Many Germans were formally or informally Nazis in their words and in a good many of their deeds.

Out of a population of 87 million in 1939, the German secret police, the Gestapo, numbered less than 35,000, or .000425 percent of the total. Surveillance, obedience, and informing on others were dependent on the willful participation of many millions of people under German National Socialism.

Today, Nazis and neo-Nazis make up a very small percentage of the total German population. The vast majority of Germans are anti-totalitarian in their thinking, they reject the notion of a one-party state, and they do not believe in race theories concerning human society. They may hold a variety of other ideas that are far from classical liberal and free market ideals, but contemporary German society is different from that of 1939 because of the ideas, beliefs, and values in the minds of multitudes of individual Germans today. The racist sins of the fathers and grandfathers have not been biologically passed on to their children and grandchildren through "the blood," independent of individual human views and values about man, society and government.

The ideas in our minds and not the DNA in our chromosomes determine who or what we are in terms of our attitudes and actions, though of course we are biological creatures. We can choose to not see human beings as "class enemies" or "race opponents" or "nationalist threats." We can choose to see our fellow human beings as individuals, each of who has their own history and experiences, their own personality and proclivities, but nonetheless a distinct and unique person to be looked at, judged, and interacted with on that basis.

The Liberal Heritage of Life, Liberty and Property

In the classical liberal heritage of ideas, every human being has an inviolable right to their individual life, liberty and honesty acquired property. The philosophical founders of classical liberalism grounded this, in general, in theology and/or reason. We are each creations of God, who breathes life into each one of us, and who in his commandments to humankind forbids killing and stealing and fraud (bearing false witness). Hence, from the beginning, God ordains a society of free and peaceful people.

Our reason, also and separately, enables us to reach a similar conclusion. Born into this world, no person in reflecting on him- or herself wishes to be murdered or plundered. Every human being wishes to have the liberty to try to survive and prosper, to pursue and perhaps achieve happiness, and to peacefully produce and acquire the means for material and cultural betterment. Not one of us wishes to be reduced to the compulsory servant or slave of another, who denies us the ability to be and act as an end in ourselves rather than a forced means to their ends. All reasonable and right thinking people know this to be true about themselves and those around them.

The rational voice inside each one of us, upon that inward reflection, says that what we want is for others to respect our own right to our life, liberty and property, but that this requires a matching respect on our part for their similar rights; through such a reciprocal respect for each other's individual rights, social peace and prosperity become possible.

The most elevated and eloquent expression of this is still to be found in the American Declaration of Independence, in which the securing and protecting of such individual's rights becomes the reason for the establishment of government to guard everyone from the plundering hands of their neighbors. And for a document such as the United States Constitution, meant to delineate and narrowly define the functions of that government so to assure that political power guards our liberty and does not become a means for denying it.

But just as the Germans of 2019 are not politically the carbon copies of the Germans of 1939, the Americans of today are not the Americans of 1819 or 1919 in terms of ideas held, government policies wanted, or freedoms cherished. Not everyone in America understands, supports, or wants what the more active and vocal progressives and new American democratic socialists say they want to see implemented in the United States. But the attention, sympathy and deference for their message in the political arena and the mass media, suggests just how far the Americans of 2019 are from those earlier Americans of one or two centuries ago.

Classical Liberal Diversity and Inclusiveness

Which gets us to the progressive and democratic socialist agenda of diversity, inclusion, participatory democracy, pluralism, and peace. These may not have been the catch phrases of the 18th and 19th century classical, free market liberals, but they represented a good part of their vision for a better world, though significantly different from the meanings and content assigned to these terms in contemporary America.

For the classical liberal, diversity is inseparable from the idea of individuals and their rights. Society is as diverse as the number of people existing in it. Every human being has a right and is encouraged to "find himself," that is, to discover and decide who they are, what they want, what peaceful avenues seem most likely to bring them closer to those goals for life. Each of use has one life to live in this earthly sojourn. And all of us should be respectful of and even understanding for the plethora of ways that human beings try to find happiness and personal meaning behind it all.

Tyranny of any sort, classical liberals argue, restrict and restrain that human diversity by controlling and confining individual human beings in terms of what they can do and with whom within the dictates of what the tyrants impose on all the others in society. The corridors of diversity are narrowed to those within the commands and prohibitions set by those with the political power to threaten others with physical force. Diversity extends no further than what serves the purposes and pleasures of those in that political authority.

In the classical liberal world of open and free markets, inclusion is both offered and fostered for all through participation in the social system of division of labor. In the arena of free exchange every member of society is encouraged and given the opportunity to find their niche of specialized productive ability as both the means to earn the financial wherewithal to obtain from others all that can better improve the satisfaction of their own ends through trade, and for all the others in society to gain from what that individual can offer to them in the voluntary reciprocity of buying and selling.

This is why classical liberals have argued for free trade, for its multitude of benefits when taken far beyond the exchanges with the village or town to incorporate every one within the same country, then on the same continent, and finally to bring together all of humanity, everywhere, around the entire world in an interdependent community of industry and commerce that includes all of humanity. What can be more inclusive that offering partnership to everyone on the planet to share what they can do to better the conditions of others as the self-interested means to improve one's own life as defined by each of us?

Here, too, is a crucial reason why classical liberals have criticized, opposed and called for the repeal of all restrictions and restraints on the peaceful and voluntary trades desired and associations wanted among all those anywhere around the globe. When governments impose barriers to freedom of exchange and association, they limit the bringing together of all those who wish the partnership of their fellow human beings on the basis of terms they mutually agree upon, rather than the prohibitions and interventions of governments that want to benefit some at the cost of excluding or limiting the possibilities that could have belonged to others, if only markets have been left free from the controlling hands of political power.

Market Participatory Democracy and Income Inequality

In the classical liberal view of society there is no better, adaptable and successful system of participatory democracy than the freedom of the competitive marketplace. There is no majority, winner-take-all outcomes in the market. The more developed and prosperous a market economy the greater the possibilities and the more the profitable opportunities to serve and fulfill not only the wants and desires of a majority of consumers, but a wide array of minority demands for a variety of goods and services.

As long as a minority of buyers are willing and able to cover the costs of production and a bit more for some private enterprisers searching for the best profit opportunities they can find given their own interests and capabilities, even relatively small niche markets will find suppliers to satisfy their demands.

As a number of economists have explained, in the marketplace people vote with the dollars in their pockets for the goods and services that they wish to have and are willing to pay for. The critic, at this point, often points out that the "voting power" in the free market is unequal, with some having far more dollars in their pockets to vote with than others.

The classical liberal has never denied this. But he asks, how is it that such an unequal number of voting dollars are present among the members of the society? The answer usually given is, either from peaceful market-oriented production or political power-based plunder.

If Joe has more dollars in his pocket than Bob or Bill, in a free, open and competitive market, the only way he could have acquired those many dollars is precisely by having produced and offered on the market something that many others in society found so attractive and desirous that they "voted" to buy his wares and exchanged to him all those dollars he has earned from peaceful and voluntary services rendered.

If I as an economics professor earn more than a checkout clerk at the supermarket, but at the same time I earn less than the corporate executive managing a large industrial enterprise, this reflects our respective value in the eyes of our fellow human beings in the arena of market exchange, in terms of what they consider our respective talents to be worth as useful means to better satisfy their own ends.

Ethics and the Anonymity in the Free Market

This does not mean that in some moral or social sense that I am "better" than the supermarket checkout clerk, or that I stand below the ethical status of the business executive. The market does not reward people on the basis of personal "goodness" or ethical deservedness. The market – which means all of us as individual buyers and sellers – judge and estimate what a person's services are worth in terms of the ends and goals that others in society are attempting to fulfill.

In this sense, the market is neither moral nor immoral, other than in terms of asking whether the transactions and trades have been peaceful, voluntary and non-fraudulent. In buying from or selling to anyone, rarely if ever do I ask whether I consider them to be a "good person" or an ethical human being. In the general anonymity of the marketplace, I am simply evaluating how much I think what this person can do for me is worth at this moment and in this context.

This is disturbing and shocking to many critics of the liberal free market system. But this anonymity and disinterestedness of most buying and selling protects and frees most of us from the prying and manipulating eyes and actions of others in society. When the otherwise busybody moralizing meddler buys a box of breakfast cereal off the supermarket shelf he does not ask and cannot know who participated in the manufacture of that product. He does not know the sexual preferences of the participants in that production process, or what church (if any) they attend, or whether they smoke or drink, or whether they cheat on their spouse, or whether they like classical music instead of punk rock.

Each can make his own living in the corner of the market's division of labor that they find most interesting and profitable in which to work; they take home their honestly earned pay, and proceed to spend it in any way they want that reflects their values, desires and pleasures, whether or not that busybody meddler would approve if he could know it all and put his nose into that person's business.

How many of us would want others to make moral judgments about us before and as the determining factor concerning what we could work at and how much we could earn to then go about the private affairs of our own life? The general anonymity of the competitive marketplace helps to free us from the meddler.

So is there no economic injustice? No reality of ill-gotten gains? No distributions of income that reflect unfairness in society? Yes, there are within the classical liberal conception of society. But these are due precisely to the actions and interventions of the very government that progressives and democratic socialists wish to turn to and extend even more power.

The fairness and justice of the free market process is perverted when governments bestow privileges or favors, anti-competitive protections, licensing and regulatory restrictions, subsidies and bounties paid for with other people's money for the benefit of some in society at the expense of the rest of the citizenry. All or part of the incomes earned through such interventionist and welfare statist policies have been political pickpocketing through the taxing and regulatory and planning powers of any government.

The answer to these and similar problems of unjust income earnings and inequalities is abolition and repeal of all of those policies so to restore the freedom and voluntarism of all human interactions, trading relationships and associations. Monopolies and concentrations and inequalities of wealth and income only become and remain concerns when markets are not left free and open to innovative rivals interested and willing to compete against existing enterprises, and when consumers are not allowed to be fully sovereign in deciding on how to spend their own earnings, in exchange with whomever they want and at the terms mutually agreed upon.

Non-Market Concerns and Civil Society

Outside of the marketplace, having earned our incomes from rendering those services to our fellows through buying and selling, we are at liberty to make our decisions about what to do with our earnings. Here is where we may make value judgments about our fellows in terms of charity, philanthropy, good works, and helping hands for those less well off than ourselves who we consider to be deserving of our assistance when we feel called upon to do so by our conscience and senses of right and wrong as members of the wider society in which we live.

This aspect of the classical liberal conception of participatory democracy is reflected in the associations and organizations of what is widely called the institutions of civil society. People come together to advance shared interests, causes and purposes that may be beyond the abilities of one, and for the accomplishment of which people voluntarily come together.

At the end of the day, classical liberals not only consider this the more moral means of solving social problems that seem to be "beyond supply and demand," by leaving such matters to the conscious and calling of free people rather than government compulsion through the impersonal and depersonalized structures of tax-funded bureaucracies. But also the organizations and associations of civil society are far more effective means to those ends by drawing upon the advantages of decentralization, competition, and voluntarism over the generally monopoly power and decision-making of those assigned such tasks within the government. For the classical liberal these represent the true forms of participatory democracy both inside and outside of the marketplace, both broadly and narrowly defined.

The Pluralism of Freedom and Free Markets

This also captures the classical liberal idea of pluralism. Precisely by leaving all such matters outside of the prerogative and power of government, multiple avenues of trying and succeeding are both possible and allowed. Many voices may speak on any number of imaginable subjects at the same time; many minds can be set to work to investigate and search for solutions to any number of problems simultaneously; multitudes of people acting both on their own and in consort with others can advance their personal and joint purposes, each in his own way according to their individual and combined judgments; all are at liberty to live their own lives as they want in different circles of often different people, given that we each of us have multiple interests concerning which different people may overlap with whom we find it best and more beneficial to associate.

The government alternative invariably involves taking much of this decision-making, acting, and interacting out of the direct hands of people, themselves, and transfers control over all these issues and concerns to those elected into political office and those to whom authority has been delegated to act upon them through government agencies. The classical liberal considers this to be both an abridgement of each person's liberty and the closing of those pluralist avenues to possible success.

Free Market Liberalism and the Peaceful Society

Finally, for the classical liberal the marketplace of ideas, actions and association is the great arena of social peace. The fundamental premise upon which the free market liberal ideal is based precludes force and fraud from human relationships. Whether one is religious or not, the classical liberal lays downs the following as the fundamental rules of human society: you will not kill, you will not steal, and you will not cheat or defraud any with whom you interact, deal or associate. In other words, the primary societal "thou shalt not's" to be found in the Ten Commandments.

That cannot be said in the same way about the world wanted by progressives, democratic socialists, and all others wishing to maintain and extend the interventionist-welfare state. For all of them, politics becomes the central if not the single human setting for determining how people live; how much they may earn; what they may do to make that living; where they will live and in what accommodations; with whom they may associate and for what purposes; what language and words may be spoken or written or gestures used in various arenas of human interaction; and what opportunities will be yours and which may be closed to you due to majority rule or the dictates of the political correctness police.

Diversity, inclusion, participatory democracy, pluralism and peace dictated and determined by ideological tyrants and power lusting interest groups using political means to achieve their ends through governmental force and collectivist intimidation undermines and then destroys the alternative and far better world of peaceful persuasion or attractive offers in the voluntary arena of market exchange.

Once more, society is faced with the fundamental alternatives: Freedom or force? Peaceful production or political plunder? Voluntary consent or compulsory command? Personal choice or government planning? Market-based prosperity or the poverty of political planning? At the end of the day, we all will have to decide.

CHAPTER 15

FREE MARKET LIBERALISM AS THE IDEOLOGY OF FREEDOM AND MODERATION

Nowadays, many along the political spectrum seem to agree that America increasingly has become a polarized society. Ideological and public policy discourse has been gravitating more towards the extremes: progressives and the Democratic Party with a more explicitly socialist rhetoric and proposed government agenda, and conservatives and Republicans who increasingly appear to be moving in the direction of populist, and especially economic nationalism under the presidency of Donald Trump.

If such ideological extremism is politically tearing the country apart in the eyes of many, then what could and should be a "non-ideology" of compromise and moderation? This is a question that Jerry Taylor, president of the William Niskanen Center, tried to ask and answer in an article on, "The Alternative To Ideology" (October 9, 2018), in which he directly challenged the premises and policy perspective of many free market liberals and libertarians.

Mr. Taylor insisted that those who espouse a political philosopher of individualism, free markets, and strictly limited constitutional government are out of touch with reality, and make themselves irrelevant in contemporary political discourse. Having long been a proponent of libertarianism, himself, Mr. Taylor believes that he understands its asserted "weaknesses" from the "inside."

Doubting Market Solutions to Global Problems

His first doubts, he explains, emerged with his conclusion that libertarians have little or nothing to contribute to the leading problem of our time: global warming. In Mr. Taylor's view, this demonstrated to him that there needed to be answers outside the mantra of individual liberty and free markets. How else could this threat to humanity be tackled other than through extensive and combined governmental intervention, regulation, taxation, and possibly organized planning?

Like a revelatory conversion on the road to Damascus, this led to him to the conclusion that libertarianism, like other "dogmatic" and single-focused ideological perspectives, failed to admit that there are issues or problems in the world that do not and cannot be dealt with through a strict following of a policy view of free market voluntarism, based on an uncompromising attachment to individual liberty.

Furthermore, Mr. Taylor says he saw that too many libertarians ignored the reality and the fact that there are personal and social values in the world other than individual liberty. People also value "the pursuit of social justice, equity, community, virtue ... pluralism, material well being, or any number of concerns that animate people," besides the desire for unrestrained personal freedom.

Jerry Taylor decided, therefore, that he had to give up his belief in and adherence to the "ideology" of free market liberalism. Instead, he came to the awareness that what needed to be cultivated and advanced is a social philosophy of moderation and compromise. He explains:

> "Politics and policymaking without an ideological bible is incredibly demanding. It requires far more technocratic expertise and engagement than is required by ideologues, who already (they think) know the answers. It also requires difficult judgments, on a case-by-case basis, about which ethical considerations are of paramount concern for any given issue at hand, and what trade offs regarding those considerations are most warranted.

> To embrace non-ideological politics, then, is to embrace moderation, which requires humility, prudence, pragmatism, and a conservative temperament. No matter what principles we bring to the political table, remaking society in some ideologically driven image is off the table given the need to respect pluralism. A sober appreciation of the limitations of knowledge (and the irresolvable problem of unintended consequences) further cautions against over-ambitious policy agendas.

Does this mean "anything goes" in a non-ideological politics, including ideas and policies that many might consider abhorrent? No, Mr. Taylor says; there are limits to what may be accepted as legitimate policy views in the common area of democratic decision-making: "Compromise, however, has limits," he states.

"Compromise with theft, murder, slavery, or gross infringements on human dignity is indefensible ... Firm positions and tough stances are sometimes required. And when necessary, moderates must have the stomach for a fight."

The Meaning of Ideology and Its Social Relevance

Is Mr. Taylor right about the nature of ideology and moderation, and what does this imply about the free market liberal views of man, society and government? First, what is an "ideology"? The Oxford Dictionary defines it as, "A system of ideas and ideals, especially one which forms the basis of economic and political theory and policy." Also, "the science of ideas, the study of their origin and nature."

The term seems to have been first used in this way by the French classical liberal, Destutt de Tracy, in 1813 as an attempt to formulate a conception of the reality of the human condition and what it implied about the organization of a social order in response to the tyranny and terror during the French Revolution and then the dictatorship of Napoleon Bonaparte.

A starting premise to the classical, free market liberal "ideology" has been a focus on the uniqueness of the individual as a distinct thinking, feeling, valuing, and acting being. Different authors have expressed it differently, but in general there has been a common consensus that based on God or nature and man's reasoning ability, it is possible to discern and deduce an understanding of the individual human being as a unique creation or conscious entity that both needs and deserves to be seen as having an inherent right to his life, liberty, and peacefully and honestly acquired property for his survival and his betterment.

This classical liberal conception of man has never presumed or posited that man is an atomistic being separate from or not interconnected with other persons. Rather, its philosophy or "ideology" has been to ask and propose what should be the institutional arrangements that can be most conducive to respecting each human being as a free agent yet ordering the social system in such a way that each individual in pursuing his own self-interest does so, in general, in a way that can further the betterment of others at the same time.

The key moral premise is that coercion and the threat or use of violence should be prohibited or at least minimized to the greatest extent possible still consistent with a keeping of the peace among human beings. An outgrowth of this is the argument that, therefore, human interactions should be based on free association and mutual, voluntary agreement; hence, the ideal of the "free market" in which people enter into exchanges with each other through agreed-upon terms of trade.

Social Contract and Social Evolution in Classical Liberal Ideas

From the time of John Locke, the imagery of a "social contract" has sometimes been posited as the basis for interpersonal agreement concerning the origin of society and the institution of government derived from each individual's "natural right" to their life and liberty. However, this usually has been understood to be merely a form of a "mental experiment" to clarify the logic and meaning of individual liberty and the rationale and limits of government consistent with personal freedom and social peace.

The classical liberal tradition has generally appreciated that, in fact, the institutions of society and the ideas of personal freedom, private property and enterprise, the rule of law, and free commerce and trade are the results of a social evolutionary process, out of which the liberal order emerged over a long period of time. Human reflection and experience led to the articulated ideal and the codifying of the premises and practices of a free society.

Classical Liberalism as the Epitome of Moderation

For the classical liberal, the idea and ideal of the free society is the epitome of human moderation and compromise. It recognizes that the notion of the distinct and distinctive individual human being means that there is an inescapable diversity among people in terms of experiences, values, purposes and abilities. To the friend of freedom, the philosophical extremist and political fanatic is the one who is revolted by and rebels against the fact that men and women differ in what they consider the most desirable ends to pursue and the perceived best means of attaining them.

Such extremists and fanatics are those who ultimately represent an ideology of totalitarianism. That is, the attitude and insistence that all in society should and must conform to and be confined within their notion of a "socially just" or "fair" or "good" society. The method of imposing their collectivist ideal may be through dictatorship or democracy, but the underlying premise is that there is one way (or a narrowly defined set of ways) of living and associating.

Several years ago I wrote an article in which I asked, "Is the Case for Liberty Too Extreme?" I argued that:

> The free society tries to avoid extremes through the diversity of free men that it both permits and fosters. It restrains the practice of 'extreme' personal behavior because it imposes costs and consequences upon everyone who practices them, in the form of lost economic opportunity, and possibly social

ostracism by those who are repelled by it.

It also teaches the advantages of moderation – courtesy, good manners, tolerance, and 'socially acceptable' conduct – in the competitive arena of intellectual pluralism where to win an argument the only medium of exchange is peaceful persuasion. In other words, the free society nudges men toward better behavior and rational thought rather than tries to compel it. It teaches good and tolerant conduct through reason and example. It fosters compromise by demonstrating the personal costs of being too extreme in one's words and actions. And it raises the ethical conduct of society by the discovered advantages of personal improvement through time.

Are the arguments for and the advocates of liberty too extreme? Quite to the contrary. Freedom is the epitome of moderation.

Civil Society and the Market as Arenas of Moderation and Diversity
Classical liberalism does not ask that people give up or abandon their sincere devotion to notions of "the pursuit of social justice, equity, community, virtue ... pluralism, material well-being, or any number of concerns that animate people," as Mr. Taylor pointed out. What it does argue and, indeed, insists upon is that the social setting in which to advance these purposes be based on and guided by one fundamental and underlying principle: the foregoing of coercive means to attain them and the tolerance of diversity among men by utilizing peaceful and mutually agreed-upon avenues to achieve them.

For the classical liberal, the institutions of civil society are those that human beings participate in and through which to reach their chosen ends. Government necessarily imposes forms of "one-size-fits-all" once it goes beyond the "negative" though essential task of protecting each individual's right to his life, liberty and honestly acquired property.

The classical liberal recognizes that human beings do differ in terms of what they consider important and the best ways of advancing them. The pluralism of the free marketplace is precisely that it allows each individual to follow that peaceful path that he considers most attractive and opportune to improving his own life and that of others that he is concerned with.

Libertarian Solutions to Various Social Problems

Mr. Taylor suggests that free market liberals propose a free society without detailing how many of the things that various people consider useful or desirable will be possible to attain. This is historically very far from the case. Take the advocate of the welfare state. Someone may be honestly motivated by a desire to assist those who are less well off than themself. But when the friend of freedom responds that these matters should be left up to individuals and "the market", he does not stop there.

Classical liberals and libertarians have and do explain the logic and social mechanisms that are open to bettering those who are in need or who have fallen upon hard times not of their own making. Indeed, the history of the 19th century – the era considered to be the heyday of laissez-faire – saw the emergence and success of a very large number of private charities and voluntary associations. For instance, the Friendly Societies provided the means through which the vast majority in Great Britain found ways of providing themselves with medical insurance, unemployment assistance, retirement pensions, and life insurance; all without government and covering the vast majority of, especially, among the British "lower classes."

The same may be said about education. Many if not most classical liberals advocate private education and greater schooling choice. They have noted the historical successes of private education before compulsory government schooling and the means by which it would operate in our modern times. They have pointed out, likewise, the private sector means to assist during and after natural disasters.

The Tragedy of the Commons and Environmental Externalities

Mr. Taylor explained that his own doubts about the efficacy of free market solutions to social problems arose from his concerns about the reality of global warming, and not seeing any answers that did not involve encroaching upon the fundamental liberal principle of non-intervention that precluded both regulation of business or taxing policies to reduce atmospheric pollution problems.

The impression, therefore, could easily be drawn that market-oriented economists have given little or no attention to the problems of externalities. At least since the 1960s, that is, for more than half a century, problems of externalities and the "tragedy of the commons" have been a major subject area for serious study concerning the role of private property rights to "internalize" such problems through extension, introduction, or greater enforcement of private property rights.

Some of the classic essays on this theme are by Harold Demsetz and Garrett Hardin demonstrating the history and theory of the role of property rights in reducing overuse of scarce resources and related efficient economizing decision-making when the costs as well of the benefits must be more fully weighed and born by agents in the market both in the present and looking to the future.

Rivers and lakes have been, are, or can be privatized with resulting reductions in pollution or excessive harvesting of plant and animal life. The same applies to forests and wild life. Proposals have been detailed on how the same might be extended to the oceans. And the possibilities of similar enforceable private property rights in the atmosphere are possible, with the technologies available to trace back pollutants to their points of origin for legal recourse as in many other property rights disputes presented to the courts.

Without getting into the pros and cons of the heated technical and scientific debates concerning human activities threatening significant global temperature increases through the use of fossil fuels, the issue does concern policy proposals involving a reduction in the liberty of individuals and enterprises in society and must be judged and weighed in this context. Mr. Taylor too easily brushes aside the potentials and possibilities of real free market responses to global warming, if it presents the danger that many in the media and the scientific community claim that it is.

Social Humility and Limited, Decentralized Knowledge

We saw earlier that Mr. Taylor called for a non-ideological public policy approach because, "A sober appreciation of the limitations of knowledge (and the irresolvable problem of unintended consequences) further cautions against over-ambitious policy agendas." But unlike those "ideologues" espousing interventionist, regulatory, fiscal and direct planning policies to deal with environmental and other social and economic issues, the free market liberal takes Mr.

Taylor's concerns completely to heart.

Classical liberal and "Austrian" economist, Friedrich A. Hayek highlighted and strongly emphasized that individual human knowledge is not only limited, but that the knowledge of the world is decentralized and defused among all the members of the human society; it is made up of such qualities and characteristics that it is logically and practically impossible for even the most sincere and best of human minds in government and its bureaucracies to assemble, integrate and utilize that knowledge better than the multitudes of market participants themselves.

How can we know if some proposed governmental remedy for global warming, such as international taxes on fossil fuel uses or cap and trade licensing devises are the most effective and efficient tools for dealing with rising temperatures, if the proponents of the hypothesis are correct?

How can we know what costs individuals may or may not be willing and interested in bearing to grapple with this problem, if government, instead, co-opts and preempts any possible answers by "nationalizing" the problem through preventing or limiting private property solutions through internalizing of the impacts from people's energy-related actions?

How can we know if the particular "energy alternatives" currently proposed by advocates of government intervention and regulation are the ones that are the most cost-efficient or possible of positive payoff, when government policies by necessity narrow or hinder or prohibit any private enterprise answers guided by real market-driven incentives and returns?

For all of his insistence on a new non-ideological politics of public policy moderation, Mr. Taylor's proposals amount to merely more of the same. For what classical liberals and libertarians are asked to compromise is the principle and ideal of a society with minimum use or threat of force and compulsion by the government agency meant to secure people's freedom. Compromise, in this instance, is acceptance of the introduction of political coercion and paternalism into human affairs, and far more so than is already the case. Classical liberals have a far greater respect for and appreciation of real social diversity and pluralism than those with whom Mr. Taylor is asking them to compromise.

The Principled Case for Liberty is Not a Vice

Finally, Mr. Taylor states that there are some things worth standing on principle to defend, without compromise. He stated that, "theft, murder, slavery, or gross infringements on human dignity" are not open to compromise. But in many cases acceptance of these ideals originally started with and even required a "dogmatic" and "ideological" outlook and fervor.

Between two and three hundred years ago, those insisting upon the end to human slavery and its trade confronted a "diversity" of competing and institutionally entrenched views that claimed that African slaves were meant to be held in bondage according to a particular reading of the Bible; that slavery was a form of benevolent socialism that was good for those lucky enough to be the human property of other men; that it secured "jobs" and a certain "way of life" that justified its continuation in the American South; and that good money was paid for that human property and it would be unjust to the owners to take it away without just compensation.

It required a strong, uncompromising, principled dogmatism with a single focus of intention and ideological determination to oppose the slave system and insist upon and fight for its full abolition. No acceptance of value diversity was considered possible among the abolitionists with the slave masters and slave traders. "Moderation" was not a politically acceptable stance in the face of this moral evil of holding human beings in perpetual servitude by others who were permitted to use fairly unrestricted force to maintain their plantation life. In calling for the end to slavery, to use a phrase, the abolitionists declared that political extremism in the defense of liberty was not to be considered a vice.

Classical liberals consider that their defense and insistence upon a principled practice of individual liberty and competitive free markets to be no less of a moral necessity and calling than earlier demands for ending infringements on personal and social freedom that were widely taken for granted.

What Mr. Taylor considers to be unacceptable dogmatisms is for the classical liberal the just fight against the century-long collectivist counter-revolution against human liberty and the peaceful society of voluntary association. His appeal to moderation is, in fact, an appeal to give up the fight for human freedom and prosperity that only the arena of voluntary association and trade can bring about.

CHAPTER 16

SOCIETY IS NOT A FAMILY, GOVERNMENT IS NOT A PARENT

Few things are as clear as the bankruptcy of the political "left." Ranting and raving about Donald Trump and "anti-democratic" trends in the United States and other parts of the world, their own vision and vista for a "progressive" and "renewed" America is nothing but the same old statist and collectivist songs they have been singing for more than a century, now.

For instance, in one of his daily missives for "The New Yorker" online (July 14, 2017), columnist John Cassidy railed against the Republican proposals for repeal and reform of ObamaCare. But he also stated clearly his starting ideological premises:

> "It is worth restating what is at stake here: the principle that society is made up of people with mutual obligations, including the duty to try to protect everyone from what Franklin Roosevelt called the 'hazards and vicissitudes of life' such as old age, unemployment, and sickness."

Notice the underlying presumption, that it is as if society is an extended family in which everyone is presumed to have responsibilities to its other members. Clearly, in this view of mankind, it is the duty and role of the government to see that each of the societal family members contributes some "fair share" to cover everyone else's "protections" against the "hazards and vicissitudes of life."

Real Parents and Private Families

Within a real family, it is generally taken for granted that the parents set the direction and form of the chores and responsibilities that the other members of the family – the children – are assigned and expected to fulfill. First of all, the parents are the adults and are presumed to have more wisdom, knowledge and experience to know what has to be done, and to assign each child the tasks they seem able and old enough to perform around the house.

Of course, parents are not omniscient beings that always know what needs to be done, or the best way, or who, reasonably and responsibly, might be assigned those activities among the younger family members. Everyone who has grown up in a family remembers times when they resented or disliked things that they were told they had to do, and how it sometimes seemed unfair in comparison to the chores assigned or the rewards given to a sibling.

But, nonetheless, it is, normally, the parents who determine if Johnny gets the rollerblades and, if so, which ones in terms of the cost and type. Parents usually are the ones who determine at what age the child gets a cell phone or has use of a family car on a Saturday night if they have gotten their driver's license.

Plus, at a certain age, if any of the children want more than the parents can afford or think they should simply "give" to one of the children, they are told that maybe they could get some type of job around the neighborhood after school or on weekends to earn the money to buy what it is they want. Besides, the parents may consider it a good lesson in self-responsibility to have to earn the income to buy the things that are wanted and to learn how to wisely manage the money that is earned, for when they are an adult who leaves the family nest and is, finally, on their own.

It is usually considered a proper and necessary part of parenting precisely to prepare a child for independent adulthood when it is not someone else – mom and dad – who will see that "everything is alright."

Government as Political Parent

If the notion of a family is extended to the members of society as a whole, it is important to ask, "Who are the parents?" In the political setting this can only mean politicians holding political office and those who man and manage the government bureaucracies regulating and controlling the private and social affairs of the citizenry, and determining the distribution of income and wealth among the social "family" members via the tax system.

"Progressives" and others on "the left," of course, parrot some variation of the chant, "participatory democracy." But what does this actually mean? In the real world of modern democratic politics it means that coalitions of special interest groups – all asserting their representation of the "true" and "real" interests of "the people" as whole – elect those into political office who will then impose their particular sets of values and belief systems on everyone in society. This includes all those who may have voted against the promised policies of those placed in high political office, as well as those who may have chosen not to vote either out of apathy or belief that it is a waste of time.

Furthermore, our political "mommy's" and "daddy's" have something most real parents in modern, enlightened society no longer have: they have the legal or ethical right to use physical force and intimidation to get those under their "parental care" to do what those in political office want to be done.

Any real child actually abused or suspected of such treatment is often placed under the care of "Social Services" (which, itself, unfortunately, can be abusive and overreaching in pursuit of its mission). Real parents not only risk loss of custody over their child, but they may even face serious jail time. On the other hand, the abused "citizen-child" has no such means of escape when they are compulsorily made to conform to the dictates of those governmental "parents" holding the reins of legitimized political force. Instead, the abused citizen is more likely, himself, to end up in custody and face incarceration (or worse!), if they oppose or resist the fiscal and regulatory commands of the state.

The Relationship between Family and Society

The fact is, "society" is ultimately made up of individuals who, over centuries of slow and truly enlightened thought and controversy, have come to be considered to possess certain inherent and unalienable rights to life, liberty, and honestly acquired property under an appropriate system of an impartial and unbiased rule of law. Certainly, that is the philosophical perspective that guided the American colonists to declare their independence from Great Britain in 1776 and, then, implement a Constitution that was meant to recognize and secure those rights precisely from abusive, tyrannical and corrupt government.

Individuals in society form families through voluntary choices of associating themselves due to romantic, psychological, philosophical, cultural and economic and other attractions that make two people want to "be together." Out of this intimate relationship, traditionally through a formal marriage (but not necessarily anymore), children are often either born or adopted as part of the emotional and social sense of "family" and offspring.

Unfortunately, marriages or "relationships" do not always last, and sometimes end in divorce or separation. Unlike in that not so distant past, unwilling partners are no longer forced to remain in that marriage or relationship if it is no longer fulfilling in the broadest sense for both partners.

The government, however, does not allow unwilling societal "partners" and community "family" members to sever the relationship with political power. No matter how much an individual may disagree with what the government does, or the means through which it does it, or the burden that government imposes on the individual in pursuit of the political goals chosen by those in governmental authority, there is no divorce allowed.

The individual is a permanent prisoner of the "community" in which birth or circumstances have placed him, under the type of collectivist ethos espoused by someone like John Cassidy. The individual is viewed and treated as a perpetual child unable to find his own job, unable to plan his own retirement, and not intelligent and responsible enough to select and finance his own medical care. It is fitting that when the proponents of the modern welfare state first made the case for it in Bismarck's Imperial Germany in the late 19th century, they referred to it as political care for all "from cradle to grave."

Civil Society and Human Institutions

In the free society, human relationships among the broad population are not bound together by the compulsory dictates of political command, as is inescapable in the very nature of the modern interventionist-welfare state. Instead, human beings are interconnected by the voluntary associative relationships and institutions of "civil society" – the workplace, family, charity and philanthropy, church, cultural interests, and many others through which people find ways to better fulfill and improve their lives with like-minded people with whom they share ideas, values, and shared goals.

The real communities and associations of civil society are rich with diversity, variety and complexity. They overlap and interconnect people in various ways and for multiple purposes reflecting the many sides of people's lives, interests, desires and beliefs. Each of us belongs to several of them, while not to others. Each chooses which of these associations and voluntary communities of shared interest we will join and participate in. And we can change our "memberships" in them as we find our purposes, values and wants change as our experiences, circumstances and ideas change over time.

Some of these relationships of civil society may literally involve the people next door, as in a homeowners' association. Others may incorporate a wider circle of people in the larger neighborhood, as with a religious house of worship to which we may belong, or a service club like Rotary whose meetings we attend regularly or when we participate in a literary reading group that meets a couple of times a month; or when we work with charity organizations for which we volunteer our time and may give a monetary contribution within our local community. We may be involved with other parents through the local little league sports activities that our children participate in.

We also often are members of professional associations that may incorporate people and activities from across the entire country and other nations around the world. We sometimes share hobby interests with people who may live half way around the world, who we may come to know rather well through the "miracle" of the worldwide web, even though we may never actually meet face-to-face.

When I was a small boy, our family belonged to what was called the "cousin's club" that connected and kept in touch our "extended family" of uncles and aunts, nieces and nephews, and actual cousins who were sometimes three or four "removed." Once or twice a year there would be arranged a banquet dinner to which a large number of the members of our extended family would attend.

This, too, was one of the interpersonal institutions of civil society through which a wider sense of family, "belonging" and appreciation of origins and "roots" could be maintained across generations and over numerous "nuclear" families dispersed across the country. Knowing what was going on in the lives of the wider network of family members also provided useful information if something had to be done to help out, say, Aunt Minnie, who couldn't get around on her own very well anymore and needed help with some of the everyday chores of life. Or Uncle Bob, who lost his job, and someone in the family needed to take him in for a while until something else might be found for him to at least partly still financially take care of himself, even though he was, now, getting up in years.

Government "Parenting" and Dehumanized Society

But when the government takes on the role of "parent" or 'big brother" and takes responsibility for all such things, it weakens the personal and familial senses of duty and obligation most people in a free society would ethically and voluntarily feel to be "the right thing to do" to help, handle and work out with others in the narrower or wider circle of actual relatives.

People in the interventionist-welfare state soon are desensitized and even dehumanized to these matters. After all, "isn't that what government is for?" Besides, "I've paid my taxes" to pay for those "social services." And, in addition, "shouldn't that be left up to the qualified experts in the government who know how to handle these things?"

As a result, government "crowds out" through taxes and depersonalizes through bureaucratization of human concerns what should be, could be, and once was the purpose and humane superiority of those institutions and associations of civil society. Detached from the spontaneous associations of human concern in a free society, the individual is left more alone facing and dependent upon the anonymous "generosity" and eligibility constraints and dictates of the State.

Furthermore, it is through that most important institution of civil society, the free, competitive market economy, that all of those concerns expressed by John Cassidy and others are able to be met and satisfied to a far greater and better degree that when provided or imposed by political power and planning. Virtually all the shortcomings that Mr. Cassidy, for instance, sees in the current system of medical insurance and health care, and for the solution of which he wishes to turn even more intensely to government involvement, are, in fact, due to the degree and extent to which existing political intervention, command and control have prevented the full emergence and working of a market-based system of medical insurance and health care provision.

The Market Economy as a Participatory Community

The market economy brings together into one vast network of human association, dependency, and betterment the entire populations of communities, countries and continents. Those on "the left" often speak majestically about transcending the confines of narrow nationalism and political boundaries drawn on maps. Yet, no social institution succeeds in this as effectively for material, cultural and social improvement of all mankind than the free, competitive liberal market economy.

Free market liberalism creates a shared and "participatory" community through the social system of division of labor. Each individual member is free to live his own life and follow his own course as interest, desire and conscience guides him. But he is bound together with all of the others in this "family" of mutually associated demanders and suppliers. Each relies upon the productions of his global neighbors for his needs, wants, and whims from the supply sides of the market. Yet, he, in turn, can only call upon their providing him with what he demands to the extent that he has, reciprocally, earned the income to buy what he wants by, first, serving others through supplying them with what they desire. We first must be voluntary supply-side "servants" guided by the market demands of others for us to, then, be demand-side "masters" who are now served by those who supply and serve us.

At this point, Mr. Cassidy and others would ask, but what about those who due to misfortune, circumstances, or "bad luck" do not have the means to fully care for themselves because of lack of sufficient financial and other resources?

But that is what those institutions and associations of civil society partly emerge for, and can do and have done much better than when government preempts them through taxes extracted and regulations imposed that makes it prohibitive or impractical for private individuals and groups to successfully undertake the necessary tasks for these purposes.

It is the reason that classical liberals have argued for and even insisted upon constitutionally limited government. Only by narrowing the functions and responsibilities of government to those essential duties of protecting individual liberty rather and abridging it, can the members of a free society successfully be adults free of political parents who presume to know enough to tell them what to do and how to live, and what forms of peaceful association with others will be allowed or compelled.

It is why it is important to not fall victim to or leave unanswered the misguided ideas that "society is a family" and that government should be considered our perpetual caregiving "parent."

CHAPTER 17

SOCIALISM, LIKE DRACULA, RISES AGAIN FROM THE GRAVE

Many of us grew up watching movies about Dracula — Nosferatu, the Undead. Fearful of the sunlight that could burn him into cinders, Dracula lived in a coffin filled with his native Transylvanian soil by day, only to come out at night to live off the life-giving blood of the living. But to continue his unnatural existence, this human-like vampire had to kill his victims by draining them of their own blood, in the process turning them into creatures of the night, like himself.

Almost every Dracula movie ended with his nemesis, usually Dr. Van Helsing, the determined vampire hunter, finding Dracula in his coffin as the dawn was beginning to appear. He would drive a stake through the vampire's heart or open a nearby window so sunlight could fall upon the sleeping bloodsucker. Dracula's centuries-old body usually would rapidly decay into dust. The undead had now died, and the world was freed from this unholy aberration.

But, invariably, in the next film the life-destroying monster, in fact, turned out to have not been truly killed, or one of the poor humans he had turned into a vampire had taken his place to plague the living.

Sometimes Dracula initially would be portrayed as an attractive gentleman, appealing to the ladies (such as in the 1979 movie *Dracula*, starring a young Frank Langella). But soon his true, evil nature showed itself as he fell upon his human prey and made them into ungodly creatures.

Welcome to the seemingly unending cycle of resurrections of the socialist idea in renewed appealing forms.

The Original Appeal of Socialism: Utopia Now

How very appealing was the socialist idea in the late 19th and early (pre-WWI) 20th centuries! All the burdens of life and everyday work, all the seemingly unjust inequalities of material wealth observable in society, and all the uncertainties of health care and old age would be lifted from the weary shoulders of the common man with the arrival of socialism.

Humanity would be freed from the shackles of capitalist "wage slavery" and everyone would be provided with all the necessities and amenities of material existence, with all living in an equality of social justice, and oppression and tyranny abolished around the world.

What a life-draining nightmare was set loose on mankind! From the Bolshevik Revolution in Russia in 1917 through all the other communist "victories," either through Soviet conquest or domestic revolutions and civil wars like in China or Cuba, the harshest and most terrible tyrannies fell upon all the luckless peoples given a socialist paradise to live within.

Socialist Reality of Tyranny and Crushed Freedom

Civil liberties were abolished, with no speaking or writing permitted other than the official line of the ruling Communist Party. Central planning meant that the government determined what was produced, where, by whom, and in what quantities. Every person's educational opportunities, living quarters, and employment were assigned and commanded by the state in the name of the collective good.

Dissent, disagreement, or even suspected lack of enthusiasm for the advancement of the bright, beautiful socialist future (as defined and dictated by those at the helm of the "people's state") was met with arrest, imprisonment, banishment to slave-labor camps, or death by torture, starvation, or execution.

Human life was stripped of privacy; informers were potentially reporting everything anyone did or said and everyone was potentially under surveillance by agents of the secret police. Fear and suspicion were inseparably intertwined with any interpersonal relationship or association, whether in the government-assigned workplace or with neighbors in government-owned apartment complexes.

Friendships, therefore, were precarious relationships that could end up in betrayal and a knock on the door in the middle of the night from the secret police that could result in an individual or an entire family disappearing without a trace.

It was not enough for the socialist state to command and control your public words and deeds. Propaganda and indoctrination were used in an attempt to manipulate and mold how people thought about the world and themselves. The contents of the individual's mind were to be a product of the central plan as much as the types and quantities of the physical goods produced at "the people's" factories.

Human Cost and Material Poverty of Socialism in Practice

The human cost of the great socialist experiment to remake humanity for a new, collectivist heaven on earth did not come cheap. Historians of the communist experience around the world have estimated that as many as 200 million people — innocent men, women, and children — have been killed in the socialist meat grinders: 64 million in the Soviet Union and up to 80 million in China, with millions more in the other socialist societies around the globe.

Did these sacrifices for that better socialist future pay off? Did socialism deliver on its promises? In every centrally planned society, shortages, shoddy goods, and stagnant standards of living enveloped the lives of the vast majority of the citizens of these countries. Anyone who had the opportunity to visit the Soviet Union (as I did in its last years) could not help but notice the zombie-like emptiness in the faces of many on the streets of Moscow as they trudged on foot from one government retail store to another in desperate search for the basic essentials of everyday life.

Long lines of people waited at one store to purchase some poor-quality consumer item or basic food products. At other stores, there were empty shelves with no customers. All the stores were manned by listless, bored, and indifferent government employees just waiting for their shifts to end.

What else could be expected from an economic system that prevented any individual initiative or incentive to work, save, and invest, now that private enterprise had been abolished and declared the basis of exploitation and injustice? (In the last five years of the Soviet Union, the Communist Party leader, Mikhail Gorbachev, had allowed small and limited private business enterprises, and these, however few and restricted, were the only pockets of economic vibrancy.)

The Austrian economists, especially Ludwig von Mises and Friedrich A. Hayek, had shown already in the 1920s and 1930s that the nationalization of private property and the end to market competition and a market-based price system did away with the possibility of any rational economic decision-making. To reasonably determine what to produce, with what methods of production, and in what relative amounts, they explained, there needed to be some effective method of economic calculation — that is, determining the relative value of what goods consumers wanted and the most efficient ways to use the scarce means of production (land, labor, capital) to best advantage in satisfying consumer demand.

But with no market-based prices reflecting actual supply and demand conditions in changing circumstances, a centrally planned economy was in a sense flying blind. Its outcome is what Mises once entitled one of his short works on this topic: Planned Chaos.

Vampire-like, socialist regimes drained the life force out of the societies they ruled. No ambition, no drive, no prospects for a better and happier life was the material and psychological state to which socialism reduced humanity in those parts of the world in which communism had triumphed.

The only opportunities for a better life came from being one of the Communist Party bloodsuckers of the ruling elite. They had special stores, special medical clinics, special holiday resorts, special living accommodations, special opportunities to travel abroad to other socialist countries or even "the enemy" West from which forbidden goodies could be brought back home. The rest of the society was truly the exploited masses from whose meager and government-mis-directed labor those limited privileges and prosperity came for the ruling Red Draculas of the communist state.

End to Socialist Planning and Rebirth of Market Prosperity

The last decade of the 20th century saw the collapse of Marxian socialism in the Soviet Union and the captive nations in Eastern Europe that were conquered by Stalin at the end of the Second World War. The death of Mao Zedong in 1976 was followed in the 1980s with economic reforms in China that did not change the political stranglehold of the Communist Party over that country, but did introduce a variety of limited and controlled market-based institutional transformations that have brought radical improvements in the everyday lives of hundreds of millions of people.

Many underdeveloped countries in what used to be called the third world turned away from the model of Soviet-style central planning in the 1980s and 1990s and put the people on more market-oriented paths to material and social betterment. Indeed, in some of these countries, abject poverty and frequent starvation have been nearly eradicated by the introduction of freer markets and competitive entrepreneurial activity.

Dracula Rises! Socialism Once More From the Grave

But, like Dracula rising once more from the grave, socialism has been making a comeback among academics, a growing number of other intellectuals, and college students. It was reflected in the Democratic Party 2018 primary win of Alexandria Ocasio-Cortez (who was a Bernie Sanders activist in 2016) over an established Democratic incumbent in a New York City congressional district. She hails as a member of the Democratic Socialists of America (DSA).

On the website of the DSA, it outlines its promise of and hope for a new "progressive" socialist America to replace the oppressive and exploitive current American system of "neoliberalism," the left's catchall label for capitalist things they hate and wish to overturn.

The DSA's supporters insist that theirs will be a truly democratic society. A small handful of wealthy capitalists should not dictate and determine the economic direction of the U.S. economy for their own private profit. No, the country's future should be in the hands of all the people through democratic decision-making.

Workers should collectively manage factories and enterprises, and the society as whole should ensure or provide a large array of free things for everyone: health care, child care, education from kindergarten through college, and housing and transportation would all be "publicly provided to everyone on demand, free of charge." (In reality, nothing is truly free, as everything comes at the expense of something else.) Also, everyone would be guaranteed a universal basic income.

Plus, the workweek would be reduced and vacation time increased to give everyone more leisure so as to create work opportunities for any of the unemployed who might still wish to be employed even in a world of all this free stuff provided by the government. (How and who is to pay for all these free items remains an unanswered question, other than a general presumption that "the rich" will be appropriately taxed to foot the bill.)

Democratic Socialism Means the Tyranny of the Meddler

Since everything would be politicized with government involvement even more than currently in America to supply this promised life of post-scarcity existence, supposedly democratic decision-making would be extended to, well, everything. The DSA says the Senate should be abolished and the entire electoral process replaced with a system of proportional representation in more directly democratically elected bodies. There would be "civilian boards for various government services, program councils (at the national, state, and local levels) for those who receive government services, and municipal and state-level citizens assemblies that would be open to all that would be tasked with making budget decisions."

Anyone who has ever gone to town hall meetings knows there is nothing democratic about the people who show up to speak out on agenda issues and nothing democratic about the voting of the local councilmen. The number of attendees is mostly small and the attendees are bee-in-their-bonnet busybodies. They are clearly people with too much time on their hands possessing political and ideological axes to grind, with the desire, 9 times out of 10, to foster regulations, controls, and taxes on others so they can achieve their local social-engineering goals.

A handful of municipal meddlers speak out at these town hall council meetings, creating the impression through their sincerity and vehemence that they are voicing the real needs and interests of the community. Where are the vast majority of the citizens of that community? The actual majority of that town or city are going about the normal and ordinary business of life: coming home from work, spending time with their families, doing chores around the house, out shopping for food or other family necessities, or just having some down time with friends before the next day of work begins.

Private Productive People vs. Political Busybodies

This ordinary and normal majority comprises the ones producing the goods and services in the private sector, which represents the source of prosperity. They are busy managing their personal and family affairs to keep them (hopefully) in financial order; they are seeing that their houses and neighborhoods are kept in order by mowing the yard, repainting a fence, or participating in some church or charity good works out of a personal sense of right, calling, or duty.

For most of them, politics never enters the equation; but, nonetheless, their actions actually keep society running smoothly on a day-to-day basis. They represent what William Graham Sumner (1840–1910) once called the "forgotten man," who peacefully produces all the things representing the wealth of nations, which the socialist planners and regulators want to get their hands on.

To shift even more decision-making away from the private sphere of business enterprise and individual and family self-responsibility to the political arena means to transfer control over people's lives from themselves to the professional and amateur busybodies who show up at those government meetings and influence the way the elected representatives vote.

Those elected representatives don't mind a bit having the power and authority to make such decisions, since the money they decide how to spend is the trough from which they buy the support of those whose votes they need to stay in office. Plus, their power and authority allow them to increase the duties of the local bureaucrats, who easily find ways to use the regulatory and redistributive powers placed in their hands to serve their own interests, both career and ideological.

The more control is transferred out of the hands of the private citizenry in the form of private enterprise, voluntary associations, and personal responsibilities concerning those affairs of everyday life and into the hands of these "democratic" socialists, the more the tyranny of the pressure group cliques and the more the community know-it-alls end up running everyone's life.

Extend that from the affairs of municipal administrations to the state and federal governments, and soon there is little that happens that the political regulators and social planners would not be in charge of, and far more intensively than they are already.

Similarly to how Dracula's attractive smile was transformed into bloodsucking fangs draining away the life of those initially mesmerized by him, the Sirens' call for "free" everything (which in reality someone will have to pay for) under the umbrella of democratic fairness and justice soon metamorphoses into a tyranny of politicians, bureaucrats, and "democratic socialists" determined to use the political process to impose their petty minority prescriptions for a better world on all of us. The arena of individual autonomy decreases and the prison walls of collectivist control tighten and grow higher around everyone.

Have no doubt that this includes not only health care, retirement pensions, public housing, guaranteed jobs, and minimum incomes. The new "democratic socialist" agenda, like that of the "progressive" left in general, whether its supporters choose to consciously label themselves as socialists or not, is to micromanage language, human relationships, social status, and group classifications of victimhood vs. privileged.

The newly fashionable idea of democratic socialism is nothing less than the same tyranny of all the earlier forms of socialism experienced over the last 100 years in more explicitly brutal forms, just more rhetorically enveloped in the appeal of participatory democracy than the earlier cries for a dictatorship of the proletariat.

It remains the same life-draining Dracula returned once more from the dead.

CHAPTER 18

ALL SOCIALISMS ARE ANTISOCIAL

Those who have seen the 1982 Steven Spielberg movie, "Poltergeist," may remember the scene when the little girl touches the snowy screen of her family's television and says, "They're here," meaning the evil ghostly forces bringing death and destruction. Well, they are here: socialism, nationalism, protectionism and political paternalism. The ghosts of collectivisms past have returned and their harmful effects will be the same as any experienced in that past.

We seem to be in the midst of what may be a dangerous return to the worst political ideas and policies of the 20th century. We must first understand that philosophically they all originate from a common root. The group, the tribe, the nation, the race, the social class, is declared to be superior to and all controlling over the individual members of society.

The words "freedom" and "liberation" are widely used by all the proponents of these variations on the collectivist theme, but their use, in fact, have nothing to do with either freedom or liberation. They reflect instances of George Orwell's "newspeak" in his famous anti-totalitarian novel, *1984*. The meanings of words are turned on their heads and are used in ways opposite to their original meanings. Hence, political control and manipulation means to have real personal freedom from tyranny; and complete intolerance and censorship of views and actions inconsistent with the "progressive" and democratic socialist views of the world means to have real intellectual and social liberation from oppression.

"Social" Means Personal Liberty and Freedom of Association

Let's take the word "socialism." It sounds, well, so nicely "social." But it is not. Social has and should mean the free, voluntary, and mutually agreed upon associations and interactions among the members of a community or a wider society, which may cover a portion or region of the world or encompass the entire globe and therefore humanity as a whole.

This is the meaning and connotation of the word "social" in the free market liberal tradition. It recognizes people as individuals who have certain inviolable and universal rights as human beings. They are the right to life, liberty and the possession and peaceful use of honestly acquired property. What does honestly acquired property mean? Property acquired by the individual's own productive efforts from previously unsettled and unowned land and resources, or through free exchange at mutually agreed-upon terms with other rightful owners of tradable goods and services.

"Social" in the free market liberal tradition has included the idea of voluntary and community or societal associations that people may enter into to advance common interests and concerns that may require the efforts and resources of more than one person. Activities and endeavors, in other words, that include but may extend outside of and beyond the more narrowly defined interactions of market supply and demand.

Historically, these have encapsulated the combined actions concerning competitive market interactions, as well as charitable and philanthropic activities, religious communion and peaceful proselytizing, local educational, health or ethical concerns of the members of a community. They are usually referred to as the institutions of civil society.

The Liberty and Pluralism of Civil Society

University of Chicago sociologist, Edward Shils (1910-1995) explained "The Virtue of Civil Society" (*Government and Opposition*, January1991) in the following way:

> The idea of civil society is the idea of a part of society that has a life of its own, which is distinctly different from the state, and which is largely in autonomy from it ... The term civil society [has historically] retained certain central features. First, it was a part of society distinct from and independent of the state. Where it had not yet reached the point of independence from the state, it was argued that it should become so. Secondly, it provided for the rights of individuals and particularly for the right to property. Thirdly, civil society was a constellation of many autonomous economic units or business firms, acting independently of the state and competing with each other ...

> A market economy is the appropriate pattern of the economic life of a civil society ... There is, however, much more to civil society than the market. The hallmark of a civil society is the

autonomy of private associations and institutions, as well as that of private business firms ...

The pluralism of civil society also comprises, within each sphere, a multiplicity of many partially autonomous corporations and institutions; the economic sphere comprises many industries and many business firms; the religious sphere comprises many churches and sects; the intellectual sphere comprises many universities, independent newspapers, periodicals and broadcasting corporations; the political sphere includes independent political parties. There are many independent and voluntary philanthropic and civil associations, etc... .

The civil society ... must possess the institutions that protect it from encroachment of the state and keep it as a civil society ... Essential to the functioning [of civil society are]: voluntary associations and their exercise of the freedoms of association, assembly and representation or petition. Individuals must enjoy the corresponding freedom to associate, assemble and petition. Naturally, freedom of religious belief and worship, association and education are part of civil society. Freedom of academic teaching and study, of investigation and publication are also part of the complex pattern of civil society.

These are the institutions by which the state is kept within substantive and procedural confinement. The confinement, which might be thought to be negative, is sustained on belief of a positive ideal, the ideal of individual and collective freedom.

Civil Society Offers Freedom and Securities for Liberty

A little reflection on Edward Shils' description and understanding of the nature of civil society makes it fairly clear that such a community of free individuals who are associating voluntarily for commonly shared values, purposes and ends is fundamentally inconsistent with all forms of political collectivism. The ideological and policy agendas of socialism, nationalism, protectionism and political paternalism inescapably involve and require the compulsory and coerced imposition of one or a group of governmental plans, regulations, and redistributive purposes on the all the member of the society.

The personal freedom of civil society implies the liberty of the individual to set his own goals, purposes, and ideals. To have the personal discretion and recognized political right to pursue them in any way that he considers best, most advantageous and likely to bring about the desired and hoped for outcomes. The individual is also at liberty to form any and all types of peaceful and voluntary associations and agreements with others that he considers useful for the achievement of some of those wanted ends.

The institutions of civil society, as Edward Shils highlights, are meant to offer wide latitude of pluralistic opportunity for individuals to find the best means to their desired goals. As Shils emphasized, the market economy is essential to and at the core of a vibrant and functioning civil society. It is within the arena of free market production and exchange that each individual has the liberty to find or create what he considers the best way to earn a living. He is then at liberty, based on the value others have placed on the services he has offered to them and for which they have paid him for some job done, to freely spend what he has earned as he desires on the things that have importance and value to him, in his role as a consumer.

Democratic Socialism and Its Anti-Social Agenda

The socialist regimes of the 20th century that succeeded in comprehensively imposing their designs and central plans on the societies over which they ruled attempted to abolish any and all of the preceding institutions of civil society. Shils noted this, too, with the effort under such regimes to replace civil society with the omnipotence of the state in all things. Indeed, as Shils says, "Marxist-Leninists declared themselves to be enemies of civil society."

Today's democratic socialists insist that they have nothing to do with those others in the 20th century who also called themselves "socialists." Those others were not real, or true, or the right kind of socialists. Therefore, the "new" democratic socialism should not have to carry any of the baggage of guilt by association through connection with those "bad" or mislabeled socialists of the recent past.

But listen to what our new democratic socialists want and propose? Ask yourself, if successful in bringing their plans to fruition, what would remain of the existing institutions of civil society in America? Government already monopolizes most of education from kindergarten through to the PhD. By calling for "free" schooling through all levels up to the doctorial degree, this means, in fact, that the federal government would pay for everyone's education, at taxpayer's expense, of course.

The money would now fully and completely pass through the conduit of political and bureaucratic hands. Curriculum, hiring and firing of faculty and administration, entrance requirements, standards for student retention and graduation, would be even more effectively and comprehensively overseen, influenced, and finally controlled by those possessing government budgetary power than is the case today.

If higher education is already heavily politicized in our current climate of political correctness, identity politics, and ideological bias and manipulation, this trend would be merely accelerated if there is nothing outside of the orbit and oversight of the government since everyone would have their "right" to "free" government paid for higher education.

How would this be any different in matters of medical treatment and health care? The federal and state governments already have an intrusive and highly heavy hand in the health industry and how and what it provides. "Single payer" means a single provider that determines what medical treatment and heath care services for whom, of what type, and to which extent, since the socialist state must focus on what is claimed to be good of all the members of society as a whole.

Your healthcare quality and duration of life, and that of your family, will be in the hands of the government bureaucratic managers of the medical profession, hospital facilities, and caregiving. If you sometimes feel yourself nothing but an ignored or depersonalize number for healthcare treatment under the current politicized system, just wait for full government socialized medicine under the "single payer" euphemism, and when you then become an even smaller decimal with four zeros after the dot.

Let now consider for a moment centrally planned social and "identity" political justice. Forget about how you want to live, how and what you'd like to say, with whom you'd like to peacefully and voluntarily associate for mutually desired purposes, or the way you would like to honestly and non-violently go about earning a living and spend the money you've received through free exchange. Overcoming the injustices of the past – real and imagined – will require the progressives and democratic socialists to plan the rede-signing of everyone's place, status, opportunities, and outcomes throughout society. Every claimed unearned income, unjust social status, unfair employment, undeserved "privilege" will have to be reshaped according to the notions of the good society as seen inside the heads of those in charge of the political machinery of government.

Think of all the other corners and aspects of society, whether it is the physical environment, or culture, art and the sciences, or investment patterns, or job locations, or the quantities and varieties of goods produced and supplied; each will have to be politically decided upon and imposed to make them compatible with "climate planning," racial and gender fairness, and social egalitarianism. What corner of your part of society would not be under the deter-mination and control of the state?

Democracy, Liberty, Socialism, and Civil Society

Analysts and advocates of the institutions of civil society have long emphasized what Edward Shils pointed out, that they also serve as intermediaries, as buffers, between the state and the citizen. They are the societal associations, organizations, and arrangements outside and independent of the government so that the individual does not have to become a slave to the plans and purposes of those in political power. The individual person can live free of the state; a status that shrinks to nothing when that individual is dependent upon and receives virtually all the things needed and wanted for life from the government.

But its "democratic" socialism! Its what the people want as shown by those they elect to political office with the campaign agenda that the citizen-voters have expressed their desire for. It is the "will of the people." Who can be against that, other than enemies of freedom, and oppressors who do not want the victimized to be liberating from their lives of injustice and unfairness?

But democracy is not liberty. Democracy is a political institutional means to determine who holds political office and for what period of time through a peaceful voting procedure that makes violent means unnecessary to remove or substitute those in positions of political authority and decision-making. And it is usually based on some form of majority-determining procedure.

Democracy carries with it the high respect and deference that it normally holds in most people's minds because in modern times it gained political prominence along with and more or less at the same time in the 18th and 19th centuries as the emergent classical liberal ideas and ideals of individual liberty, impartial rule of and equality before the law, economic freedom, and constitutionally limited government. Democracy, therefore, came to be considered as inseparable from and confused in many people minds with freedom. But it need not.

Democratic (classical) liberalism linked the two together because in the eyes of many of the liberals in those earlier centuries the role of democratic reform was to make those in political power more directly accountable to the people over whom they ruled. But simultaneously the liberal agenda was to restrain the responsibilities and prerogatives of the government because political control, planning, regulation and redistribution were considered abridgements of the personal freedom of the individual to control, plan and regulate his own life, partly through those voluntary associations and interconnecting relationships of the institutions of civil society.

Democratic socialism, on the other hand, remains socialism, a concept that insists upon and demands that the "political" is to replace the "social" as understood as meaning individual self-governing in conjunction with the voluntarism of the peaceful community of free human beings. In this understanding, socialism is inherently anti-social.

Democratic socialism coercively confines and constrains all those living within what a majority or a coalition of minorities making up a voting majority wish to have imposed on the entire society. Notice that come the political triumph of progressive, democratic socialism, everyone will have to accept and be limited to a higher education funded by and therefore fully under the oversight of the federal government. No one will be able to break out of the government plan as the single payer or provider of medical and health care throughout the country. Each person's income, wealth, position and status, and opportunities for personal betterment will be forcefully straightjacketed within what those in governmental power deem to be the politically correct, the identity politics right, and the socially just.

The pluralism and peaceful competitions of the institutions of civil society with the underlying individual freedom that it represents and helps to secure, is replaced by political monopoly and coercion through the powers of government to insist upon one size fitting all for anything and everything that such a democratic socialist regime considers to be properly within its orbit and responsibility.

Democratic Despotism Comes in Many Varieties

Some authors in the past have referred to democratic despotism or totalitarian democracy. Once the anti-social agenda of socialism is in power and implemented, it can, at the end of the day, be nothing but despotic and totalitarian. Because it is either individuals making their own plans and coordinating their plans with those of others through the voluntary agreements of the market and those institutions of civil society, or it is the plans of some imposed on others through the use or threat of political compulsion. It comes down to freedom or tyranny, whether or not that tyranny has come to power through the use of bullets or votes dropped into a ballot box.

While I have focused on socialism, the others that I referred to, nationalism, protectionism, and political paternalism, are all variations on the same theme. The Swiss classical liberal economist and political scientist, William E. Rappard (1883-1958) long ago explained in an insightful essay on "Economic Nationalism" (1938) that, "Nationalism, then, is the doctrine which places the nation at the top of the scale of political values, that is above the three rival values of the individual, of regional units and of the international community ... The individual subordinate to the state," is the hallmark of political and economic nationalism.

All that socialists argue about against nationalists and other forms of collectivism is for what purposes shall the coercive powers of the state be used in making all in society conform to some single or network of governmental plans that all are expected to obey and follow, if negative consequences are not to befall any individuals who attempt to act outside of the socialist scheme for that politically engineered bright and beautiful future.

Free market liberalism is the social system of a civil society based on and protective of personal liberty and human betterment. Socialism is the anti-social system of politics over people, governmental power instead of peaceful and free association, and a handful of imposed political plans instead of a pluralism of as many plans as there are people in the world. Where is the freedom when one political plan replaces our many personal plans? What is liberating when the state becomes the political master and we are expected to be the obedient citizen servants? Which one of these worlds – democratic market liberalism or democratic planning socialism – do you want to live under?

CHAPTER 19

THE MARKET DEMOCRACY VS. DEMOCRATIC SOCIALISM

Warnings are frequently heard nowadays that "democracy" is currently under threat, and with a demise of democracy will come a loss of liberty. Indeed, democracy and freedom are frequently heralded as being synonyms for one and the same concept. An important question, however, is what do these concepts mean, and are they in fact synonymous?

Maybe a useful place to start is with a famous lecture delivered in Paris 200 years ago in 1819 by the French classical liberal, Benjamin Constant (1767-1830), on "The Liberty of the Ancients Compared with that of the Moderns." Constant's purpose was to distinguish the meanings of freedom and democracy in ancient Athens in comparison to his own time in the early 19th century. It highlighted the difference between the freedom of the individual versus the freedom of the political collective.

The Democratic Tyranny of the Ancient Greek World

Constant argued that among the ancient Greeks liberty meant the right of the free citizens of the city-state to equally and actively participate in the political deliberations concerning the policies and actions of their government. The Individual could freely speak, debate with his fellow citizens, and cast his vote for the policies he considered best for his city-state to follow. But once any such decisions had been collectively voted on and approved by the majority, the individual was a slave to that majority's will. Or as Constant expressed it:

> [The liberty of the ancients] consisted in exercising collectively, but directly, several parts of the complete sovereignty; in deliberating in the public squire, over war and peace, in forming alliances with foreign governments; in voting laws, in pronouncing judgments; in examining the accounts, the acts, the stewardship of the magistrates; in calling them to appear in front of the assembled people; in accusing, condemning or absolving them.

> But if this is what the ancients called liberty, they admitted as compatible with this collective freedom the complete subjection of the individual to the authority of the community ... All private actions were submitted to a severe surveillance. No importance was given to individual independence, neither in relation to opinions, nor labor, nor, above all, to religion ...

> Thus, among the ancients the individual, almost always sovereign in public affairs, was a slave in all his private relations. As a citizen, he decided on war and peace; as a private individual,

he was constrained, watched and repressed in all his movements; as a member of the collective body, he interrogated, dismissed, condemned, beggared, exiled or sentenced to death his magistrates and superiors; as a subject of the collective body he could himself be deprived of his status, stripped of his privileges, banished, or put to death, by the discretionary will of the whole to which he belonged.

The ancient Greek political system, as interpreted by Constant, can easily be defined as a form of democratic totalitarianism. The political philosopher, Jacob L. Talmon once defined totalitarian democracy as recognizing "ultimately only one plane of existence, the political. It widens the scope of politics to embrace the whole of human existence. It treats all human thought and action as having social significance, and therefore as falling within the orbit of political action." Democratic politics, in other words, envelops all of human existence because social participation is the defining characteristic of every human life.

Benjamin Constant's "Modern" Meaning of Individual Liberty

This is in contrast to what Benjamin Constant, in his 1819 lecture, explained to be the alternative conception of liberty, what he referred to as the "modern" one, by which he meant the idea of liberty in the, then, new classical liberal ideal of the early 19th century. The modern notion of liberty, Constant argued, emphasized the autonomy and independence of the individual to peacefully live his life as his chose and found to be best, whether or not others in the society agree with him or dislike the courses of action he has decided to follow. Said Constant:

First ask yourselves, Gentlemen, what an Englishman, a Frenchman or a citizen of the United States of America understand today by the word 'liberty'. For each of them it is the right to be subjected only to the laws, and to be neither arrested, detained, put to death or maltreated in any way by the arbitrary will of one or more individuals. It is the right of everyone to express their opinion, choose a profession and practice it, to dispose of property, and even to abuse it; to come and go without permission, and without having to account for their motives or undertakings. It is everyone's right to associate with other individuals, either to discuss their interests, or to profess their religion which they and their associates prefer, or even simply to occupy their days or hours in a way which is most compatible with their inclinations and whims ...

Free men must exercise all professions; provide for the needs of society ... Commerce inspires in men vivid love of individual independence. Commerce supplies all their needs, satisfies their desires, without the interventions of the authorities. This intervention is almost always – and I do not know why I say almost – this intervention is indeed always a trouble and embarrassment. Every time collective power wishes to meddle with private speculations, it harasses the speculators. Every time governments pretend to do our own business, they do it more incompetently and expensively than we do.

Constant, it should be added, did not consider political liberty, in the sense of free participation in democratic deliberation concerning governmental affairs, to be unimportant. Very much to the contrary, in his view. But democratic politics was narrowed to those matters involving the effective securing and protecting of the rights of every individual to life, liberty and honestly acquired property. As such, political democracy was of secondary importance because the vast majority of issues affecting people were in the private domain of individual choice and voluntary association through the institutions of civil society, including the marketplace of buying and selling at mutually agreed-upon terms.

Again, as Jacob Talmon expressed it in his study of, *The Origins of Totalitarian Democracy* (1952), (classical) liberal democracy sees the "essence of freedom in spontaneity and the absence of coercion ... It recognizes a variety of levels of personal and collective endeavor that are altogether outside of the sphere of politics."

The recent renewed appeal of and call for "social democracy" or "democratic socialism" are really a call for a return to the political liberty of "the ancients," as explained by Benjamin Constant. It is a desire for a far greater "socialization" of everyday life in the arenas of economic production and distribution. Before pursuing this, let us remind ourselves of how liberty operates in Constant's sense of "the moderns."

The Liberty of Consumer Choices in the Market

As consumers, each of us makes our own personal and individual decisions. A useful imagery is when anyone of us goes shopping in the supermarket. Each of us rolls our own shopping cart down the store's aisles, and picks and chooses the particular items we wish to buy and take home.

Some of us will select products that others have not chosen at all. Even when there are similarities in our choice of items that we put in our, respective, carts, the relative amounts often vary, reflecting our likes and dislikes and the particular uses for them on a regular or occasional basis. We each decide on our own planned budget for buying food out of our earned income, with some spending a lot more on groceries and related items than others do.

In addition, we are free to change our minds whenever we like and are willing to incur any costs connected with the change in our consumer preferences. That I bought breakfast cereal yesterday does not preclude me from buying ham and eggs for my morning meal next time I do my food shopping. If I'm tired or disappointed with the car I've been driving I might have to wait to save for the down payment needed for a new or used car, or wait for the expiration on a leased car; but, again, I do not have to purchase the same make and model when I am in the market for a new vehicle and finally decide which one I would like to have.

We each individually decide where we wish to live and work. We do our own personal searches for employment opportunities guided by our own values, preferences and interests. What job we take out of any that may be available and possibly offered to us, is our own choice. Likewise, where we live – the geographical location, be it an urban area or rural, a house or apartment, owned or rented – are decisions each of us make as individuals.

Now, of course, our options and opportunities are not totally unconstrained. It depends upon prospective employers finding our education, skills and experience to be those they are looking for in needed employees at a given moment in time. Our ability to negotiate the salary we would like to have is also constrained by how much a possible employer considers our labor services to be worth in his enterprise, and in relation to what others in the labor market might be willing to accept, given their desire for gainful employment as well.

But just as there is usually more than one supermarket or grocery store vying for our consumer business, there is usually more than one employment opportunity available to us, though not necessarily for the job we might most desire, or the more preferred location, or at the salary we wish someone would be willing to pay us. But there is normally more than "one game in town," so over time we each have degrees of ability to pick and chose more to our liking than if there was none, or only one.

Liberty of Producer Choices in the Market

On the supply-side of a free market, anyone with a bit of drive and determination and some start-up capital that he has saved or borrowed from someone is able to try starting his own business, or pursue a particular profession or occupation. The fact that consumers are not locked into having to do business with and buy from any one producer or seller means that each producer and seller can attempt to offer a better and less expensive product than any of his rivals who are also competing for the same consumer business.

What product to produce and with what features and characteristics are greatly within the discretion of the individual private enterpriser. He can experiment with differentiating his product, with trying to devise better and less expensive ways of producing and marketing it than his rivals.

Freedom of Choice in the Civil Society of Peaceful Association

In such a free society we are at liberty to form associations, clubs and groups for virtually any purpose and interest that we might have in common and share with others. This includes professional associations, sports clubs, religious congregations, or philanthropic and charitable endeavors to assist those individuals or advance those causes we consider worthy of our support. If we need a facility to house such an organization we can either rent an existing location from its owner with whom we reach mutually agreeable terms, or we can purchase or hire the land, labor and materials to build the facility we want.

The "Democratic Pluralism" of Market Liberty

If we wanted to express it this way, we could say that the Constant's "modern" conception of liberty represents a form of "democratic pluralism." The patterns of market and social outcomes reflect the preferences and active choices of all the members of society, as each member has been free to make his own decisions without the consent of a majority of others.

These social outcomes are a pluralistic representation of "the will of the people," in that a wide and diverse set of desires, wants and values simultaneously are fulfilled. The fact that, say, Cheerio's and Wheaties are demanded by a significant majority of the consuming public does not preclude a minority from satisfying their desire for ham and eggs in the morning, or for a bowl of hot cereal with a side dish of grits, instead.

As long as a minority of consumers have enough dollar "votes" to make it profitable for some producer(s) to see an opportunity from serving smaller or niche demands for various goods and services, they often will be fulfilled. The development and application of new technologies that have enabled the production and marketing of eBooks, and video and audio streaming have dramatically widened the number of multiple and diverse wants and likes that can be simultaneously catered to, regardless of how small that minority might be, or how large and perhaps disapproving and noticeable a majority can be.

Personal Choices Constrained by Democratic Socialism

But what if we returned to something more on the lines of the ancients' notion of liberty, as explained by Benjamin Constant? I would argue that this is, in fact, what the call for democratic socialism or social democracy actually entails. Private property in production, marketing and sales would be, if not abolished and transferred to the State, then at least heavily hampered and regulated by the State.

Not the individual private enterpriser, but the voting majorities of the citizenry through their government representatives would determine and decide what goods would be produced, to whom would the output be distributed, and at what nominal prices (if any!). If the majority deems the eating of meat to be animal genocide by human beings, the individuals who do not share this view and desire to continue eating meat products would find themselves unable to do so, since the means of production through which one product or another can be produced would be owned or controlled by the citizens of the society as a collective whole.

If you think that cancer research is more important than additional wild life areas or homes for the elderly, your income and wealth will be allocated and used not according to your own values and desires, but as the majority has deliberated and decided. Housing would no longer be fully privately owned and sold on the market based on competitive supply and demand. Instead, where you lived, with how many rooms and accompanying amenities, and at what rent (if any!) would be decided by the majority of your fellow citizens as manifested by the housing construction and allocation through the authorities acting on behalf of "the people."

If the majority of voters were persuaded that Harper Lee's posthumous work, *Go Set a Watchman* (2016) was sufficiently "racist" in its undercurrent that it threw into doubt the reputation of its author, then a majority might consider any further printing and sale of her earlier, *To Kill a Mockingbird* (1960) to be "hurtful" to those negatively portrayed in the later novel.

If it were countered that a social democracy would be dedicated to respecting the civil liberty of freedom of the press and ideas, the book need not be banned; but given the heavy competing demands for the resources out of which books are manufactured, the government's allocation of resources simply might be curtailed enough such that the, de facto, result would be the same as a publishing ban.

We saw that in the freedom of the marketplace the individual is free to change his mind about what to buy, how to live, where and for whom to work with relatively wide latitude of discretion, given general the constraint that he lives in a world of other people.

Under Democratic Socialism, Individuals Controlled by Majorities

Under a regime of democratic socialism, for an individual to have the opportunity for any such changes in many aspects of life, it will be necessary for him to influence and change enough other minds that the next time when voting is held on these issues, new decisions will be made about these everyday matters.

But what if the individual is not able to successfully change other's minds in sufficient numbers? Then many individual's on the minority side of the debates, decisions and voting will be compelled to live within and under the desires of the unchanged majority. Then, any new attempt to change government policies must wait until the next round of voting, usually years away.

In the real world of even the most sincere democratic socialists, the will of the people that add up to a majority of voters will, like now, be composed of minority interest groups who will form coalitions with each other to have the greatest combined votes on election day, so their respective wants and desires are served at others' expense who are not fortunate to have the needed numbers in the voting booth.

If current politics under "democratic" crony capitalism seems corrupt with favoritism and redistributive benefit for floating majorities who use the system for their own advantage at the expense of consumers and taxpayers, this would be multiplied many times over when virtually nothing could be done in society without voter consensus and approval, with the outcomes determining the place, position, and status of everyone in the society.

Beware Those in Politics Who Wish to Take Care of You

We will have returned to the political liberty of the ancients where democratic majorities tyrannize over personal liberty. As Benjamin Constant warned:

> The danger of ancient liberty was that men, exclusively concerned with securing their share of social power, might attach too little value to individual rights and enjoyments ... The holders of authority ... are ready to spare us all sort of troubles, except those of obeying and paying!

They will say to us: what, in the end, is the aim of your efforts, the motive of your labors, the object of your desires? Is it not happiness? Well, leave this happiness to us and we shall give it to you. No, Sirs, we must not leave it to them. No matter how touching such a tender commitment may be, let us ask the authorities to keep within their limits. Let them confine themselves to being just [in the enforcement of impartial rule of law]. We shall assume the responsibility of being happy for ourselves.

Benjamin Constant's warning against democratic collectivism and defense of individual liberty and competitive market pluralism – what he called the benefits of "commerce" – remains as true today as when he delivered that lecture to an audience in Paris two hundred years ago in 1819.

CHAPTER 20

TYRANTS OF THE MIND AND THE NEW COLLECTIVISM

The current counter-revolution against liberty is being fought on a number of fronts in American society. One is on the college and university campuses across the country, where the ideology of "political correctness" is strangling the principle and practice of freedom of speech and the ideal of intellectual controversy and debate.

Critical to this campaign against free expression and open exchange of competing and opposing ideas is the capture of the language through which this campaign has been instigated and the linguistic characterization of its protagonists.

We need to remember and reflect upon the fact that it is through our language that we think about ourselves, our relationships to others, and the general social order in which we live and that we share with those others. Words do not simply define or delineate the names of objects, individuals, events or actions. Words also contain and connote meanings that create mental imageries, emotions, attitudes, and beliefs in people that influences and colors how they see themselves and the world around them.

The Nazi Manipulation of Minds Through Language

For an example of this we may turn to Victor Klemperer (1881-1960), a German Jew who survived in Nazi Germany outside of the concentration camp system because his wife was not Jewish and she stood by and defended him throughout the Second World War. Several years after the defeat of Hitler and the National Socialist regime in 1945, Klemperer wrote a book called *The Language of the Third Reich* (1957). A professor of romance languages at a university in Dresden before Hitler's rise to power in 1933, he was especially attuned to the uses and nuances of words and their contextual meanings.

He kept a detailed and truly fascinating diary about daily life during the Nazi era in Germany, the full contents of which was published many years after he passed away, under the title, *I Will Bear Witness: A Diary of the Nazi Years* (1995). He drew upon these meticulous observations in writing *The Language of the Third Reich* in the 1950s. Klemperer argued that virtually everyone in Hitler's Germany was a Nazi – whether or not they considered themselves to be National Socialists, including many of the victims of the regime (including German Jews).

Why? Because they had been captured by and had adapted in their thoughts and beliefs the ideas and ideology of their Nazi masters. They found it difficult to think about life and morality in any other way; that is, to reason in a way independent of the language of words and political phrases reflecting the Nazi conceptions of man, "race" and society. In their minds, Klemperer was suggesting, they were no longer self-governing human beings, but slaves of the regime since they thought and acted in terms of the lexicon and logic of Hitler's National Socialism. Said Klemperer:

> Nazism permeated the flesh and blood of the people through single words, idioms and sentence structures which were imposed upon them in a million repetitions and taken on board mechanically and unconsciously ...

> Language does not simply write and think for me, it also increasingly dictates my feelings and governs my entire spiritual being the more unquestioningly and unconsciously I abandon myself to it ... Words can be like tiny doses of arsenic; they are swallowed unnoticed, appear to have no effect, and then after a little time the toxic reaction sets in after all.

Klemperer said that it was not that the Nazis made up very many new words, though they did in some cases with intentional design. But what was far more invidious, he argued, is that through their own particular uses of existing words, over and over again in their propaganda, speeches and publications, they changed the meanings and contexts of these taken for granted words of the German language.

The Nazis, through this method, made words have only one meaning, the collective or shared meaning serving the Nazis' purposes. "Making language the servant of its dreadful system it procures it in its most powerful, most public and most surreptitious means of advertising," Klemperer explained, and went on:

The sole purpose of the [Nazi use and form of language] is to strip everyone of their individuality, to paralyze them as personalities, to make them into unthinking and docile cattle in a herd driven and hounded in a particular direction, to turn them into atoms in a huge rolling block of stone ... Where [Nazi language] addresses the individual ... where it educates, it teaches means of breeding fanaticism and techniques of mass suggestion.

The Soviet Control of Thought Through Language

No different in this ideological technique of bending language to their purposes was the communist regime in Soviet Russia. Russian historian, Mikhail Heller (1922-1997), highlighted this aspect of the socialist planned society in his insightful work, *Cogs in the Wheel: The Formation of Soviet Man* (1988).

From the time of Vladimir Lenin with the coming of the Bolshevik Revolution in November 1917 through the near 25-year reign of Josef Stalin, to the Soviet leaders at the end of the regime in 1991, language was made to serve the means and ends of the socialist system. Heller explained:

Lenin developed a special way of writing that made it possible to establish the 'formula-slogan' in the mind of the reader or listener ... Then, as the most important compositional element, there is the use of repetition, by means of which a rectangle is formed which concentrates the attention, narrows the field of possibilities, and squeezes thought into a tight ring from which there is only one exit ...

Total power over the Word gives the Master of the Word a magical power over all communications. Soviet speech is always a monologue because there is no other party to talk to. On the other side is the enemy. In the Soviet language there are no neutral words – every word carries an ideological burden ... That is why in Soviet language the same words are repeated over and over again, until they become a signal that acts without any effort of thought. The effect of set phrases and slogans is also assured by their always being repeated in absolutely the same form ...

The Soviet language became the most important means of preventing people from acquiring more knowledge than the state wished ... Soviet speech lost its freedom. The language was put together out of slogans and quotations from the Leader [Stalin] ... The crushing, unquestioned authority of the Leader's word is the result to a large extent of his right and power to name the Enemy ... The word that signifies the enemy must be striking, easy to remember, implying condemnation by its very sound, and always imprecise, so that everyone who at a given moment does not please the Leader can be included under it rubric ...

From "Socialism" to "Liberalism" to "Progressivism"

The same totalitarianization of words and ideas can be seen to be at work in the language of the progressive and radical "left" in America today. Just how successful this has been can be seen in getting people both to forget the past and accept the title "progressive" for all those who desire a further collectivization of contemporary society.

The fact is, those who have taken on the mantle of "progressivism" today were the socialists of a hundred or more years ago. They were certain and confident that such things as Marx's "laws of history" were making a socialist planned society inevitable and inescapable. But "socialist" soon came to possess too many negative connotations such as central direction and command of everyone in society under what was likely to be a dictatorial political regime.

So, socialists undertook the linguistic sleight-of-hand to transform themselves into the new and "true" or "progressive" liberals, wishing merely to fulfill the unfinished political program of the older, 19th century "individualist" liberals who only spoke of "negative" freedoms from coercion and interference by other private individuals or governments.

The unfinished new "progressive liberal" agenda required the fulfillment of "positive" freedoms through governmental guarantees to a wide variety of redistributed benefits for the "needy," the "exploited," and the toilers of the earth who were the "real producers" of all things, but who were unjustly treated and abused by "the rich," the "capitalist owners," the greedy profit pursuers who cared nothing about the "little guy" on whose back these capitalist exploiters rode to their unethically acquired wealth.

And when "liberal" became, itself, a criticized and unpopular word due to negative attacks by political conservatives and others, the word "liberal" was jettisoned and replaced with simply "progressive," meaning a person looking forward for the achievement of more "social progress," connoting what used to be considered a "socialist" program of a hundred years ago – welfare redistribution, and extensive government control and regulation of economic and social life.

But to accuse a "progressive" of being a socialist or interested in advancing portions of a traditionally socialist agenda, has been made into a demonstration that the proponent of such an argument is a "right-wing extremist," a "hater of the poor," an opponent of "social justice," if not worse. All of which serves as a linguistic trick to prevent anyone from taking such a critic seriously in terms of the logical and historical basis of his accusation and argument because to take it seriously shows that such a person, himself, has fallen victim to "reactionary" ideas outside of legitimate and acceptable political debate. Discussion closed.

From "Class Warfare" to the New Race Collectivism

The core social concept in traditional Marxian political economy has been the notion of the "class struggle." Society is divided into two main "social classes" defined as and identified by whether an individual is or is not an owner of the means of production. If he is such an owner, then he is a member of the capitalist "exploiting class." If he is not such an owner, then he is a member of the exploited and oppressed and victimized workers' class.

Property ownership determined the social status and place of any and every individual person in the society. What the individual believed, how he personally acted in his social and economic interactions with others were essentially meaningless. You were praised or condemned based upon your "class status" in the society. You were either a "class enemy" or a "social comrade."

Today, the Marxian conception has been modified and transformed into the new notion of irreconcilable social conflict: the beneficiary of 'white privilege" versus the sufferer of "white oppression." Instead of your status relative to the ownership of productive property determining your classification of social "saint" or social "sinner," there is the new race collectivism.

Being "white" condemns a person as an implicit and explicit beneficiary of a social and economic system ("capitalism") that has been placed at the service of a limited segment of the human community to gain power, position and wealth for itself at the expense and cost of all those other "people of color" everywhere else around the world.

That so many "white people" either fail to understand this or oppose admitting it demonstrates just how embedded "white racism" really is in modern American society, the new race conflict advocates insist. Failure to accept this new race collectivist argument is taken to be, ipso facto, proof of the racist mindset that the "progressive" opposes and is determined to overthrow by virtually any means.

The Individual Lost in Collectivist Classifications

What is the individual's own background? Did his ancestor's ever own African slaves? Were any such ancestors "pro-slavery" or "anti-slavery"? Did those ancestors come to the United States after slavery had ended in America? Were they, themselves, immigrants escaping oppression and discrimination in the "old country" and advocates of equality of rights for all in their new land of America?

How has the individual standing accused of "white privilege" merely due to the pigmentation color of his skin acted in his own personal life toward others? How has he earned his own place in society, through fair detailing on what remains of a free market in the United States or through "crony capitalist" favors and benefits from the government? These questions are never asked, and any attempt to offer answers to them is rejected as smoke screens and rationalizations for maintaining "white privilege."

Individuals are submerged within and reduced to social categories defined and imposed by ideologists dreaming their own utopian dreams of a socially engineered world reflecting their notion of a new race- and ethnic-conscious society. This not only dehumanizes individuals who by accident of birth happen to be the descendants of Caucasian parents, but this does it no less to those who may be black or Hispanic. You are a "victim" as a "person of color." You are not able to transcend your own accident of birth to be a thinking, willing, acting individual guided by your own standards, benchmarks and goals, and able to successfully traverse the trials and tribulation of life. You, too, are an inescapable captive of your race, with only a "progressive" government able to guarantee you a "just" place in society.

The Family Resemblances Between the Old and New Collectivisms
How familiar it all sounds to those Nazi assertions that everything undesired and undesirable in German life was due to the machinations and intrigue of "international Jewry." The failure of so many others in the world to see the invidiousness of Jewish manipulation and exploitation demonstrated the extent to which "the Jew" had succeeded in his control of the social and economic affairs of the world, and how many others were either their unwitting victims or the degenerate accomplices of their attack on "civilization" and race purity.

And how similar to the Soviet method of debate and argument stopping: He is a lackey and dupe of the capitalist exploiters, and therefore should be ignored or condemned. Her refusal to admit the justness of the socialist cause shows that she "must" be in the pay of the capitalist bosses, and thus her arguments should be rejected as special pleading. His arguments against communist and socialist planning should be discounted and ridiculed because he is simply a "red baiter" trying to demagogically arouse emotional resistance against those interested in "social justice" and "world peace."

On some American campuses, now, how similar are the techniques of the "Red Guards" during the Cultural Revolution under Chairman Mao in China during the 1960s and 1970s. Mobs of shouting, bullying and physically attacking young thugs spouting meaningless and ideologically vacuous phrases from the "little red book" of quotations from Chairman Mao, to mentally and physically crush any and all who failed to parrot the Party Line or who were the objects of Chairman Mao's political purges and personal vendettas against real and imaginary opponents.

And at the core of it, the same use of language, repeated and repeated, over and over again, in short, clear phrases connoting "bad things" that merely by being labeled as such stands as accusation, condemnation and implied deserved punishment of the "just wrath" of – the National Socialist German people, the Soviet Socialist toiling masses, the "unprivileged" race victims of "white privilege."

Academia, the New Race Collectivism, and Word Tyranny

A distinct difference between the proponents of this new race collectivism compared to the 20th century episodes of German Nazism or Soviet socialism is that this linguistic totalitarianism and word indoctrination is being advanced and imposed without any direct coercive and monopoly apparatus of governmental power.

Instead, the "headquarters" and "front lines" are in academia, especially in some of those institutions of higher learning that are oases of intellectual autonomy from accountability or challenge due to primarily or heavily taxpayer funded salaries, programs, and curriculums. Freed from the world of market-based work and reward and blessed with lifetime tenure, those academics employed on these islands of educational socialism have the "safe spaces" within which there can be cultivated, to use George Orwell's phrase, "some ideas so absurd that only an intellectual can believe them."

The assertion and repetition of "white privilege," "the one percent," "social justice," "racist," "gay-basher," "LGBT-hater," "gender insensitivity," etc., have had numbing effects on private and public discourse. It has produced degrees of self-censorship out of fear that the wrong word, the misplaced phrase, the wrongly understood witticism, or an unintentionally offending double entendre will bring down an avalanche of criticisms and threats to one's job, social status, or acceptance among professional and informal circles in society.

Similar to the robot-like, expressionless faces seen in the videos of crowds of people in some scenes from North Korea, the politically correct world of American progressivism and the new race collectivism threatens to drain human interaction of spontaneity, banter, and the real and relevant diversity of views, voices, and modes of expression and argumentation. Increasingly, people feel that they have to be "walking on eggs," never knowing who might take anything said or done as an offense against some ethnic or racial group or person; and the offender finding himself in the dock of social condemnation and ostracism.

Another technique of the new race collectivism and progressivism is to take what is normally accepted as reasonable and appropriate modes of polite and courteous behavior and turn it into a weapon to serve their own agendas. We all know and usually attempt not to intentionally say or do something that will offend or be embarrassing to someone we are associating with in some social setting. We just know it's "not the right thing to do." And if we see someone going out of their way to, in fact, act in this improper manner, we find it inappropriate and "not right," even if we remain silent and don't do anything in response to it.

The new race collectivists and progressives have learned to use this notion of proper etiquette and good manners that acts as a break on most of us in the social arena as a weapon to silence and beat down anyone or anything not consistent with their worldview and political agenda. Anything said or done inconsistent with their ideas and ideology is "hurtful" to some oppressed minority or subgroup in society. It shows an insensitivity and misunderstanding of that group's experiences, history, culture or degree of suffering caused by – "white privilege," or "the capitalist system," or ...

Made to feel guilty in thinking some thought, saying some word, or expressing some idea, and fearful about the consequences from doing so, an increasingly successful Orwellian-like thought police of politically correct "newspeak" is imposed on people in almost every circumstance of social life.

Making the Past Serve the Ideological Purposes of the Present

In George Orwell's novel, *1984*, the anti-hero, Winston, works in the Ministry of Truth. His task is to go through the pages of old newspapers and rewrite the articles in them to make events and statements made in the past consistent with and supportive of the government's current Party line. The words and events of the past are made to conform to the ideological "truths" of the present.

Here, too, is another trick and technique of the new race collectivists and progressives. Historical events and the people who lived in that past are remade to fit the "truth" of these new totalitarians. When Jefferson wrote in the Declaration of Independence that all human beings are created equal and have certain unalienable rights among which are life, liberty, and the pursuit of happiness, this was all "really" code words and rationales for a society of white racism.

If James Madison helped to author a constitution for the United States that had as a leading purpose restraints on the passions of potential individual rights-violating majorities that would threaten a free and prosperous society, this is "really" the institutionalization of the power of an oligarchy of the "the rich" to thwart the progressive will of the majority of "the people" for "social justice" against the exploiting "one percent."

Oh, how similar to Stalin's method of rewriting the actual history of the Russian Revolution to make himself, a relatively minor player in those events, into the right-hand comrade of Vladimir Lenin in assuring socialist victory. And what a family resemblance to the other Stalinist tool of making the past conform to the politics of the present, when following a purge those sent to the labor camps or to their death had all positive mention of them deleted from books and magazines, and all pictures of them airbrushed out of old photos.

Everyone who believes in any of the liberal values of freedom of thought, freedom of speech, freedom of association, in freedom of exchange of ideas, must oppose and prevent this new race collectivism and its accompanying "progressive" linguistic totalitarianism from imposing a new dark age of diminished human discourse.

The wit, charm, creativity, and humanity of words and the ideas expressed through them, must not be stunted and then petrified by those who wish to reduce individual human beings to collectivist categories of ideological control and command. Liberty of thought, deed, action and association is too precious to be lost to these latest coercing and intimidating thugs of the human mind.

CHAPTER 21

COLLECTIVISM'S PROGRESS: FROM MARXISM TO RACE AND GENDER INTERSECTIONALITY

By many objective signs and indicators the world is becoming a far more materially comfortable place. Over the last thirty years, tens of millions of people have been raised out of poverty in various parts of Asia, Africa and Latin America. At the same time, new technologies have been transforming communications and conveniences of everyday life. Yet, present political trends in America and other places in the world seem to be suggesting a far different story.

Wherever degrees of market freedom exist anywhere around the globe there are amazing successes in creating wealth, opportunity and personal choice. But among many intellectuals and paternalistic ideologues every such improvement in the human condition is matched with condemnations and attempts to smother personal and economic liberty.

Statist Trends Around the World, Including America

For instance, the Chinese government and Communist Party leadership are proudly hailing its own brand of authoritarianism as a political model for the world, based on the silencing of disagreement and dissent combined with government guidance and planning of economic development for restored "national greatness." The European Union continues to fracture, with revolts of nationalist and populist movements in many of the member countries opposed to the centralized planning bureaucracies and political elites headquartered in Brussels, but which desire to implement many of the same types of government policies only at the local levels of national control and command.

In the United States, political divisions seem to be growing even deeper between the progressive "left" and the Trumpitarian conservatives, with each side vying to transform America into their respective images through use of the state. The progressives want to use the government to impose a straightjacket of "politically correct" words, actions and attitudes. The Trumpitarian conservatives are determined to build "walls" against people and goods that might enter the country, while following their own version of America continuing to play policeman around the world. In the meantime, the U.S. government continues its path along worsening fiscal irresponsibility as both Democrats and Republicans in Congress "compromise" with each other to gain deficit-busting increases in both domestic and military spending

All of these trends, I would suggest, are instances of the fact that as we approach the end of the second decade of the 21st century, the world is, again, in the grip of a wave of anti-individualism and anti-liberalism. In fact, it is merely a continuation of the same counter-revolutionary trend that has been at work for well over a century to reverse the achievements of 19th century classical liberalism. It is the same old collectivist wine poured into new political and cultural bottles.

Collectivism's Counter-Revolution Against Liberty

Classical liberalism and the ideal of a free, open competitive market society were already under attack by conservative, socialist, and nationalist forces in the middle and last decades of the 19th century. Though expressed differently, all of these counter-revolutionary movements emphasized the group before the individual, the submergence within and the submission of the person to the collective – whether that collective was called the hierarchical order of the aristocratic society, or the "workers of the world" united to impose socialist planning on mankind, or an ancestral call and appeal to tribal lineage of national blood and language.

The most repugnant, violent, and brutal of these competing collectivisms – Soviet communism, Italian fascism, and German National Socialism – all were gone by the end of the 20th century (though some of the Soviet offspring still rule parts of the world, in such places as China, North Korea, Vietnam, Cuba and Venezuela). But the collectivist genus, of which communism, fascism and Nazism were merely species, persists and threatens, once more, to possibly prevail.

Freedom, Tyranny, and the Postwar Interventionist State

The post-World War II global struggle between the United States and the Soviet Union brought out certain defining features between a free society and a totalitarian one. It was visualized in such contrasts as that between West Berlin and East Berlin, especially after the building of the Berlin Wall in 1961.

In West Berlin, there was a vibrant market-based material and cultural recovery, along with wide and respected civil liberties, after the destruction experienced by the German people due to their active or passive support for and obedience to the Nazi regime and the cataclysmic war that Hitler brought down on all of Europe. On the other side of the Wall, in East Berlin, was a drab, grey and dictatorial system, with its ever-present secret police, which was imposed on the East Germans by Stalin and those who followed after him in Moscow, with much of the rubble and ruin of the war still surrounding the East Berliners in the bright and beautiful East German socialist state. Who could deny the contrast between these two worlds separated by a Wall built to keep the captive people of communism inside and the ideas and hopes of freedom outside?

But in the West, the market-oriented economies during those post-1945 Cold War decades were not truly free markets, as understood in the classical liberal tradition. They were economies enveloped within and hampered by varying degrees and forms of government regulatory intervention and redistributive welfare statism. The interventionist-welfare state may have been more extensive and intrusive in a number of Western European nations compared to the United States, but they were all managed, manipulated and partly planned societies within democratic political regimes.

The Left's "Shock" over the Crimes and Collapse of Soviet Socialism

Nonetheless, the fall of the Berlin Wall in 1989 and the collapse of the Soviet Union in 1991 were "shocks" to the emotions and the ideology of many of those on the political left in the Western world.

For most of the seven decades following the Bolshevik Revolution in Russia in 1917, the socialists, progressives, and modern American "liberals" had all yearned for the success of the great experiment of "socialism-in-practice" in the hope of a government planned "better world." In the middle decades of the 20th century many of them were apologists and mouthpieces for Lenin's and Stalin's Russia. Reports and eyewitness accounts of terror, tyranny, and mass murder at the hands of the Soviet regime were often denied or ridiculed as anti-socialist "red baiting" or the false tales of disgruntled opponents of "the new Russia."

After the revelations of "Stalin's Crimes" following his death in 1953, the brutal suppression of the anti-Soviet uprising in Hungary in 1956 and the Soviet invasion of Czechoslovakia in 1968 to crush "moderate" socialist reforms, many on the left in the West had their hopes and dreams of the Soviet model completely shattered. Instead, given the complementary failure of socialist central planning to bring either prosperity or freedom to those countries in the Soviet and socialist orbits, the democratic socialists in Europe and the progressives in America gave up their heart-felt ideal of ending "capitalism" and replacing it with the planned economy. Their fall back position by the 1970s was for a heavily regulated and more redistributive system to assure "social justice."

With the end of the communist system in the Soviet Union and Eastern Europe, and the shift to market-oriented reforms in places like China, it seemed as if only "capitalism" was left standing, embodied in America's political, economic, and military dominance of the world. The political and cultural progressive left retreated even further than before into the cloistered halls of higher education. They could sulk and lick their ideological wounds, while continuing to sit in their intellectual ivory towers chanting incantations that capitalism was evil, communalism was just, and the "oppressed" and "exploited" still needed liberation. And they could share their abiding "faith" in a collectivist better world to the clusters of students who passed through their college and university classes, with those young and innocent minds waiting to be remade with a "raised consciousness" concerning social justice.

Old Marxist Wine in New Collectivist Race and Gender Bottles

But the 21st century was no longer the "harsh conditions" of the industrial revolution in the early 19th century, nor the "bad times" of the Great Depression in the 1930s. America and Western Europe, especially, were highly "middle class" societies with standards of living even for the poorest that were unimaginable for the kings and princes of past times. Good or at least reasonable pay for most, comfortable daily lives with new technology-generating amenities constantly easing the chores of everyday life for larger circles of the population, and generally wide areas of personal freedom and civil liberties for almost everyone.

So who were the oppressed, the exploited and the "marginalized," the "suffering masses" yearning to be freed from the injustice of capitalism? Enter the new variation on the old Marxist theme. For most of the last two hundred years, the socialists and communists insisted that the great human conflict centered on "social classes." But how do you sell "class warfare" when most in society view themselves as and financially are "middle class," and while those in the lower rungs of the income categories want nothing more than to become middle class themselves – maybe even rich, one of the "one percent"?

So the traditional socialist class warfare was jettisoned, and in its place there was offered the new race and gender warfare. The

Marxists of old used to insist that the failure of the proletariat to fully understand their exploitation by the capitalist bosses was due to their being indoctrinated with a "false consciousness" that they were "free" under capitalism, while all the time they were "wage slaves" not even knowing the extent to which they were the victims of the unjust social system of private ownership of the means of production.

A New Race and Gender-Based "False Consciousness"

Now the false consciousness was to believe that racism in Western society, if not eradicated (after all there will always be some stupid people with foolish ideas), at least was dramatically reduced compared to the past, with attitudes and actions by most people far more consistent with the American ideal of judging and treating others as individuals. All the while, racism, it was asserted, is in fact pervading the society, keeping "people of color" down for the benefit of those who were "privileged" merely by their "whiteness."

The same applied to gender and sexual orientation. More women in the workplace and in a growing number of positions of authority and responsibility with salaries reflecting that status hid from view the reality of sexist and misogynist attitudes that were "really" keeping women in second place and leaving them open to all forms of physical and psychological abuse. Legal niceties about same-sex marriages and relationships created the lie that homophobia was not actually haunting every corner of society.

Anthropologists and psychologists will tell you that the power of magic is to get a person to believe something to be true that is objectively not the case. Convince someone that a witch doctor sticking a needle into a voodoo doll made to look like them will cause them pain, and that person may, under the power of suggestion, feel as if they were experiencing pain. As the hippies of the 1960s used to say, "It's all in your head, man."

Get people to believe that any experienced disappointment, every personal failure, any slight by another person (whether actually intended or unintended) is a demonstration of the pervasive and inescapable existence and practice of racism, gender discrimination or sexual orientation bigotry, and some people are made into viewing themselves as the inescapable victims of white and male and heterosexual oppression, everywhere and every day.

Individuals Submerged Within Race and Gender Intersectionality

Furthermore, this new variation on the collectivist theme insists that everyone's identity and sense of "self" is bound up with their classified gender, race and sexuality. These define you, determine who you are, and establish the meaning and context of your life. But what of the person who denies this, who opposes this, who rejects this, and who thinks of him- or herself simply as a thinking and acting individual, or who appreciates that they may be, by accident of birth and circumstances, a particular race, or gender, or person of a certain sexual orientation, but considers these to be of secondary importance in terms of their own self-identity and purposes in life?

Then this is their form of "false consciousness" from which they need to be reeducated and liberated. They are a self-hating enemy of who they "really are," who has been brainwashed and manipulated to serve the interests of the white, male, heterosexual oppressors of humankind.

Plus, there is "intersectionality." It seems that there are many complex forms of gender and race discrimination and oppression. You may be oppressed for being a woman. Or discriminated against for being black. Or you may be oppressed and discriminated against because you are black and female. Or you may be "marginalized" by others because you have a physical handicap. So you may be oppressed, discriminated against and marginalized because you are black, female, and handicapped. Or you may be gay and humiliated and made fun of. So you may be black, female, handicapped and gay and, therefore, a victim of all these abuses and "aggressions."

Each of these "intersections" has their own category of meaning, experience, oppression, discrimination, abuse and "marginalization." And others, even abused "black sisters" may not fully know "the troubles you've seen" because you are female, black, but also handicapped and/or gay. And, of course, a white woman can only really understand one fraction of what this other person goes through because, though a women, she is white and therefore has had some degree of "privilege" due to not being a "person of color."

You can't keep up with all the permutations of abuse, oppression, and discrimination without a detailed and complex intersectionality scorecard! Nor can you know the forms and types of "white privilege" unless you have a similar scorecard of unjust opportunities or benefits you may have no idea that you, as a "white person," may have been enjoying without even realizing it or wanting it.

You get five points for being black, female and gay; but you only get three points because while you may be gay and handicapped you are a white female. As a white, heterosexual male with only a stutter, you get one point for the speech impediment but minus nine for being totally otherwise white privileged. The mind gets dizzy with all the intersectionality calculations and possibilities.

The focus on collective groups and "rights" in the context of these discussions of "intersectionality" submerges from view, attention and weighted significance in the social analysis one other small minority: the individual. It ignores or downplays how the individual person views and classifies himself, how he judges and evaluates the nature and meaning of the actions of others and his own actions toward them. And what he considers important, meaningful and relevant in the social setting in which he chooses and acts.

Censoring Discourse to Dictate Identity

Just as the old Marxists used to call upon all workers of the world to unite against their capitalist chains regardless of their particular ethnic, linguistic or national backgrounds, so, too, the new race and gender collectivists insist that all victims of all forms and permutations of white, male "privilege" must stand united as one force of resistance and liberation. An offense against one oppressed or "marginalized" group is an offense against all; even though the members of one such oppressed and marginalized group may never really know and understand the other. That is why it requires being "non-judgmental," and "sensitive" to the "feelings" and experiences of all other subgroups in the wider, generic category of "oppression," as each subgroup defines these things for themselves.

The communist states insisted that they needed to block out and prevent all unapproved Western ideas from entering the socialist paradise, so capitalist propaganda could not undermine the educated and reeducated minds of the Soviet people about the glories and superiority of socialist life. The new version is the declaration by the race and gender collectivists that all "hateful" or "offensive" or "fascist-type" ideas must be censored and suppressed from having a hearing in various "public spaces." And, if necessary, any person attempting to utter the forbidden words and ideas may be physically challenged and ejected. Welcome to the latest version of ideological thuggery.

Confusing the Meaning of Words for Collectivist Ends

In addition, the progressives and race and gender collectivists have been highly successful in manipulating the meaning and use of words, and to make concepts that are different to seem as if they are synonyms. Thus, the word "discrimination" has been transformed into a synonym for "oppression."

"Discrimination" means to "distinguish between," and to prefer, value or act differently toward one defined group or set of things compared to another. Thus, for example, I "discriminate" against all writers of romance novels since I choose to never buy their books and, thus, limit the income they might otherwise have earned if I bought their works. I "discriminate" against Nazis and communists because I refuse to intentionally bring them into my circle of friends, and thus I "restrict" them from the benefits they might have wanted to obtain from my company.

"Oppression," on the other hand, normally connotes the use or threat of some form of violence or legal prohibition faced by an individual or a groups of individuals classified with certain characteristics. Slavery was oppression. Segregation laws were oppression. Laws penalizing consensual homosexual behavior were (are) oppression. Ending oppression involves prohibiting private acts of force or its threat toward others, and the repeal of laws and other legal restrictions preventing individuals defined as possessing some type(s) of group characteristics from peacefully pursuing their own affairs and/or in voluntary association and interaction with others.

Ending oppression requires education and legal action (that is, repeal of restrictive or prohibitory laws). Ending discrimination requires education and reason and persuasion that the criteria used by individuals in their choices and actions are incorrect or misplaced. Laws against discrimination can only coerce people in a different way, by prohibiting or insisting on their acting in certain ways toward others that by necessity reduces and limits their own peaceful choices and actions. To compel me to interact with someone with whom I'd rather not is no less oppressive than preventing me from peacefully interacting with someone whom I would like to for some personal and mutual advantage.

Restoring America's Individualist Roots

How did we get here? It is because we have travelled a long way from those founding American ideas of individual rights and liberty. From a society that accepts that individuals may think and act in many different ways, including how that individual views himself and relates to and associates with others for various purposes that gives value and meaning to their life. But it remains the individual who is the conscious, thinking, choosing, and acting building block from and upon which all that we call "society" emerges and takes its patterns and forms.

We must retrace our steps, and return to our roots in philosophical, sociological and political liberalism and individualism. We have to recapture our understanding and appreciation of who and why the individual is important and that any associative identifications that an individual makes should emerge out of his own reflections and judgments concerning the meaning of and purpose to his life. They should not be imposed on him by collectivist ideologues wanting to straightjacket him into categories and classifications not of his own making and to which they wish to confine and condemn him, and, indeed, through which to oppress him. Otherwise, we are heading for another dangerous and damaging episode in the history of mankind.

CHAPTER 22

"IDENTITY POLITICS" THREATENS THE OPEN AND FREE SOCIETY

America started a "great experiment" in human history, that being the ideas of individual freedom and limited government. All of history before this assumed that the individual was subservient to the tribe, and governments had nearly absolute power over people in the form of ruling kings and princes.

Today, again, there are counter-revolutions against this great experiment in human liberty. In China it takes the form of an asserted alternative to Western constitutional democracy that claims the superiority of an authoritarian model (on a Marxian foundation) under which political power is concentrated in the hands of one party and one leader. To assure "unity" and one over-arching plan for Chinese "national greatness" reclaimed, it utilizes a vast surveillance state that watches, controls, arrests, and imprisons or kills any and all who offer criticism, dissent, and resistance to Beijing's "Big Brother" State.

In the Middle East, thousands of Muslim fanatics gravitated

to the banner of the "Islamic State" with its totalitarian insistence of one true faith, one true theological doctrine, one true path to salvation. Like far too many other religious callings of the past around the world, the Islamic State called upon the redeemed and the righteous to us fire and sword to establish that one true faith over all of humanity. Brutality and mass murder were the keys to the kingdom used by those of the Islamic State who arrogantly asserted knowing how to get to a heaven on earth.

In the West, and especially most visibly on American university and college campuses, and among a seemingly growing number of academics and intellectuals, is the claim that the founding American principles were all a ruse, a smoke screen, for the perpetuation of racism and gender oppression, along with social class exploitation.

The Danger of Identity Politics – Past and Present

"Identity politics" is the latest revolutionary collectivist banner under which the enemies of philosophical, political and economic individualism are marching to create their own variation of a bright, beautiful new world. But you can be certain that if triumphant their victory would herald an end to that American experiment in human liberty. All the precious freedoms articulated in the Declaration of Independence and codified in the U.S. Constitution would be threatened with extinction.

The assault on freedom of speech and the press is already entrenched on many campuses around the country. The thought control thugs shout down, intimidate, and threaten or use physical violence against any and all who attempt to talk about ideas, policies, or views inconsistent with or contrary to these latest totalitarians of the mind. The only legitimate speech or publicly published words are those that reflect the lexicon and ideological content of the leaders and the enthusiastically chanting mobs of frenzied students who demand the end to all views and values other than their own.

Have we not seen all this before? Leading up to and then following the rise to power of Adolf Hitler in Germany, there were large gangs of Nazi thugs who would break into and brutally break up the meetings and speeches of opposing groups. Young Nazi fanatics terrorized and attacked those designated as "race enemies." Were these not the proponents of a version of identity politics? Were you a member of the oppressed and humiliated "pure" German race demanding liberation and rebirth, or were you one of the exploiting and blood-sucking minorities, especially the "degenerate" and "racially impure" Jews?

What about the Red Guards in the China of the 1960s and 1970s? Revolutionary cadres made up of thousands of Chinese students ran wild while holding and waving in their hands the "little red book" of the quotations from Chairman Mao, and mindlessly repeated the vacuous phases and sayings of Mao Zedong's take on Marxism and communist power through the barrel of a gun. The humiliation, the brutality and even the murder of parents, teachers, professionals and anyone else, even poor ignorant peasants, unfortunate enough to be classified as an "enemy of the people" in the irrational hysteria of Marxist class conflict overlaid "with Chinese characteristics." Was this not a form of identity politics? Into which "social class" were you born and lived: oppressed worker or oppressing capitalist?

The demands of America's identity politics proponents that statues be pulled down, symbols of the past be removed, and buildings and streets be renamed all have their family resemblance, as well. From the time of the Russian Socialist Revolution in 1917, the communists wherever they came to power initiated their campaign of eradicating all traces of the "evil" and "bad" past by blowing up churches, destroying architecture, and changing the name of any cities, streets or buildings that reflected the dark era of capitalist exploitation that Marxism was relegating to the "dustbin of history."

The Nazi leaders and mobs did their version of this in 1930s Germany. The bonfires of books were meant to reduce to ashes any memory or knowledge of ideas and authors not a part of the identity politics of German National Socialism; an aspect of this Nazi plan for a new and better "master race" was extended to the burning of the bodies of the millions of the "racially inferior" who were killed, so no trace would be left of them either.

Was this not identity politics in the extreme? Just as was the murder of tens of millions of "class enemies" in the Soviet Union, with millions more of such "class" identified "enemies" sent to work, starve and die in the slave labor camps of Siberia or Soviet Central Asia? Individual human beings were reduced to and classified by the collectivist identity politics of race or social class, a group identity classification that sealed your fate, separate from who or what they were as a distinct individual person.

Making the Past Fit the Identity Politics of the Present

The Marxists and Nazis reduced human history to preconceived narratives of either class conflict or race warfare through the ages. What did not fit the ideological narrative was either ignored or twisted to conform to the identity politics story line meant to explain all of human existence down to the present. The practitioners of America's new identity politics are now doing the same. Everything that has happened on this planet is forced through the prisms of race or gender identity.

The ignorance, error, or outright lying reaches a level of near total disbelief. It is sometimes claimed, for instance, that if not for white racism slavery would never have existed. In fact, slavery has been one of the most universal human institutions since the beginning of recorded history. Ancient Greeks enslaved other Greeks; the ancient Romans, as they conquered and expanded their vast empire, enslaved peoples from many ethnic, linguistic and religious backgrounds. The same was true among Asians, Africans, and in the America's among the Aztecs, Mayans, and the Incas of Peru.

African tribes enslaved each other as a result of their tribal wars; black African chieftains would sell conquered slaves to Arab slave traders who would bring their human cargo to the coasts of Africa where those slaves would be sold at auction and transported to the "New World" of the Americas. At the same time, white Europeans were common among the slave populations of the Muslim world until not that long ago. The very word, "slave" is derived from "Slav," meaning a variety of the peoples in Eastern Europe who were conquered and held in bondage by other Europeans.

Beginning in the 1500s slavery was given a new area of employment with the "discovery" of the Americas and the transportation of increasingly large number of Africans by the Portuguese, the Spanish and then the English. The accounts of the slave ships that crossed the Atlantic are horrific in their brutality and inhumanity of treatment. And with the growth of a partly slave-based economy, especially in what became the southern states of the new United States, it was not too surprising that the white slave owners developed race-based rationales for their "peculiar" institution, often attempting to derive it from Biblical interpretations. In addition, in the first half of the 19th century Southern authors such as George Fitzhugh argued in his books, *Sociology of the South, or the Failure of Free Society* (1854) and *Cannibals All! Slaves Without Master* (1857), that slavery was a "benevolent socialism" under which slave masters far more tenderly cared for their human property than the selfish capitalist factory "slave masters" of the North who paid barely subsistence wages to their "free" workers and cared nothing if they starved and died.

The Idea of Liberty and the End to Slavery

But it was also among Europeans, and especially among the British, in the second half of the 18th century that there emerged an active, organized and finally successful anti-slavery movement that brought about the end to much of the slave trade across the Atlantic, and then the abolition of the institution of slavery throughout the British Empire by an Act of Parliament in 1833. These individual Englishmen, who by accident of their birth happened to be "white," argued that slavery was an abomination against God as revealed in their Christian faith; all men are born equal children of God, and which mortal man, no different from all others in the eyes of God, should presume to lord over some of those others as if they were God? There is only one Master of all human beings, and He rules in Heaven.

They spoke eloquently and movingly against the cruelty and barbarity of the treat of captured Africans by the slave traders and the slave masters. Given the indignities and ignorance the masters imposed on their human property, was it any wonder, the anti-slave advocates said, that the African seemed to some to be so less human and civilized compared to whites, when the slave owners prohibited all forms of literacy and learning for their property, and treated their slaves more like abused animals than fellow human beings? The humanity and humanness of Africans was no different than that of Europeans, they insisted, if only they were set free to live normal human lives.

The anti-slavery sentiment had a parallel growth in the United States. Abolitionist groups among Northern whites slowly grew in number and fervor during the decades before the Civil War, with public outcries against their Southern white fellow countrymen. Northern whites demanding the end to this immoral institution undertook rallies, meeting, publications, and political campaigns. There were pro-slavery advocates in the North, too, and abolitionists (white and black) risked physical assault and murder when especially vocal and determined in their opposition. Others risked arrest and imprisonment in working with the Underground Railway moving runaway slaves to Canada where they could not be extradited back to their Southern owners.

This is not to downplay or marginalize the efforts and actions of free blacks in the North or the courage and character of those runaway slaves who risked being sent back to the South by publicly telling their personal stories to arouse the conscience of more Northern whites against the institution from which they escaped. Or the often-pervasive degrees of racial discrimination that blacks in the North faced even in those states that had long before abolished slavery.

But in this environment of "political correctness" in which "whites" as a collective category stand condemned and accused of responsibility for "racism" and slavery, historical accuracy requires that it be remembered that the movement that finally brought a global end to the legal institution of slavery began in Europe and spread to America. That many individuals who were "white" took public stands and fought (sometimes with their lives) for the final triumphant end to slavery on both sides of the Atlantic.

Individual Rights as Key to Free People from Bondage

Why did they do so? Why did these multitudes of people speak out against this ancient institution and run the risk and experience the condemnation and threatened assault by their fellow human beings who defended slavery? In a word, LIBERTY.

The 17th and 18th centuries had seen the emergence of an articulated political philosophy of individual freedom and constitutionally restrained government. John Locke's *Two Treatises on Government* (1690) expressed this new social ideal that the individual possessed certain inherent and inseparable human rights: to his life, his liberty and his honestly acquired property. The individual owned himself, and was neither the property of a tribal group nor an absolute king. Locke insisted that man's life and liberty were given to him as a gift from God, but he also argued that our human reason is able to reflect upon our own nature as human beings and our condition in the world.

Our reason can demonstrate the intuitive "self-evidence" that each of us both needs and desires freedom to survive and prosper. That this includes the peaceful appropriation of physical property by the use and application of our mental and physical labor to transform the natural objects in the world into useful things to sustain and improve our lives. However, sometimes, other human beings do not respect an individual's right to his life, liberty and property, and he may not be able on his own to fend off the attack.

So people form associative relationships for mutual defense and securing of justice, which goes under the name of "government." But this government is meant to be a guardian of our individual liberty, not its abuser and violator, and is limited to and restrained in its powers by written or unwritten constitutional demarcations that define the permitted actions by those who hold political office.

Once such an idea was set loose on the world and came to be understood, believed in, and defended by a growing number of people, it demonstrated to be a force of its own that demanded logical and consistent application, however long the resulting process might take. Yes, the early Americans tolerated or even continued to support the enslavement of one portion of the nation's population. But just as two objects cannot successfully occupy the same physical space, so too, two logically incompatible ideas could not permanently occupy the same social space.

How could political leaders and most of the citizenry declare that theirs was a land of liberty, of peaceful and voluntary association and exchange, of opportunity for all to live their own lives peacefully as they chose in following their own personal purposes, while some human beings held others in permanent bondage? A lie cannot be perpetually lived, no matter how hard a person or people may try.

Either there is liberty or there is slavery and tyranny. The ideals expressed in the Declaration of Independence and codified in the U.S. Constitution's Bill of Rights have forced people living in this country over the years and the decades to more consistently live the words they say their country is supposed to be all about, in this case, when it came to ending slavery and extending equal rights and protection under the law to all people residing within the boundaries of the United States.

The New "Identity Politics" Would Mean the End to Liberty

Neither the Declaration of Independence nor the Constitution speaks of "rights" in terms of racial, gender, or social class "identity." They recognize only INDIVIDUALS, with their individual rights before the law and protected by an impartial rule of law, above which are no individuals or special groups. That people and politics often do not always reflect the ideas and ideals espoused should not come as too much of a surprise. But the purpose and role of those ideas and ideals is to serve as the benchmark of comparison from which to judge and evaluate the reality of men's words and deeds. That individual human beings fall short does not detract from or suggest the hypocrisy or deceitful "smoke screen" of these ideas and ideals. It merely means that "the flesh is weak," and we are all called upon to more fully practice what we preach.

But the new advocates of "identity politics" would erase from public discourse, discussion or understanding these noble and historically monumental ideas of individual liberty and rights, and constitutionally limited government by the linguistic slight-of-hand of excluding them from the academic and public arena by labeling them with the condemnatory "hurtful" words of "racism" or "racist" and "sexist" or "homophobic."

What would a triumphant world of the new identity politics look like? You would no longer be an individual allowed to life your own life as you peacefully find most likely to bring you happiness and personal meaning. You would be classified and categorized from birth as belonging to a racial, ethnic, linguistic, or social group or class. Your life opportunities, therefore, would be defined and dictated by how the political process determined what station and status your "identity" group should hold and be allowed to benefit from.

Your words and language use would be permanently "policed," judged and potentially condemned for anti-social thoughts defined by whether they were "hurtful" to some other politically identified racial, gender, ethnic, or linguistic group in your society. You would be subject to "re-education" to clean your mind and its thoughts of "hurtful" ideas that demonstrated your hidden and insensitive racist and sexist outlook. Indeed, linguistic gender insensitivity on your part might even result in imprisonment, as a recent piece of legislation in Canada suggests could happen to the unlucky person who commits a gender "word crime."

Who you could associate with, for what purposes and under what terms would all be subject to approval and command of a government designed to impose a society of "identity politics," rather than under the current Bill of Rights that recognizes freedom of speech, the press, religion, association, property, and protection against self-incrimination. In the world of identity politics it will be necessary, like under communist regimes, to have public sessions of self-criticism so to free the individuals from their word and deed "crimes"; but how could this be accomplished if a person cannot be intimidated and forced to admit and confess his "thought crimes," that is, to "incriminate" himself before others?

Here is why it is, in my view, that the identity politics orchestra-tors and their mindless mobs of youthful followers so vehemently find it necessary to condemn and reject the philosophical foun-dations and constitutional basis of the American experiment in freedom. How else do you undermine the institutions that stand in your totalitarian way than to assert that they are to be condemned as racist and sexist rationales for an unjust society? And, therefore, not open for discourse or discussion, having been exiled from the debate over America's political future.

The victory of identity politics in America will be the death of the idea and ideal of human liberty, with its respect for and a value to the individual human being who is not meant to be a slave in the hands of another version of the collectivist dream of tribalism and human sacrifice on the altar of one more utopian nightmare.

CHAPTER 23

THE NIGHTMARE FAIRYLAND OF THE GREEN NEW DEALERS

When a small child runs around waving their arms saying, "I'm a bird, I'm a bird," we often will say what a cute and creative imagination they have. If an adult runs around doing the same, we usually say that that person needs help because they are clearly out of touch with reality. Anyone who takes the time to read the proposed Green New Deal legislation can only conclude that the authors are living in a fairyland that is also deeply out of touch with reality.

Read through the list of desired and, indeed, demanded activities and goals the congressional sponsors say they want the federal government to take on and solve over the next decade. It resembles a child running around the toy store saying, "I want that, and that, and that, and that, and ..." while all the time completely oblivious to the fact that everything they want costs money that their parents do not have in unlimited quantities.

They may very well throw a temper tantrum when they are told that not everything they want can be had, or at least not right now all at the same time. What the child is not yet fully cognizant of is the existence and meaning of scarcity, costs, and trade-offs. Food, clothing, a room in which to sleep, and various other nice things just seem to be there from their parents. So why can't they just have all these other things as well, and just for the asking?

The Green New Deal's Grab Bag of Desired Things

House of Representatives Resolution 109 (February 7, 2019), "Recognizing the Duty of the Federal Government to Create a Green New Deal," has a long list of sponsoring congressmen and women who seem to be not much different than that child in the toy store. I want an end to climate change; and I want an end to poverty; I want an end to social injustice, and an end to racism, sexism, and ethnic discrimination; I want a fossil fuel-free environment with renewable energy sources and high-speed railways; I want everyone to have a good, well-paying, secure and meaningful job, guaranteed by the government; I want everyone to have good, inexpensive government-supplied housing; I want everyone to have a free education all the way to the PhD; I want well balanced manufacturing and agriculture provided by government support and subsidies; I want happy and respected indigenous peoples; and I want guaranteed and comfortable government-secured retirement pensions for everyone; plus, I want everyone to have a well paid and guaranteed vacations.

In addition, each of the sponsors of the legislation say, I also want labor unions to have the power and ability to determine work conditions and set wages; and I want all the groups in society, and most especially the ones that I consider to be underprivileged and under represented and not treated nicely, to all sit at the political table of governmental decision-making and make sure that everyone of these designated and assigned groups gets what I know they want and deserve. And I also want the U.S. government to be the guider and financial provider so the rest of the world can do the same. And I want the federal government to do it NOW, before the oceans rise, the sky falls, and greedy capitalists who don't care about anything other than their selfish profits destroy all living things on the planet.

Then with beautiful little birds chirping in the air against a clear blue sky, we will all live happily ever after in the Green New Deal paradise. The End.

Ignoring Criticisms to Pursue Political Purposes

A variety of critics have pointed out that the potential financial costs if the U.S. government attempted to implement all of this would likely run into the tens of trillions of dollars, looking over the next few decades. Others have calculated that the possible dollar environmental benefits between now and the end of the 21st century most likely would be way too small to justify the lost aggregate growth in the overall American economy over the next 80 years. And still others have reminded people of the dangerous loss of personal freedom and decision-making that would result by shifting to the required government central planning if the Green New Deal were to be fully implemented.

That most of the politicians who have signed up in support of the Green New Deal seem unconcerned by these consequences should not be too surprising. First, they are spending other people's money, that is, money to be taxed from the American people or borrowed with future taxpayers expected to foot the bill. Besides, once you are talking in terms of trillions of dollars it loses all sense of reality. Who can even picture in their mind what those kinds of sums really mean? It all seems like play money in a Monopoly game.

Second, all those politicians suffer from electoral near-sightedness. Their vision extends no further than the next election, which for these members of the House of Representatives is only two years after the last election, which means they were already running for re-election even before they were sworn into their term of office in early January 2019. Their mindset is that of "Après nous, le deluge" – After us, the flood. The full, long run effects of vote-getting short-run policies will only emerge much later, possibly long after many of them are no longer in office. And if they are still in government when some of those longer run consequences start to appear, well, who will go back and check their voting record from decades earlier to prove that its really all your fault? The finger can be so easily pointed in other directions.

Third, far too many of them are guided by an ideological zeal that is accompanied by a power lusting for remaking the world in their own image. Which one of them does not suffer from the hubris of the would-be social engineer, the redesigner of society according to their own presumptuous conception of how people should live, work, and interact with their fellow human beings? Nary a one demonstrates any modesty or hesitation in believing that they know better how humanity should live than all those actually living out their individual lives in the world according to their own lights concerning what would be best for them and their families.

Few Politicians Know the Meaning of Bottom Lines

According to the Congressional Research Service in their December 2018 profile of members in the House and the Senate, less than 40 percent of all members of the House of Representatives and fewer than 30 percent of those in the Senate had any prior experience in business. Before winning their Congressional positions the large majority had careers in state or local government offices, or in the law profession, or in teaching.

Many in Congress have had little or no experience in running an enterprise, satisfying customer demands, meeting employee payrolls, or assuring that a company's bottom line remains in the black in the face of market competition. This does not mean that law or teaching are not worthy occupations, or that they preclude someone from having a good understanding of the market process or the value of securing individual liberty; after all, I'm in the teaching profession, myself. But those who have operated a business are likely to be more aware of the reality and workings of financial costs and benefits, uncertain investment decision-making, the need for inescapable trade-offs, and personal risks of success and failure that occurs in the world of competitive private enterprise.

Of course, having been a businessman before entering politics does not assure that someone is immune to the power lusting or social engineering bug, nor does it prevent such a person from easily falling into the mindset of spending other people's money. Even those who claim to be pro-free enterprise, individual freedom and limited government too often show themselves cut from the same political cloth as any others running for or holding political office. Indeed, those businessmen who end up in political positions too frequently seem badly infected by the interventionist and welfare statist viruses.

Green New Dealer's Scarcity-Free Fairyland

But it is not really surprising that those who have most enthusiastically signed on to the Green New Deal are those in the "progressive" wing of the Democrat Party, and especially those who are the self-declared democratic socialists among them. Only a socialist can still believe that government planning can solve all the problems of the world. That merely commanding resources and directing people can take care of humanity's economic and social shortcomings, and all within a decade of setting it all in motion.

Read through House Resolution No 109, and not once do you find any reference to limits, scarcity, trade-offs, costs, or consumer choice and private enterprise decision-making. Like a throwback to the Stalinist five-year plans of the 1930s, great transformations will be conjured up out of the ground: new infrastructures in the form of roads, transportation, buildings, energy, and production will be redesigned and introduced in every corner of society with merely the will and command to free the world of fossil fuels and their effects. Though to be fair, they have shown greater modesty than the Stalinist enthusiasts of that earlier time; the Green New Dealers have given themselves a decade to perform these miracles, rather than within the frame of a Soviet-style five-year plan.

They admit at several points that there may be the constraints of what science and technology will allow to be physically achieved; but they also propose the necessary government funding for research and development so that even nature should not serve as an inescapable obstacle to Utopia. The government experts will surely know which technologies deserve support to meet the targets and goals laid out in the economy-wide encompassing Green Central Plan.

Nor should there be any concern about the money for all this because that is what taxing the rich and government borrowing are for; and last but certainly not least, the money to pay for it can always be created, since that is what central banks are for. The latter especially may have to be used, since America is also to be the guider and subsidizer for similar Green Plans in the other parts of the world. Who said American progressives and democratic socialists don't believe in making America great again? What could be greater than Americans paying for all that may be needed to save the entire planet? If that does not make you proud to be an American!

Listen to their responses to those who challenge their Green Plan. Again, like the immature child, they pout and stamp their feet that the only problem is that "the rich" don't want to pay up what they "owe" society. Or the racists and sexists want to maintain the existing social order of things so they can have the power to oppress the victims of their exploitive profit seeking. If not for the enemies of "the good" all would be possible without limit or natural constraint.

Green Planning and the Abolition of Rational Calculation

Is it really necessary one hundred years after the publication of Austrian Economist, Ludwig von Mises's famous essay, "Economic Calculation in the Socialist Commonwealth" (1920), to point out that it is not enough to physically or technologically know what you would like to do or achieve? It is fundamentally essential in a world of inescapable scarcity of the means to attain our various desired ends to know in value terms what are the competing and most highly valued uses for which the limited factors of production might be applied.

How will the Green New Dealers know if they have invested too much in a high-speed railway line in Nebraska compared to one in Idaho? Or how will they know if either one has been worth it at that time and in those places compared to solar panel constructions in North Dakota or wind turbines in Mississippi? How will they know whether a government housing project in Boston has really been "affordable" in comparison to a new "free" medical clinic in Tucson, Arizona? How will they know any of this in relation to a vast and complex variety of consumer items that citizens all around the country would have wanted and have been willing to buy, if their incomes had not been taxed and there had been a competitive free market in the production and sale of finished consumption goods?

The answer is, there will be no real and meaningful answer. Without a private competitive market for the means of production (land, labor, capital) upon which private enterprisers offer factor prices based on their alternative entrepreneurial judgments about the types and quantities of consumer goods that market demanders might be interested and willing to buy in the future at particular anticipated prices, there is no way to know if the means at society's disposal (that means all of us as individual buyers and sellers) have been cost-efficiently used to attain as many of the alternative and competing ends we would like to see possibly achieved.

But the proposed Green New Deal implicitly does away with a functioning, competitive price system. Instead, what the Green New Dealers offer is a free-for-all of political plundering through interest group horse-trading and pandering. That's what they say in the proposal: "A Green New Deal must be developed through transparent and inclusive consultation, collaboration and partnership with frontline and vulnerable communities, labor unions, worker cooperatives, civil society groups, academia, and businesses." The government, labor unions, and stakeholder groups will also acquire equity ownership in the private enterprises that, clearly, now will be producing for environmental sustainability and social justice outcomes rather than for self-interested profit guided by market-based prices to satisfy consumer demands.

Green New Dealers Ignore How Little They Really Know

Is it also necessary 75 years after the publication of Friedrich A. Hayek's classic essay, "The Use of Knowledge in Society" (1945) to remind people who should know better that it is the height of arrogance to presume that the designers of the Green New Deal and any others appointed to detail and implement such a grand epoch in American central planning, that there is more dispersed, decentralized and ever-changing knowledge possessed in the minds of all of humanity combined than any group of social engineers can ever hope to master, integrate and coordinate to solve the various "problems" of society?

Here, too, is an instance of the infantile ignorance of the Green Social Engineers who believe that, like Olympian gods high above the ordinary mortals of humankind, they can shape, remake, and direct the appropriate and best future for not only all those in the United States but the entire population of the world. Straightjacketing everyone within the confines of the contours of the Green Plan means that the minds of hundreds of millions of people are prevented from deciding how best to use what they know that many others do not, and in ways that in the competitive, price-guided market process enables all to benefit from what everyone else knows.

The Green New Deal Leads to Planned Chaos

With the implementation of the Green New Dealers' dreamland, America will begin the transition from a system of price-guided production serving and satisfying market-based consumer demand to what Ludwig von Mises called the "planned chaos" of waste-creating surpluses of unneeded and wrongly made goods along with life-frustrating shortages of desired and essential consumer items and producer commodities.

No longer singularly directed by competitive prices, the forms and types of production will increasingly be determined by the political dictates of the coalition of "inclusive" groups participating in the democratic decision-making of remaking America into the Green World of the future. But precisely because of the direct and indirect supply-chain interdependencies of one sector of the economy on a multiple of others in a social system of division of labor, resulting imbalances and distortions in one sector will have its inescapable spillover effects on many others.

A component part needed for one production process is lagging in availability due to manufacturing delays in the factory supplying that part because its own energy supplies are dependent upon faulty solar panels caused by inferior inputs allocated to its own manufacture under the Green Plan.

In another part of the country highways are crisscrossed with newly installed electric car powering stations, which are under utilized or not used at all because far fewer electric powered automobiles have been produced than the Plan had planned for. Or the traffic flows in that area of the country have turned out to be far less than the Green Planners had projected due to other mismatches between central plan and local realities.

The types of competitive, market-based flexibilities in resource allocations and production adjustments in the face of unexpected and changing circumstances that are always occurring and constantly adapting the supplies to the demands in a system of private, free enterprise under the incentives of profit and loss are all lacking under the Green Plan.

Prices and wages cannot adapt to the changed and changing circumstances because various politically connected stakeholders in these imbalanced corners of the economy insist on preserving their socially just standards and locations of living; while numerous historically "victimized" groups insist that any change that does occur must protect or improve upon their existing material or social status in society; to not do so will imply continuing residues of racism, sexism, and social injustice. And there are, of course, the diehard Green New Deal ideologues who will insist that personal sacrifices must be made, accepted, and even happily supported because there is no going back to "capitalism." It's either the Green Plan or an end to the planet.

With each passing day, every passing month and year, the dislocations in the economy grow with accompanying acrimonious accusations, buck-passing rationalizations and excuses, and grandiose political justifications for the increasing shortages, decreasing qualities, and lagging achievements in all the Green Plan had promised to supply.

There is disgruntlement and outspoken complaints by more and more people; here and there groups of consumers and workers and disappointed members of old or new victimized groups publicly demonstrate with anger and insistence that something better be done. They are met with the Green Planners promising plan corrections and social improvements, along with accusations about shadowy and dangerous enemies of the beautiful Green World being built.

The Demise of "Democracy" Under Green New Deal Planning

Which raises another important question: Once the Green New Deal is actually in affect and controlling over all of society, what then happens to "democracy"? What if "the people" have second thoughts in election years 2022 or 2024 or 2026 or 2028? What if other voices challenge the premises and the policies of the Green New Dealers? If planetary existence and social justice for all time are at stake, can our democratic socialists allow the fickle and wrong-headed voting decisions of some of "the people," alter the collectivist course that has been taken?

Surely, it would be irrational to permit the central plan to be dismantled, to backslide into chaotic and petty profit-motivated self-interest, to undo all that "the revolution" had and was attempting to achieve? The socially just "People's Will" cannot be allowed to be reversed because of some people's misinformed and misguided voting whims under the influence of "sinister interests" swaying them against their "true and real" interests?

Oh, we have heard all this before, and no doubt, if they were to come to power, we would hear it all once more. But, but ... it can't happen here! Not America! Think again. The logic of central planning undermines the institutions and the spirit of liberty. By concentrating power and decision-making in the hands of those in government, the Green New Deal form of central planning, like all other forms of socialism, first weakens and then eliminates autonomous centers of choice and association.

Green Planning Equals Political Plunder

The "democratic" socialism about which its new proponents almost lyrically sing is really be an extended political plunderland of all those groups listed in the proposed legislation whose leaders will get together and decide how much of other people's money, social positions, and future life opportunities will be divvied up among their assigned followers at the expense of others in society. It is a gangster politics of coercively imposed outcomes that reduces both victims and recipients of redistributed booty to the status of slave-like dependents of those in governmental power who are determining their fates.

In spite of the colorful rhetoric of the common good, the general welfare, and social justice, the political arena is populated with those hungering for political power, with those wanting to take from others what they cannot peacefully acquire, and with those who dream dreams of remolding the human matter of society into a "better world" of their fanciful imaginations.

Everyday democratic politics is corrupt and wealth-inhibiting enough in the context of the modern interventionist-welfare state. But if the Green New Dealers have their way, this will be taken to an entirely new and more destructive level as one Great Plan for global salvation is imposed on everyone, everywhere, with no avenues of escape in our age of electronic Big Brother surveillance and control. Once embarked on, history suggests that such implemented central planning systems are very difficult to reverse without great and costly hardships on nearly everyone in society.

CHAPTER 24

WHY NEO-LIBERALISM IS REALLY NEO-SOCIALISM

If there is one common enemy that all opponents of individual liberty, free markets, and limited government seemingly can agree upon it is the "evil" of Neo-Liberalism. Everything that is hated in an open, competitive market society is summed into that word and condemned. The problem is that actual free market liberalism has nothing to do with its "Neo-Liberal" caricature and is being used as a rationale for abolishing what remains today of a free market society.

The idea of need for a "new" or Neo-Liberalism did not arise out of the ranks of the proponents of laissez-faire as an attempted reformed justification for unrestrained and unregulated markets. Instead, it emerged from those who wished to do away with the relatively free market system of the middle and late 19th century as it was still widely in existence, especially in countries such as Great Britain and the United States.

The German Historical School and the Modern Welfare State

One important strand of this came from the intellectual influences of the German Historical School that was made up of social philosophers and economic historians who held sway at many of the leading universities in Imperial Germany in the second half of the 19th century. They rejected the ideas of the Classical Economists of the 18th and early 19th centuries, including those of Adam Smith. They denied that there were "laws" of economics true and valid for all people, at all times, and in all places. In their view each historical period had its own economic "laws" and accompanying appropriate set of institutional relationships between markets and the State.

They said that economic policy decision-making should be based on "opportunism" and "pragmatism." The role of the State was to oversee and balance the interests of the "social classes" to assure a fair, equitable, and loyal nation that would not threaten political unrest and revolution that would undermine the harmony and destiny of Germany in its path to being a great power among the nations of the world.

To assure such social balance and stability, especially beginning in the 1880s and 1890s during the time when Otto von Bismarck was German Chancellor, a series of "social reforms" were introduced that included a national health care system, government funded pension plans, government regulations in the workplace, and protectionist tariffs to foster and guide the directions of domestic industry to serve the interests of "society" rather than merely the profit pursuits of private owners of business enterprises. These interventionist policies included government support for cartels and monopolies considered essential to making Germany "great again."

German Professors and American Progressivism

With few universities in the United States offering doctorial degrees at that time, a good number of American graduate students flocked to Europe to earn their PhDs. Of course, some went to Great Britain or France, but a significant number of Americans pursuing advanced degrees in philosophy, political science, economics, and sociology went to study at German institutions of higher learning.

Here they sat at the feet of many of the leading members of the German Historical School. They were taught, for instance, that the economic theories of earlier thinkers such as Adam Smith or David Ricardo were unrealistic abstractions not touching the historical facts in which actual societies existed. They were told that the path to insights on economic and social matters would only come through an inductivist focus on social and economic historical "facts" on the basis of which conclusions might be reached concerning relevant social and economic institutional relationships in the past and the present.

The lesson to be learned, they insisted, was that while in one historical period economic policies of free trade might be relevant and appropriate, at other times government interventions in both domestic and foreign trades might be both necessary and desirable for the good of society as a whole. The British doctrines of free enterprise and free trade were merely a means for capitalists in that country to exploit the people in other lands who were not as yet as economically developed as Great Britain. Free trade, the German Historicists insisted, was just British "imperialism" in the disguise of freedom of trade.

When the American graduate students who had absorbed the German Historicists' ideas returned to the United States, they became the intellectual vanguard of the emerging "Progressive" movement. The older free market liberalism of a "let-alone" policy by the government had to be set aside for a more "positive" role by the political authorities.

What was needed was a new, progressive liberalism that regulated industry, limited business "bigness" through anti-trust laws, and ameliorated the hardships of the "working class" through government health care, workplace safety and wage laws, and public housing and government guaranteed living conditions. It was under their impetus that many of the federal-level regulatory agencies came into existence before and after the First World War. Those who had studied in Germany before 1914, or their students they had taught at American universities, swelled the ranks of the growing number of federal employees in Washington, D.C. under Franklin Roosevelt's New Deal in the 1930s.

The "New" Freedoms of Political Paternalism

Here are some of the words of Frederic Howe, a leading figure in the early 20th century Progressive movement, and who served in Roosevelt's New Deal Administration. This is from his book, *Socialized Germany* (1915), and was meant to serve as a model for America:

> The German state has its finger on the pulse of the worker from the cradle to the grave. His education, his health, and his working efficiency are matters of constant concern. He is carefully protected from accident by laws and regulations governing factories. He is trained in his hand and his brain to be a good workman, and is insured against accident, sickness and old age. While idle through no fault of his own, work is

frequently found for him. When homeless, a lodging is offered so that he will not easily pass to the vagrant class."

Frederic Howe admitted that under this German welfare-state system, with its pervasive controls and regulations, "The individual exists for the state, not the state for the individual." But he insisted that in this German welfare state paradise, people did not lose freedom; they, rather, gained a different kind of freedom.

> This paternalism does not necessarily mean less freedom to the individual that that which prevails in America or England. It is rather a different kind of freedom ... This freedom is of an economic sort ... Social legislation directed against the exploitation of the worker and consumer insures freedom in many other ways. It protects the defenseless classes from exploitation and abuse.

Furthermore, Howe explained that the principle guiding the policies of the welfare state was expediency:

> In the mind of the Germans, the functions of the state are not susceptible to abstract, a priori deductions. Each proposal must be decided by the time and the conditions. If it seems advisable for the state to own an industry it should proceed to own it; if it is wise to curb any class or interest, it should be curbed. Expediency or opportunism is the rule of statesmanship, not abstraction as to the philosophical nature of the state.

Here is part of the explanation for the change in the meaning of "liberalism" from an idea and an ideal of individual liberty, with freedom of domestic and international enterprise under constitutionally limited government, into the new American connotation starting in the 1930s that liberalism now meant a socially active government through an extensive interventionist and welfare state. This new, or "Neo-Liberalism" has been and is the government regulatory and redistributive state under which we currently live.

Neo-Liberalism Pragmatism and Critics from "the Left"

Joining this Neo-Liberalism of pervasive political paternalism in the post-World War II period was the idea that "ideology" as a system of abstract ideas about freedom and the role of government in society had to be set aside as being out-of-date, with pragmatic "compromise" determining the needed changing course of government policy. There were no philosophical Archimedean points from which to evaluate the meaning of human liberty or the institutions to sustain it. The right policy, it was argued, was a matter of the changing "democratic" consensus based on what seemed to be needed at any moment in time.

Of course, those more radical strains on the political "left," beginning in the 1930s, labeled this is as "social fascism," that is, an attempt to save the capitalist baby by only emptying out the laissez-faire bathwater. Hence, the notion by both supporters and leftist critics of New Deal liberalism and other policies later building on it, that it was all designed to "save" capitalism, and not to destroy it. And this was considered a black mark on the existing order of things.

The supporters spoke of having the best of both worlds: private enterprise but with a paternalist system of government regulation and redistribution to assure "social justice." The more left-of-center opponents charged that it was all a cover-up to keep the capitalist "exploiters" in control of the means of production with a candy coating over the retained social injustices.

"Neo-Liberalism" Meets Public Choice

The world we live in, in America, does reflect the ideas and policies of Neo-Liberalism, but it is not the classical, or free market, liberalism that the new, more radical "progressives" and democratic socialists attempt to portray it to be. It is the creation of their intellectual and ideological ancestors of just a few generations ago during the 20th century.

Rather than admit that the political-economic system in the United States is the result of the very interventionist-welfare state which they mislabel as free market capitalism, they try to protect the rationale and logic for the regulations and redistributions they want by pejoratively calling it the very thing their own intellectual predecessors created, a "Neo-Liberalism" that undermined and replaced the classical, free market liberalism of the past.

Their dream of the socially just system of political paternalism has become the reality of almost everything that Public Choice theory has warned us about. Public Choice theory is the application of the logic of economics to the political process. The "false consciousness" of all the talk about the "public good" and the "general welfare" is stripped away, and what we discover that we are left with are real flesh and blood human beings who run for political office and do so by offering interest group voting blocs "other people's money" through regulatory restraints on the competition of rivals or by direct government contracts, or numerous "transfers" of wealth and income through the institutions of the welfare state.

Then there are the bureaucrats who have vested interests in defending their bureaus, agencies, and departments to assure budgetary allocations that fund their salaries and enable them to spend ever-more money to justify their existence. A system of political privilege, plunder, and power, generates a host of interest groups guided by material or ideological motives and purposes to acquire incomes and revenues through the government they are not able to obtain through the peaceful and voluntary interactions of the marketplace and the institutions of civil society.

Joseph Stiglitz's "Progressive Capitalism" Equals Socialist Planning

One of the recent voices making these types of accusations against the market economy is Columbia University economist, and Nobel Laureate, Joseph Stiglitz, who offers an agenda for "After Neoliberalism" (*Project Syndicate*, May 30, 2019). He says that there are three competing economic policy agendas for America: "far-right nationalism, center-left reformism and the progressive left." Donald Trump represents far-right nationalism; center-left reformism is the Neo-Liberalism of the likes of Bill Clinton, and the progressive left is reflective of the vision in the Green New Deal.

Notice the sleight-of-hand. The free market system that leaves capitalists free to destroy the planet and plunder their fellow man are the Clinton Administration policies of the 1990s (along with those of the former British Labor Party leader, Tony Blair). Unbridled capitalism is now the "middle of the road" interventionist-welfare state of the Democratic Party during the last decade of the 20th century.

So what does Joseph Stiglitz want? Well, to begin with, he labels his agenda, "progressive capitalism." He conveniently avoids the word "socialism." Yet, he makes plain that the central planning of the U.S. and indeed the global economy that is called for in the Green New Deal proposed legislation captures his economic vision of America's future. How Orwellian: democratic socialism is now progressive capitalism. I love Big Brother, I love Big Brother, I love ... as long as we don't use the "S" word. It is good to know that Professor Stiglitz is following in Frederic Howe's footsteps, considering that the use of words should be guided by "expediency" and "opportunism."

Stiglitiz's Fantasy Fear that Government is Getting Smaller

Professor Stiglitz is deeply bothered that for forty years, he says, America has been following a Neo-Liberal agenda of lower taxes, deregulation, and reduced government spending. He must live in an alternative universe with a substitute Planet Earth containing a different country called the United States, because what he says is not the America the rest of us live in.

You just need to read through the Congressional Budget Office's "Overview of the Budget and Economic Outlook: 2019-2029 (January 28, 2019) to discover the reality rather than Joseph Stiglitiz's fantasy land. For the period 1969 to 2018, federal government taxing and spending were, respectively, on average, 17.4 percent and 20.3 percent of Gross Domestic Product. The difference between what Uncle Sam has taxed and what he has spent reflects the annual budget deficits for most of the last fifty years that has now created a national debt of nearly $22.5 trillion.

By the end of the coming ten years, the CBO projects that the federal government will be taxing 18.3 percent of GDP and spending 23 percent of GDP, or a 5 percent increase in taxation and a 13.3

percent increase in government spending. The gap between these two numbers explains why the CBO is also projecting the return to annual $1 trillion deficits as far as the fiscal eye can see, with the national debt increasing by close to an additional $10 trillion during the next ten years.

In fiscal year 2019, federal spending on entitlement programs will make up $2.7 trillion out of a total budget of $4.41 trillion. In ten years time, if the CBO estimates are correct, entitlement spending will come to $4.6 trillion out of a 2029 total federal budget of $7.04 trillion. While total government spending will be 60 percent higher in ten years than today, entitlement spending will have increased by 70 percent by 2029. This hardly suggests that government has been or will be suffering from a severe austerity diet, or that entitlement spending is be axed to death over the next decade, under current legislation and the prevailing politics of the country. Earth calling Professor Stiglitz in his alternate universe!

As for government regulation over the private sector, the Competitive Enterprise Institute estimates in its latest "Ten Thousand Commandments" report (May 2019), that the cost of regulatory compliance is around $1.9 trillion a year. And the number of pages in the Federal Register comes to almost 70,000 pages of rules and regulations that private business must meet. This $1.9 trillion dollars in compliance costs is equal to about 10 percent of the county's GDP, and is about 43 percent of what the federal government will spend in 2019.

Stiglitz's Agenda for the Planning of His Choice

So what does Professor Stiglitz want? It is the same old grab bag of bigger, more intrusive and controlling, and more costly government intervention and redistribution. Let him speak for himself:

> Governments have a duty to limit and shape markets through environmental, health, occupational-safety, and other types of regulation. It is also the government's job to do what the market cannot or will not do, like actively investing in basic research, technology, education, and the health of its constituents.

> A comprehensive agenda must focus on education, research, and the other true sources of wealth. It must protect the environment and fight climate change with the same vigilance as the Green New Dealers in the US and Extinction Rebellion in the United Kingdom. And it must provide public programs to ensure that no citizen is denied the basic requisites of a decent life. These include economic security, access to work and a living wage, health care and adequate housing, a secure retirement, and a quality education for one's children.

Here is the same arrogance, the same hubris, the same "pretense of knowledge" that the interventionist-welfare statist "Neo-Liberals" have been advocating and implementing for more than one hundred years with increasing presence within the American economy and society. But let us call this all for what it really is: this is Professor Stiglitz's "Neo-Socialism." That's what the Green New Dealers are all about, which he is clearly endorsing as the road (to serfdom) that he wants America to continue going down.

The battle between what he calls "Neo-Liberalism" and his "progressive capitalist" Neo-Socialism is not an ideological conflict between friends of economic liberty versus the champions of the command and control society. It is a contest between those who want the government to continue doing all the same interventionist and welfare statist policies it has been doing and what Joseph Stiglitz – social engineer, central planner, and social coercer – wants that government to do.

He wants to pick the industries and jobs in America rather than Donald Trump or Bill Clinton; he wants to decide the fair and just distribution of income instead of traditional Democrats and Republicans; he wants to implement that grand central plan to "save the planet," instead of the more restrained responses to what he considers to be the climate crisis facing the globe. In other words, he wants to be advisor-in-chief to the right occupant of the White House who will listen to Prophet Stiglitz instead of all those false prophets representing "right-wing" nationalist statism and "left-of-center" Neo-Liberal interventionist "establishment" statism of the current Washington consensus powers-that-be.

When Professor Stiglitz says at the end of his article that his Neo-Socialism (oh, excuse me, his "progressive capitalism") is the only alternative to the failed Neo-Liberalism of our time, he is merely saying: let me impose upon you the economic planning schemes that I consider the good, fair and just ones for you, in place of those other command economy coercers who want to take you down "wrong" collectivist paths compared to mine.

What is lost in all the "Neo's" this and the "Neo's" that? It is that what society needs is that true free market liberalism that calls for the end to all planning schemes, whether comprehensive "democratic" socialism or in the form of piece-meal interventions and redistributions. The real free market liberalism that would solve or avoid most if not all of Professor Stiglitz's social concerns, if he would just learn to leave people and their market and social interactions alone from the grasping and meddling hands of those in politics who constantly presume to know how to plan our lives better than we ourselves.

CHAPTER 25

HAS LIBERAL MODERNITY MADE AN INDECENT SOCIETY?

He dressed decently and had a decent meal before going to work. He showed some common decency toward his next-door neighbor. He did the decent thing to do. From these examples, you might conclude that the word decent refers to following some rule or standard of conduct, or behaving in some proper and ethical way toward others; and you would be right according to most dictionary definitions. But listening to some, to act decently requires you to be a tribal collectivist.

Turn to, say, the Merriam-Webster dictionary, and you discover that the word, "decent," means to act appropriately; to conform to standards of propriety, good taste, or morality; to follow or achieve some agreed upon standard or benchmark; to show moral integrity, kindness and goodwill in interactions with others.

All these refer to the nature of the conduct, but not to the content. It all depends upon what the specific standard may be and the particular code of ethics expected to be followed in one's own actions and towards others. But according to Umair Haque, a London- and New York-based consultant who writes frequently about what he considers to be wrong with individualism and free-market capitalism, most people in the United States lack a proper sense of decency and have a fundamentally flawed and indecent social behavior because they have turned their back on the ethics of group-oriented altruism.

The Sharing, Caring Society of Tribal Man

In a recent article on, "Why Decency is the Most Powerful Idea Human Beings Ever Had," (*Eudaimonia*, March 28, 2019), Mr. Haque argues that our ancient human ancestors who lived in small tribal bands, at an admittedly primitive standard and quality of life compared to ours, were, nonetheless, ethically far superior to us in our modern world with all our advanced science, technology and comforts for everyday life.

You see, they cared about each other; while far to many of us do not care about our fellow human beings. Oh, their ancient diet was barely subsistence, the tools they used may only have been stone knives and a stick, medical practice may have been the witch doctor sprinkling incense and reading the entrails of the goose, and education was only a tribal elder telling tales to the young folks around the fire because they had no written language. But what they had was a collectivist ethics of communal caring and sharing. And that made them light years ahead of us socially, even though theirs was a way of living now long gone in the past, says Mr. Haque.

Our ancient ancestors placed needs of all the members ahead of their individual wants and desires. Theirs was an ethics of communal sharing, and not personal taking. Food, medical care, education may have been simple and backward by the standards of our contemporary life, but no one said, "This is mine, you cannot have it." Collective production had its match in fair and just collective distribution. Here was a system and a way of living that was grounded in an ethics of decency, Mr. Haque insists:

> Our distant ancestors were better people than us, in my estimation. They cared about one another, respected one another, in ways we do not – and simply do not seem to even think about anymore. They cared about a very great deal: each other, their young, their old, their environment, their past, their future, their little societies. And it strikes me these days – just how different we have become ...

> They were kinder, better, gentler to each other, sharing what basics they did have in fairer, truer, and smarter ways, because they had something we lack: the deep wisdom of decency.

The Supposed Indecency of Modern Man

Modern man, by which Mr. Haque means self-interested man in market-oriented liberal society, only wants more for himself, and at the expense of others through lying, cheating, stealing, defrauding, with no concern about the weak, innocent and plundered who are left behind. Individualist, market-based society, regardless of its scientific and technological achievements, is inherently immoral, indecent, and even fundamentally evil. In Mr. Haque's words:

> We are the only people I can think of who take care of nothing at all – not their young, not their old, not their land, not each

other—only caring for themselves ... We don't care about anything but ourselves – and even then, we only care for ourselves in increasingly stupid, backwards, narrow-minded, evanescent ways ...

We don't believe it's important to share what we have made and accomplished in fair, equitable, and reasonable ways. We believe that all the gains should go to the rich, to the powerful, to the cruel, to the abusive. Maybe not you – but certainly enough of us. We don't remotely [have] the same quality, nuance, insight, standard, power of morality, ethics, truth, that even our distant ancestors had ...

It's true that we've made technological progress. But it seems to me that we have made profound, ruinous moral regress, too, along the way ... Nobody in history, really, so far as I can see, has been as indecent as us. As obscene, selfish, abusive, cruel. Our indecency is unmatched.

Can you think of anyone – anyone at all – else who didn't take care of their young, old, neighbors, selves, or environments? Who didn't give each other education, healthcare, retirement, childcare, and so on – in the ways that they could afford, in the forms they could achieve? ... We are not enlightened and civilized people.

Small-Tribe Socialism Kept Humankind Poor

For thousands of years humankind lived and survived in small bands as hunters and gathers, as nomadic travelers moving according to the seasons, following the animal herds for their meat and skins, and searching not only for waterholes but on the lookout for other rival bands that were also foraging for subsistence, either to avoid or plunder them.

Mr. Haque admits that these bands were often authoritarian, certainly non-democratic, and frequently warlike. But everyone knew the other, and each had their expected and required place in the tiny community in terms of efforts and activities. They were, no doubt, forms of small roving islands of primitive socialism traveling over areas of the earth in the quest for the primordial basic needs of life.

But why did humans live for so long like this? Why did it take so long for elementary tools and means of material and related improvement to be developed and take hold to ease the difficulties of existence? In these small bands it may be assumed that everything was circumscribed for all members of the tribe in terms of actions, attitudes, responsibilities and restrictions. Innovation, differentiation, and experimentation, as well as any significant dissent or disagreement would have been looked upon with suspicion and social disapproval.

Chieftains and witchdoctors would have imposed the rules of conduct and implied communal "ethics." Paternalistic belief that order and obedience were essential for the tribe's survival against natural and human threats, as well as power-lusting and personal preservation of position and status within the tribe, would have been the motives for the chiefs and witchdoctors to instill and inculcate peer pressure acceptance of the group's heritage of moral norms, including submission to the chief and the witchdoctor.

Poverty and Constraint Under Tribal Collectivism

A collectivist ethics of obedience and group responsibility, enforced by the physical retribution of the chief, as well as the superstitions and fears surrounding the magic of the witchdoctor, would have assured that traditions, customs, and imposed obligations to others in the tribe were maintained. As a result, intellectual and technological progress would have been arrested for untold generations among the tribes that survived.

The ethical decency to which Mr. Haque so nostalgically harks back and hankers for a return to in his own time, represents a small-band socialism of fear and superstition, matched with stagnation and poverty. How many individuals would have thought of or had the incentive to imagine new ways of doing things when the rulers and their tribal peers would have frowned upon and shunned any threatened break from the established way of doing things? And why demonstrate greater than average skill and ability in better and more productive performance, when any of the positive results must be shared out in some assigned equal proportions to all in the tribe, without your personal agreement or permission?

Little wonder that thousands of years went by with little improvement in the human condition much above subsistence poverty, in a setting of group ethical pressures and primitive political constraints. The present-day technological and medical availabilities that Mr. Haque so easily shrugs off as simply taken for granted, would not have emerged if there had not been the appropriate changes in the social and institutional norms that made them possible.

Even more, if the world had stayed frozen in the collectivist "decency" ethics that he most longingly desires, it is doubtful if Mr. Haque would even be alive today. The world's population probably would have remained stationary, no doubt, numbering only in the millions rather than the billions of people who are alive now. Mr. Haque's ancestors most likely would have died of starvation, disease, injury, or murder in the conflicts among the "decent" socialist tribes in some earlier time. Mr. Haque would never have existed to make the case for a social system that would have made it likely that he would never have been born.

Progress Through Ending the Tribal Sharing Mentality

But, in fact, what is decent about a society in which humanity is condemned to a life of abject poverty, because any new idea or possible way of doing things differently and better is doubted, denigrated, and discarded as destabilizing the "just" and "fair" order of things? Few will to try to get ahead of the other tribal members when they know that anything they bring into existence through their own mind and effort will have to be shared with all the others in the tribe whether they wish to or not, and on the basis of the collective's standard of fair and decent, and not their own.

Human progress began when individuals found ways to openly or in the interstices of the social system in which they lived to keep some or most of what their intellect and labor had successfully created and produced outside of the existing ethical order of things. Progress began when the individual at least partly escaped from the stranglehold of the "decency" ethics of tribal socialism.

And that gets us to a fundamental question, why should collectivist sharing based on an ethics of tribal altruism – that the needs and interests of the group come before the individual's own judgment and assessment of how to dispose of the fruits of his own mental and physical labors – be considered the right ethical norm and standard of decency and the decent society, about which Mr. Haque speaks?

It has taken a long time in the West to at least partially overcome the ethics of collectivism. A thinker like Bernard Mandeville (1670-1733) shocked many in the polite society of his time in the early 18th century when in his poem, "The Fable of the Bees" (first version 1705, revised extended version 1714), he gave to it the subtitle, "Private Vices, Public Goods."

What? The "decency" of the "public good" based on the individual's sacrifice of his one personal interest and desires was to be turned on its head, with self-interest proclaimed as the sources of human industry and social betterment? Children were forbidden to and severely chastised if found to have read this immoral and most certainly "indecent" piece of poetry when it had first been published.

John Locke on Individual Rights and Limited Government

Here in very stark terms was an economic aspect of the natural rights philosophy articulated only a few years earlier by John Locke (1632-1704) in his *Second Treatise on Government* (1689). Each individual has a natural right to his life, liberty, and honestly acquired property (either through first settlement and development, or peaceful and voluntary trade).

Individualism, as a philosophy of man, society and government was not an abridgement of or an embarrassment to a more decent collectivist human ethics. No, very much the opposite. "Society" is a community of free and sovereign individuals, each at liberty to preserve and better their lives in any peaceful way that they find most advantageous in terms personally chosen ends and selected useful means.

All human relationships and interpersonal associations, therefore, should be based on the mutual respect of voluntary consent and free exchange. No man should be forced to be the slave of another, and no man should have his life violently taken by someone through an act of aggression. Alas, human beings are too frequently short-sighted and aroused in their emotions to always act reasonably in their dealings with others.

Thus, governments are formed among men to secure and protect their individual rights and liberty from the aggressions of other human beings. Government's role, therefore, is a "negative" and defensive one, Locke argued. Its duties do not include compelling and commanding the members of society to act and live contrary to their own, respective, ideas and conscience. Reason and persuasion are considered to be the essential and morally limiting methods to move people to live and act and associate in ways differently then they were peacefully choosing to.

It was nearly 90 years later, in 1776, when Adam Smith detailed and clarified the nature and workings of a "system of natural liberty" for improving the human condition through an increase in *The Wealth of Nations*, as Smith entitled his famous book. When a society has a social system of division of labor, and if the institutions of that society recognize individual rights to personal freedom and private property, permits open and free competition, and bases all interactions on voluntary exchange, then, as if by an "invisible hand," each individual in pursuit of his own self-interest would best serve it by directing his productive efforts to improving the circumstances of others at the same time.

To acquire from others what they have that we want, we must offer them in trade something that they may value more highly than what they currently possess that we desire from them in trade. It is worth repeating some of Adam Smith's famous words on self-interest and mutual betterment:

> "Man has almost constant occasion for the help of his brethren, and it is in vain for him to expect it from their benevolence only. He will be more likely to prevail if he can interest their self-love in his favor, and show them that it is for their own advantage to do for him what he requires of them.

> "Whoever offers to another a bargain of any kind, proposes to do this. Give me that which I want, and you shall have this which you want is the meaning of every such offer; and it is in this manner that we obtain from one another the far greater part of those good offices which we stand in need of.

> "It is not from the benevolence of the butcher, or the brewer, or the baker, that we expect our dinner, but from their regard to their own interest. We address ourselves, not to their humanity, but to their self-love, and never talk to them of our own necessities but to their advantages."

Prosperity Through Freedom

It would not be too surprising if Mr. Haque, at this point, said something like: "But you see that is just my point. While men are pursuing their self-interests with little direct regard for their fellow man anymore, what will happen to the "social" dimension of humankind, that earlier decency concerning the wellbeing of others who are our fellows in the wider community of humanity?"

Nothing has done more for the wellbeing of our fellow human

beings than the freeing of the individual from the constraints of the collective tribe, so he has the liberty and the latitude to apply himself as he thinks best to advance his own personal circumstances, precisely because in that system of natural liberty about which Adam Smith and others spoke, all are made better off through the unintended consequences of human action.

The technologies, medical and other advances in science, the improvements in the material and cultural aspects of humankind that are rapidly eliminating poverty from the face of the earth have been made possible through the individualism that Mr. Haque dislikes and clearly would like to eliminate.

Freedom Fosters Voluntarism in Civil Society

In addition, it was in the United States, especially during those decades in the 19th century that came closest in some parts of the country to that practice of unrestrained individual freedom that Mr. Haque considers the essence of American "indecency," that there also blossomed the institutions of civil society that concerned themselves with wider community interests outside of simple market supply and demand.

Is this a figment of the imagination of an "apologist" for classical liberal individualism? Here is a description of that rugged individualist epoch in American history and the accompanying "decency" of a free people precisely because these matters were not considered the concern of government.

It is precisely in a free society that there is likely to be cultivated a sense of social participation and personal responsibility for a part of the society on one's own shoulders. This arises not out of a misguided sense that you owe the world because you have been more successful and better off than others around you as an obligation of sacrifice. But because the free human being properly, "decently," understands that he lives in a wider society in which if individuals do not concern themselves with certain common affairs no one will.

We can go back in time to ancient Greece, and Aristotle's observation that when men are allowed to own property and keep the fruits of their labors, the very prosperity they may experience tends to awaken a generosity in them of sharing some of their good fortune with others out of a sense of benevolence towards one's fellow men.

Another instance of Mr. Haque's confused misunderstandings is his assertion that individualism and capitalism generate plunder, privilege, corruption, and disregard and abuse of others in society. If anything, these are elements embedded in the more politicized system that he wants humankind to go back to. When it is possible to advance one's self-interest through use of government regulations, redistributions, and spending, individuals and special interest groups will be drawn to the dirty and indecent political trough of crony capitalism. It was these corruptions and constraints on individual freedom and a freer market economy that Adam Smith was opposing when he called for that system of natural liberty, under which government was to be restrained to being a protector of life and property, not an active accomplice in the pursuit of political plunder for some in society.

The Ethical Decency of the Liberal Market Society

What can be a more decent society than one in which each and every individual is viewed and treated as an end in him- or herself, and not a coerced means to someone else's ends? What is a more decent conception of the human being than a social system based on the premise and practice of voluntary consent and peaceful mutual consent in all interpersonal relationships and associations, inside and outside of the market arena of supply and demand? Where is a sense of benevolent decency towards one's fellow human being more likely to be cultivated and encouraged, than in a social setting in which all such "good works" or common community interests require the free choice and willingness of each participant of their own accord?

Like too many others, Mr. Haque confuses "society" with the state or the political authority. So when he refers to introducing greater social decency in human relationships he does not mean what has just been suggested, that is, the voluntary institutions and associations of civil society; instead, what is implied is a compulsory giving and doing imposed by political power under an arrogantly presumed paternalism.

Real and true human decency is based on and grows out of free association and chosen voluntarism. Compelling people to be "decent" through government taxing and spending in fact drains decency from human relationships. What is decent about depersonalized bureaucracies that siphon off the honestly earned income and wealth of the private producers in society, and then determine on the basis of political pull and power manipulations who will get what and in which amount?

The last thing that humanity needs is a return to the tribal and primitive collectivism of Mr. Haque's fantasyland of communal decency through forced doing and giving. The right road to the decent society is individual liberty, free association and the self-interested actions of free people in the open and competitive market economy.

CHAPTER 26

THE PLAGUE OF MEDDLING POLITICAL BUSYBODIES

Who knows what might be better or best for you? You or those in the government? We all make mistakes and misjudgments, but who is most likely to have a wider and deeper appreciation of your wants and desires, you or a bureaucrat in an often-faraway government agency? Who is more likely to have an insight into the options and opportunities for achieving your wants and desires, you or a handful of politicians focused on their own goals and political purposes?

Expressed in this general way, most of us would say that each of us knows the answers to these questions better than any politicians or bureaucrats. If I am your next-door neighbor, and I proceed to impose my views on you about the ends you should pursue and the best means to attain them, most likely you would resent and resist this insistent know-it-all busybody interfering in your life. Who am I to tell you what you should live for and how to do it?

When People Want Others' Opinions They Ask

We do frequently turn to the advice and informed opinions of others. We consult with the medical doctor about an illness we may have and the treatments to over come it. We hire financial advisors to suggest how best to invest our money for the future. We contract with an inspector to evaluate the structural soundness of a new or existing house we are thinking of buying. We turn to a neighbor to find out his experience about a lawnmower or car or a dishwasher they have bought, when we might be in the market to buy one of these ourselves.

We also consult publications such as *Consumers' Report* on the quality and reliability of various goods we might be interested in purchasing. And certainly today, we turn to the Internet to find out the evaluation of multitudes of others in society who we may never know or meet about their experiences and conclusions concerning goods and services we are thinking of buying. In all of this, we decide what advice and judgments and by whom seem most reasonable and relevant to solve our problems and use as guides in deciding on our own courses of action.

How much information and knowledge is worth getting before making our decisions on these and many other things is decided by each of us as consumers and producers. Some people do meticulous and detailed searches in making such decisions, while others seem to "shoot from the hip" in deciding how, what, and when to do something.

Everybody is a Better Judge of Their Own Circumstances

Each person weighs for him- and herself the (marginal) costs and (marginal) benefits in how best to make a more or less informed choice, based on the importance that choice has for them and the value they place on the cost of time and resources that would have to be taken away from other things to be more informed before making any particular decision.

Entrepreneurs and private enterprisers also have to make these decisions: how best to apply their business abilities and acumen in deciding into what corner of the market to invest their time and resources, and to apply their talents in organizing and directing the business for which they are taking on responsibility. This includes the technologies and resources to use, the capital equipment to acquire, and the workers and labor skills to hire and employ.

Whether it is the consumer's choice or the enterpriser's investment and business decision, the cost of a failed or less than hoped for success falls upon the individual having made those choices and decisions. Surely, then, the person who runs this risk has the nearest and dearest motive and incentive to try to get it more right rather than more wrong.

Errors, mistakes, incorrect judgments, and disappointed outcomes are inescapable in the real work of imperfect human knowledge, and ever-changing circumstances in the physical and social world. With all this considered, could anyone or any institution do it all better than each individual in society, for themselves?

The Danger of Each Claiming to Know How Others Should Live

It is certainly true that we often look at others and think to yourselves, how could this person live like that? How can they think that "that" is worth spending and wasting their time in trying to achieve? What is going through that other's person's mind in thinking that "this" means or method is the best one to reach some end or goal?

And you know something? You might be right and that other

person might be wrong. But by what right can you assert the right to interfere with their life and their actions? First of all, if you believe that freedom has any value, it must include at its core the right of each person having the latitude and liberty to make their own choices and decisions – even if it includes them making their own mistakes and experiencing their own disappointments, which they might have not made if only they had had the "wisdom" to listen to you.

Once you go down the road to imposed paternalism – even though you have the best of intentions and feel very, very confident that you are right about what that other person should do – where do you, or me, or any other person draw the line? It is an inescapable potentially slippery slope. The reason being that there is no reason that others will think that the place you want to draw the line beyond which the individual should not be coerced into the "right" choice or decision, will be where they will consider it the right place to draw that line; or there may very well be some who do not draw any line, believing that there is no choice and decision being outside of potential outside intervention and control.

Second of all, once the meddling busybody premise is accepted and it is considered legitimate for me to paternalistically intervene in your life and reciprocally legitimate for you to paternalistically intervene in my life, we reach the peculiar conclusion that we are all informed and intelligent enough to direct other people's lives, but we are not competent to oversee and guide our own, respective, lives. We are incompetent to plan and implement our own decisions, but we are wise and informed enough to do so for others. Surely, if we are not component to plan our own individual lives, it seems not too unreasonable to conclude that the same human short-comings lead to the conclusion that we are not wise and knowledgeable enough to plan the lives of others, as well.

From Private Busybody to Political Meddler

So who, then, can or could claim that they possess this extra-ordinary capacity to plan their own lives and those of others? In the past the answer to this has come in one of two ways: an individual or elite who have claimed that "history" or some "higher power" or some "special intuition" has been given to them to see, understand, and know what ordinary human beings have not been privileged to be able to know and understand.

Or, the meddlers have been raised to such power and authority through the democratic electoral process with the "will of the majority" claimed to legitimize them taking on such political responsibility through government enforcement. This raises the question as to how it is that the citizens of a society are informed and knowledgeable enough to democratically appoint those who will then be expected to tell them how to live and interact with others, but they are too unformed to do that living and those interactions based on their own personal decisions? I am not capable of being self-governing over my own affairs, but I am somehow knowledge-able and informed enough to appoint those who will govern over and command me.

Nonetheless, the arrogance and hubris of such presumptions of knowing how to guide and direct other people's lives never seems to reach an end. No matter how many failures and disappointments from such paternalism in the past, it seems that there is always a new crop of economic and social policy busybodies to assert their ability to do the meddling – and this time get it right.

For instance, Harvard University professor, Dani Rodrik, and Charles Sabel, of Columbia University, have said that government must institute "An Industrial Policy for Good Jobs" (*Project Syndicate*, May 8, 2019). They insist that America must go beyond the existing network of government interventions and redistributions with a "new set of 'productivist' measures that intervene directly in the real economy, targeting the expansion of productive jobs."

Professional Meddler's Plans for a More Productive America

The problem, they say, is that the focus of the current interventionist-welfare state is to regulate the existing structure of industrial and investment activity, and redistribute wealth within the existing patterns of employments and wages. The "next level" is to introduce government policies that transform industry, investment, and work and wages into those avenues that represent the more productive and higher valued employment opportunities of the future.

Risks and uncertainties, you see, hold back and tie down private enterprises on their own. They stay in the more or less current niches of production and employment or only move in new directions too slowly and cautiously to enable the economy to really take off and improve the conditions of the working population. They admit that knowing what is a "good job" is not always easy and not completely unambiguous. But even so, the task of the next generation of meddling busybodies is the following:

> First, by legislation or other means, the government commits to address the problem of bad jobs, creates an interagency body to review and prompt improvement of regulatory responses, and provides funds and authority for voluntary programs.

Second, regulators currently overseeing areas directly affecting job abundance and quality – vocational training, agricultural and manufacturing extension, standard setting, and the like – introduce governance mechanisms that not only induce innovation, but also anticipate the need for support services to help vulnerable actors comply with increasingly demanding requirements. The requirements could take different forms, including specific employment quantity targets and/ or standards.

Third, where current regulatory authority doesn't reach, the government creates volunteer, public-private programs to advance the frontiers of technology and organization, or – perhaps more important – provides support services and possibly subsidies to help low-productivity/low-skill firms move to the advanced sector. Finally, conditional on the success of voluntary arrangements, the scope of these practices would gradually be made obligatory for non-participating firms, starting with mandatory submission of credible plans for improving the quality and quantity of jobs.

The Political Meddler as Central Planner

Here we have the economics busybody who presumes to know where businesses should invest and in what technologies to enhance what they define as the more "productive" methods of production to increase the value of workers and the wages they may earn as a result. They wish to use the power and tax-funded financial means at the government's disposal to subsidize, direct and target how the actors on the demand and supply sides of the marketplace will use their wealth and private enterprises concerning the application of their investable property.

Businesses will be obligated to set goals, demonstrate success in pursuing them, and answer why they have only gone so far along the politically directed road and not further in creating the investments, technologies, and jobs that Professors Rodrik and Sabel consider best for the good of the society as a whole.

Notice that at first they propose "voluntary" government-business partnerships to test the social engineering techniques for improving, as they say, the qualities and quantities of the jobs that they consider the most desirable. But having gotten into their central planning "groove," they then say that the government's reach will extend beyond those private enterprises that at first "freely" decided to collaborate with these political planners to "be made obligatory for non-participating firms."

In other words, the end goal of our planning paternalists is the command economy, the government-directed market, with all businesses required to follow the planner's investment and employment directives and, presumably, under some type of punishment if the imposed targets are not met. And be sure, if any private enterprises failed to meeting the targets it will be declared to be another instance of a demonstrated "market failure." A new proof that government will need to far more directly take control over such enterprises to fulfill the technological and employment targets because profit-motivated self-interest cannot be trusted to improve the quality and quantity of those most productive and value enhancing jobs in the American economy.

The Arrogance of Knowing What Best for Others

The arrogance and hubris of a Professor Rodrik or a Professor Sabel is no different, I would argue, than the neighborhood meddlers and busybodies who say they know how we should live, how we should act, how we should associate with others. They would, likely, claim but they are not like the nosey old biddy in the house next door who watches everything you do, gossips about all the wrong things you are doing in your life, and who tries to get others on the block to condemn and pressure you to conform to how the meddling busybody thinks you should behave.

Dani Rodrik is, after all, a Harvard University economist and Charles Sabel is a Columbia University law professor. They are, well, the experts building and playing with their mathematical and statistical models of the economy and the legal structures of the society for inducing certain forms of human conduct rather than others. They are implicitly presuming, I would suggest, that because they are trained professional academic social meddlers, they know what has to be done and how to impose the right industrial policies to generate the jobs that they think to be good and best. They are, after all, "qualified" social busybodies as opposed to merely neighborhood amateur ones.

If the Political Meddler Gets It Wrong Others Pay for It

But who bears the costs if they get it wrong? Will they lose their academic tenure? Will they be shunned and ostracized by those in their economic and legal fields? Will they be required to wear sackcloth and ashes as penance for making the conditions of their fellow man possibly worse than if they had left their intervening hands to themselves?

No. They will rationalize the disappointment and failures by pointing to the selfishness of the businessmen who did not do what they were told; they will argue that they just need more data and more discretionary authority and control to get it right; they will never admit the they were guilty of what Austrian economist, F. A. Hayek, called, a "pretense of knowledge" in believing that they could know more and better than the multitude of market actors and social participants who possess the divided and dispersed knowledge that the economic planner can never know and successfully master.

In the image of small town life where the meddling busybody may be irritatingly and incessantly putting their nose into other people's business, the right response by the target and victim of such presumptuous intrusions is to tell that neighbor to mind their own business. They should keep their advice and comments to themselves, unless they are asked for. And they should stop trying to churn up trouble in the neighborhood with their constant attempts to cause trouble with their unasked for invasions into other people's affairs.

Social and economic policy meddlers and busybodies should be told the same thing. They should keep you interventionist and planning schemes to themselves. If businessmen investing and risking their own capital need advice about how best to employ it, they can ask chosen consultants for assistance. If workers want or need help in deciding what human capital may be best to invest in in terms of education and training, they can find their own sources of information and advice.

Tell All Meddlers to Mind Their Own Business

Who asked for Professors Rodrik and Sabel's advice? And if that advice is so useful and valuable to private sector investors and employees in the marketplace, why do they need to be peddling their meddling to the government, an institution that forces courses of action on people rather than persuading them through reason and voluntary choice?

It is time for more people to see these political meddlers and busybodies for what they are: arrogant and irritating people who seem to spend too much of their lives believing they know better than everybody else. And when others in society won't listen to them and follow the advice of their own volition, they turn to government and those manning the seats of political power to make the rest of us do what they want us to do – and always in the name of doing it all for our own good.

We ought to see them and call them for what they really are: compulsive coercers who just cannot leave the rest of us all alone. Maybe it's an uncontrollable addiction for which they need medical treatment and psychiatric help – but please, not at taxpayers' expense!

CHAPTER 27

REASONS FOR ANTI-CAPITALISM: IGNORANCE, ARROGANCE, AND ENVY

Why is the free market liberal economic system so widely disliked, hated and opposed? Given the success of the competitive market economy to "deliver the goods," it presents something of a paradox. An economic system that has either radically reduced or even in some instances virtually eliminated poverty, that has created widely available opportunities for personal, social and material improvement, and has abolished traditional systems of political privilege, plunder and power-lusting, is still considered by many to be an evil and unjust social system.

One would think that the market economy would be hailed as the most important social institution that humanity had stumbled upon in all of human history. Let's not forget that for most of that history the condition of man was to use British philosopher, Thomas Hobbes's, famous phrase, "poor, nasty, brutish, and short."

The Transformation from Poverty to Freedom and Plenty

Humanity existed for thousands of years at a level of existence that was at or sometimes even below bare subsistence. The images still shown on our television screens of starving, diseased and seemingly hopeless children in what used to be called "third world" countries, with appeals for charitable giving to save those young lives, was, in fact, the general condition for the vast majority of human beings everywhere around the globe just a few centuries ago.

But such circumstances have been diminishing in degree and extent in a growing number of places in the world, first in Western Europe and North America starting in the 19th century, then in areas outside of "the West" in the 20th century, and now in the 21st century in more and more parts of Asia and Africa and Latin America. It is not impossible to imagine that before the end of the 21st century abject poverty may very well be a thing of the past for practically all of humankind.

What has made this transformative process possible over the last two or three hundred years – a blink of the eye in terms of all the time that human beings have been on this planet – has been a political philosophy of individualism and an economic system based on market-based and -oriented relationships. The idea and spirit of individualism heralded a cultural shift that moved society away from a view that the individual human being was an object of control, manipulation and sacrifice for a wider collective group or tribe. And that an individual had a right to peacefully live for himself, pursuing what he considered to be in his best interest for himself and those he cared about. Slavery and servitude were replaced with the belief that human association should be based on mutual benefit through voluntary exchange.

The new science of political economy, symbolized by the publication and growing impact of Adam Smith's *The Wealth of Nations* (1776), drew attention to the fact that freedom, peace, and prosperity could be combined by harnessing personal self-interest to the simultaneous betterment of others through the institutions of the free market economy. As if by an "invisible hand," advancing one's own circumstance also brought with it an improvement in the conditions of those with whom one interacted in an arena of competitive supply and demand.

In spite of the astonishing success of functioning market economies in enlarging freedom and prosperity for now billions of people on this blue ball revolving in space around the sun, free market liberalism ("capitalism") stands criticized and condemned wherever it exists to one noticeable degree or another. Why?

Anti-Capitalism Arising from Ignorance of Economics

I would like to highlight at least three of the reasons for the persistence of anti-capitalist attitudes and arguments. They are ignorance, arrogance and envy.

The first and most common one among a large number of people in society is ignorance of the nature, logic and workings of a functioning and competitive market economy. Most people rarely reflect on the how and why of what brings about the material and cultural quality of everyday life, especially as experienced in North America and most of Europe. It is just taken for granted that all those goods and services appear everyday in the shops and stores regularly visited or that, now, are simply ordered online and which then appear in a very short period of time at our doorsteps.

Nor do many people understand what can easily become the

negative effects from various government policies. Why not a minimum wage law? Shouldn't everyone have a "living wage," a "fair" wage for a decent life? It takes some effort of following through several chains of logic to fully appreciate that artificially setting the hourly wage above where a competitive market had or would establish it may result in the unemployment of those whose labor skills in the workplace may be viewed as being worth less to an existing or prospective employer than what the government dictates must be paid to them. Thus, a minimum wage may price out of the market some of the very people such legislation was designed to help. Their standard of living and life opportunities, therefore, may be worsening, whatever the "good intentions" of the minimum wage advocates.

Neither do people always understand that attempting to maintain domestic businesses and jobs through protectionist tariffs that raise the cost of importing various foreign-made goods may actually hurt the employment and profits of many more than supposedly are helped with these barriers to international trade. If foreign suppliers of goods earn fewer dollars from doing business in America, this reduces their financial ability to purchase American-made goods they might have wanted to buy, thus negatively impacting export sectors of the U.S. economy. Such import tariffs also mean that American consumers have fewer goods from which to choose and tend to pay higher prices for the same goods that they now end up purchasing from government-protected American producers and sellers. In the long run, everyone tends to be made worse off from government policies designed to give special benefits to some small segments of all those employed in the economy-wide social system of division of labor.

Educating for Economic Literacy

While such ignorance makes it easy for far too many to fall prey to misguided and counter-productive economic policy ideas, in principle ignorance can be corrected with informed education about the workings of a free market system. People can be assisted to see both the direct and indirect effects resulting from different economic systems – capitalism, socialism, the interventionist-welfare state – and why and how it is that only open, competitive free market systems can supply both freedom and prosperity, especially when the market system is effectively bolstered by a philosophy of individual liberty and rights in an institutional setting of impartial rule of law that assures freedom for all and special favors or privileges for none.

I know from personal experience in the college classroom that if presented in clear, relevant, interesting and persuasive ways, the ideas and importance of free market liberalism for assuring a "good society," is teachable and learnable. It does not mean that every student coming out of an economics class leaves a free marketeer at the end of the semester. But the limits and absurdities of many, if not most, government interventions can be understood by most, and many can appreciate the benefits of the competitive economic system.

This is especially so, from my experience, when the case for the free market is offered in an "Austrian" economic framework that emphasizes the limits of individual human knowledge, the role of the pricing system for coordinating the actions of multitudes for economic wellbeing through economic calculation, and the inescapable impossibilities of government planners and regulators to ever know enough of all the complex, dispersed and decentralized knowledge of the world, upon which any modern society is dependent, to ever successfully do better than the free market economy.

Economic Education Begins with Self-Improvement

The other educational task is to share the philosophical and economic ideas of the free market society with others with whom we interact in our daily lives, when it seems appropriate. No one likes a pushy know-it-all, but over lunch or dinner, for instance, when political or economic policy ideas arise in conversation there are sometimes opportunities to offer one's own "two cents" about freedom, the free market and the role of government in society.

But as Leonard E. Read (1898-1983), the founder and longtime first president of the Foundation for Economic Education (FEE) always emphasized, changing the world only happens one person and one mind at a time. And the person and mind over whom we can have the most influence to think rightly on such matters is ourselves. Therefore, making the case for freedom to others begins with the self-education and self-improvement of ourselves in knowing, understanding and learning to effectively articulate the principles of liberty and free market liberalism.

Anti-Capitalism from Intellectual and Ideological Arrogance

The second cause for much of the anti-capitalist sentiment in our society is human arrogance. We each are susceptible to hubris, the belief that we know how others should live and act better than those others themselves. However, those who are most frequently guilty of such arrogance are the intellectuals of modern society. Some of the more classical liberal-oriented minds of the 20th century drew attention to this, including Joseph A. Schumpeter and Friedrich A. Hayek.

The peculiarity of successful free market liberalism is that it has generated enough prosperity that it enables to be sustained an entire segment of the population who are able to devote themselves simply to the pursuit and propagating of ideas. They include schoolteachers, college and university professors, authors of "serious" and "popular" journals, magazines and newspapers, and books.

When a writer of a newspaper or magazine article or editorial piece, says at some point that "critics" or "experts" say, invariably among them are "the intellectuals" whose role in the division of labor is to interpret, analyze, and challenge the ways things are and how they might otherwise be for the better. Most such intellectuals, if one is frank and direct, have lived in "ivory towers" of academia or in the general informational media a good part or even all of their lives. They know little or nothing about the actual day-by-day working of a business, meeting a bottom line to meet an enterprise's employee payroll, or the need to focus on the consumer satisfactions of others to avoid a loss and maybe earn a profit.

Their knowledge of "capitalism" is usually derived, and sometimes exclusively, from reading the earlier and other contemporary critics of the market economy. Businessmen are "exploiters" of workers, "plunderers" of the planet, the greedy "cutthroats" who would sell their own mother for an extra margin of profit, and who reduce all of human life to a financial bottom line. They care nothing for "society," and make their employment decisions based on racist and misogynist prejudices and biases.

This cultivates an arrogance and hubris in many such intellectuals, the "social critics" of the human condition, that if only they were in charge or if their advice was followed by those holding the reins of political power and decision-making, how much better could the world be made.

De Jouvenel on Three Reasons for Anti-Capitalism

The French social philosopher, Bertrand de Jouvenel (1903-1987), once discussed, "The Attitude of the Intellectuals to the Market Economy" (1951). First, for them the market economy is "disorderly," that is, they look at the outcomes of the market and assert how much better would be the patterns and relationships and results of society if only there was someone in charge – the government planner, regulator, redistributor – to generate the "socially just" and economically moral outcome that clearly the market does not and cannot provide when left to its own unfettered devices.

The second criticism is that the market economy exalts and satisfies the wrong values. Surely, we don't need another brand of toothpaste or a new and improved pair of sneakers when the society's resources (through government control and redistribution) could be better applied to "feeding the hungry," or subsidizing planned parenthood, or paying for more college classes on why genders are imaginary categories imposed by white, male capitalists to abuse the weak and "marginalized."

And, third, de Jouvenel, said, there is the implicit resentment by many intellectuals that the market economy places them at a disadvantage. What is that disadvantage? That the market rewards people for catering to the everyday, "lower" wants of the uninformed and manipulated consumers, rather than they, the intellectuals, who devote their lives to the "big ideas" – the beautiful, the just, the good, the better – but who have little or none of the recognition or income of the billionaire businessmen who has made his fortune by persuading easily manipulated homeowners that they really needed his "designer" bathroom sink faucet. How morally depraved that the man who could have been the world's next great music composer has to lower himself to earn a living in the market economy writing catchy television commercial jingle songs.

School Privatization to Reduce the Arrogance of the Intellectuals

Institutionally, one of the most important long-run remedies to the continuing cultivation and inculcation of such anti-capitalist attitudes and ideas into young minds is the privatization of education, from kindergarten through the university PhD. As long as these types of intellectuals can live on other people's tax money in sequestered academic islands of educational socialism, they will never be ousted from their protected realms of near monopoly control over the minds of one generation of students after another.

How many parents would want to directly pay for so many of the asinine college and university courses, especially in the social sciences and humanities, that have often become little more than ideological indoctrination camps in the ideas of "political correctness" and collectivist "social justice" fantasies? Market-based educational competition would soon test whether or not these are the ideas that parents and students want offered and experienced among the academic curriculum choices as steppingstones to after graduation careers. And whether such groupthink notions that passes for "postmodern" deepness, would be the cultural literacy that those paying for their own and their children's educations would really desire.

The first step toward introducing real intellectual diversity into K-12 education would be the ending of teacher licensing in all private and current choice-based schools. Teachers' unions and education degree mills presently have a monopoly on who gets to teach those young and impressionable minds long before some of them may go on to college. Open market competition for teachers would offer different techniques for teaching and the content of what was taught.

The ultimate and essential step is the end of all mandatory government schooling. All primary and secondary schools should be privatized, either by handing the schools over to the existing teachers and employees and tell them they are now fully responsible for demonstrating to parents that their curriculum and teaching methods will, in fact, educate their children and prepare them for the future. Or the schools might be privatized through selling them off at public auction to single stand-alone companies wanting to buy them, or to private school chains wanting to offer a brand name of potential excellence and quality either regionally or nationally.

The full privatization of schooling and education would offer the best long-term avenue for the creation and the cultivation of an alternative community of intellectuals and teachers more aware of, more oriented to, and more sympathetic towards the nature and workings of a market system. This will never occur as long as government monopoly-licensed teachers in taxpayer-funded schools can have such huge control over the ideas offered to the youth of the country.

Anti-Capitalism Arising from Socially Destructive Envy

Finally, the third cause for anti-capitalist attitudes and resentments is envy. The German sociologist, Helmut Schoeck (1922-1993), in his classic study on, *Envy: A Theory of Social Behavior* (1966), made a point of distinguishing between jealousy and envy. Jealousy refers to a desire or wish that the success or good fortune of another had been yours, instead. You may consider that the other person's success or good fortune was rightly or justly earned or not, but your reasoned and emotional response is that he has achieved or acquired something that you would like to have or that in a fairer world could or would have been yours.

Envy is something different, Schoeck said. In this instance, the envious person begrudges the success or achievement of another. It is a desire or wish not so much that the envier had obtained that success or achievement, but rather "that the best kind of world would be one in which neither he, the subject, nor the object of his envy have them ... One begrudges others their personal or material assets, being as a rule almost more intent on their destruction than on their acquisition." Indeed, and perversely sometimes, "The envious man is perfectly prepared to injure himself if by so doing he can injure or hurt the object of his envy."

Ayn Rand (1905-1982) offered a similar idea of envy in her essay on, "The Age of Envy" (1971) in which she argued that the envious person is one who hates "the good for being the good." Or as she said in *Atlas Shrugged* (1957), the enviers "do not want to own your fortune, they want you to lose it; they do not want to succeed, they want you to fail; they do not want to live, they want you to die; they desire nothing, they hate existence."

Both Schoeck and Rand emphasized that the envious person senses or believes that he could never successfully do or achieve what the object of their envy has attained. He hates and resents the other precisely because the other's success is a slap in the face pointing out or reminding the envier of his own more limited qualities or capabilities. If I cannot do it, then no one should have the ability to do it with the resulting rewards.

Ludwig von Mises also offered a version of the same idea in his short book, *The Anti-Capitalistic Mentality* (1956). In the free market system success or failure is more greatly determined by one's own demonstrated ability. In the pre-capitalist systems of society, you were born into a social caste or class that was defined and enforced by law or rigid custom. Never rising to a higher station in life, or a higher income, could be said to not be your fault. You are a "victim of the system." The serf was tied to the land and forced to follow in the footsteps and the same status that was imposed on his father before him.

Under capitalism, there is always, of course, chance, or the bad luck of poorly choosing whom one's parents turn out to be, or often just the bad timing of being in the wrong place at the wrong time. But far more than under other social systems known in human history, the free market system offers the individual far more latitude and liberty to determine his own fate. You have greater freedom to pursue an education, select a profession or occupation or line of work, to decide on trying to become a successful enterprising entrepreneur, to save out of income to start a business or partnering with others in doing so, and competing with more established firms if you think you can better satisfy consumers.

But it also means, Mises observed, that it reminds a person that any disappointments in life or failures to go as far professionally and financially as one had hoped falls mainly on oneself. Some find it hard to accept and deal with this. It is easier to say if not for greedy capitalists, or if not for the harsh coldness of the profit system, or if not for dog-eat-dog competition, I would have been more successful.

From Resentment to Envy to Social Destruction

But the resentment and blame game that Mises considered part of the anti-capitalist mentality, only becomes the destructive emotion of envy when, as Schoeck and Rand said, some people so resent the nature and the outcomes of the free market system that they would rather see other's poor than themselves possibly better off or rich; would rather undermine the opportunity for anyone to have a chance for success than live in a world in which they could try but clearly don't believe they could succeed; and would rather see the enslavement of all than deal with the burdens of being free themselves.

Envy, as Helmut Schoeck also observed, is an ancient affliction that has always plagued the human psyche. During many periods of history, envy has been an emotion that social pressures have required the individual to repress or keep hidden away in his heart, being unbecoming of healthy human beings and destructive of society if let loose upon the world.

But in our age of collectivism in its various ideological manifestations, paternalistic arrogance and the dark sickness of envy have been able to raise their ugly heads in the latest campaign against free market liberalism. From former President Barack Obama's insistence addressed to successful businessmen that they did not really "make it," to the demand that the "injustice" of inequality must be undone by pulling down the "one percent," or to the battle cry that "white privilege" dictates the radical reconstruction of all forms of human association and interaction to a lowest common dominator of group status defined by race and gender, "social critics" and social engineering elites demand to remake society in their own delusional images. While the envious would rather destroy human society as it exists than accept a reality inconsistent with their dreams of frustrated tribal justice.

Only a renewed philosophy of individualism and free market

liberalism can turn the world away from these three reasons behind the anti-capitalistic mentality of our time.

CHAPTER 28

FREE MARKET LIBERALISM IS NEEDED MORE THAN EVER

The famous New York Yankees baseball team player and manager, Yogi Berra, is credited with the saying, "It's déjà vu all over again." He is also credited for claiming, "I really didn't say everything I said." Never were both of these truer than in our era of reborn defenses of and demands for more government intervention, redistribution, and planning.

Many of us assumed, or at least certainly hoped, that after the disastrous social, economic, and human consequences of centrally planned societies during the 20th century, and the generally abysmal failures of and corruptions resulting from government interventions in the economy that there might arise a reawakened appreciation for and understanding of a truly liberal, free market society.

Over the last several decades, humankind has been witnessing a dramatic and amazing end to poverty in more and more parts of the world, along with the availability of unimagined technological inventions for a growing number of the billions of people on this planet. But instead of an appreciation of how partly freed up market forces have made this all possible, especially in those areas formerly known as the underdeveloped third-world, the counter-revolution against human liberty seems to be picking up steam, once again with the call for "democratic socialism," a Green New Deal, and massive increases in the welfare state's "entitlement" programs and beyond.

Furthermore, friends of freedom are burdened with a highly successful propaganda campaign by those on the political "left" who have misrepresented and insisted that the economic system under which we all live is one of free market capitalism. In reality, one hundred years of continuing growth in and intrusiveness of government's power and reach long ago transformed the modern economic system into something very different from what the proponents of economic liberty have historically called for and defended.

The Meaning of Free Market Liberalism

Let us remind ourselves of some of the basic ideas that we have been discussing in the previous chapters. What is a liberal or free market society? Since the time of Adam Smith in the 1770s, it has been generally understood that a free market economy is one based on the recognition of a wide latitude of individual freedom in matters of both consumer and producer choice. These free choices occur within an institutional setting of private ownership of the means of production (land, labor, capital), in which human transactions and associations are based on voluntary consent and mutually beneficial exchange.

The open and competitive interactions of all the participating demanders and suppliers generate the terms of trade for all that is bought and sold. These, in turn, provide the structure of market prices that coordinates the interactions of those multitudes of individual participants in the, now, global social system of division of labor. Production is initiated by private enterprisers, by entre-preneurs, who direct their businesses in the quest of profits and the avoidance of losses.

The only social means at their disposal to do as is to direct the enterprises under their ownership and control into the manufactur-ing and offering of those goods and services that consumers and other demanders are willing to buy from them, instead of the wares also being offered on the market by their peaceful and competitive rivals who are pursuing positive returns over incurred costs as well.

The Role of Government Under Free Market Liberalism

The primary duties and responsibilities of government under free market liberalism are those of protecting each citizen's individual rights to their life, liberty and honestly acquired property, along with the enforcement and adjudication of freely entered into con-tracts, and guarding the members of society from the aggressions of domestic criminals and possible attackers from outside the country through the defensive use of police and the armed forces.

Free market liberals have debated among themselves about what other roles and duties even a government meant to primarily secure rather than violate liberty should or should not undertake. This has usually concerned government spending and involvement in education, infrastructure expenditures, specific regulatory respon-sibilities, and certain minimal welfare-related expenditures.

But the underlying premise in the case for the liberal free market economy is that individuals should be considered as ends in themselves and should not be compelled to be the means to others' ends through the use of coercion or threatened force. And to this end, all avenues for private initiative and voluntary association should be considered the desirable means for solving social problems before any serious consideration of government involvement is ever undertaken. Laissez-faire is the default position, unless otherwise demonstrated with strictly compelling reasons and evidence.

The "Let-Alone" Principle

In support of such a "let-alone" principle of no government social or economic intervention, since the time of Adam Smith it has been taken for granted that individuals are in general better informed about their own wants and desires and the surrounding circumstances in which they must make their everyday decisions than politicians and bureaucrats who not only lack the totality of all the knowledge possessed by the respective citizens, but have their own purposes and interests that may have little to do with those over whom they rule.

Indeed, the premise and logic of "The Let-Alone Principle" was concisely articulated by the American economist and astronomer, Simon Newcomb (1835-1909), who taught at Johns Hopkins University, in an 1870 article with that title:

> That each individual member of society should be left free to seek his own good in the way he may deem best, and required only not to interfere with the equal rights of his fellowmen ...

> The let-alone principle may be regarded either as a declaration of rights or as a maxim of political policy. In the first case, the principle declares that society has not the right to prevent an individual who is capable of taking care of himself from

seeking his own good in the way he deems best, so long as he does not infringe on the rights of his fellowmen.

In the second case, the principle forms the basis of a certain theory of governmental policy, according to which the political system is most conducive to the public good in which the rightful liberty of the individual is least abridged ...

It needs only a consideration of first principles to make it plain that the main object of government is the protection of minorities, especially those most powerless minorities, individuals ... It makes little difference to the minority or to any particular individual whether [his] rights are disregarded by a despot, a highwayman, or a majority of his fellow-citizens, wielding the powers of government ...

The real point in dispute between the friends and the opponents of free government and individual liberty is simply this: Is man a being to be taken care of, or is he able when protected in his rights to take care of himself better than any governing power – congress, king, or parliament – can take care of him? The advocates of universal freedom claim that, if each individual is protected in the enjoyment of his individual rights as a responsible member of the community, he can take care of himself, and manage his own affairs and his share of the public affairs better than any other one else can do these for him.

Socialism Means Government Power, Planning, and Tyranny

For most of the last two hundred years, a socialist or planned economy has meant a political-economic system under which the government owns and manages all of the physical means of production (land, resources and raw materials, factories and capital goods). The socialist government has responsibility for the planning and directing of all economic activities concerning what goods and services will be produced, where and when, and with what combination of inputs to produce certain centrally planned quantities of outputs. Finished goods and services are to be distributed by the government to the citizens of the planned society in some manner reflecting an asserted conception of social justice and equity.

Under such a planned economy, by logical extension, the government is the only employer of all those looking for or commanded to work in the socialist society. This also includes the government determining the location and living conditions for all those employed, since, as the monopoly producer of all things, the government must produce and allocate housing, amenities, amusements, medical and health care, retirement funding, all sources and types of information and schooling, as these end up being incorporated within "the plan" and according to some declared notion of social "fairness."

The 20th century was littered with the tragic reality of socialist centrally planned societies in practice. The real individual human beings became nothing and the mystical collective "masses," became everything. The ever-vigilant secret polices of the Marxist regimes were always on the outlook for imaginary "enemies of the people," and constantly undertaking paranoid searches and arrests for anti-socialist "wreckers" and traitors whenever the contradictions, inconsistencies, and failures of the central plan had to be blamed on anyone other than those who were the ruling dictators and social engineers running the workers' shining utopias.

Roundups of millions of innocent men, women and children according to central planning targets to fulfill the needs for slave labor in the Gulag camps that stretched from one end of the Soviet Union to the other; torture chambers and basement execution cells in Moscow and every regional office of the KGB; millions of intentionally starved peasants whose "crime" was unwillingness to give up their private farms to the State. Unending propaganda and indoctrination to make everyone believe the lies of how wonderful their socialist society was compared to the rest of the world and to be obedient and diligent worker bees to serve the needs of the ever-watching and all planning socialist state. The human cost was somewhere around 150 million people or more killed in the quest for the perfect collectivist world.

The Interventionist State and Pursuit of Privilege and Plunder

The interventionist-welfare state is often referred to as a "middle way" between an unhampered free market economic system and the fully centrally planned economy with little or nothing outside of the controlling orbit of the socialist state. Its stated purpose is to take advantage of the innovative benefits of the self-interested profit motive of the market economy, while tempering its effects or consequences through various types and forms of government regulations and restrictions.

Complementing these government interventions is a redistributive network of government programs meant to supply certain "socially necessary or useful" goods and services that the market, it is said, may fail to provide or in insufficient quantities and types. It is also meant to reduce claimed ethically unacceptable inequalities of income or social positions among various designated groups in the society through use of the tax code and selected regulations.

In fact, an interventionist state is merely a halfway house to a planned economy. The very nature of various forms and types of government regulations concerning prices and wages, methods of production, rules for marketing and sales, licensing restrictions and requirements to pursue an occupation or operate a business is to take the peaceful decisions and opportunities concerning all such matters out of the hands of people themselves and transfer them to those in political power.

Such government interventionist and redistributive policies have momentous influence over the economic and social circumstances of virtually everyone who is trying to earn a living or profitably open or operate a business. It should not be too surprising that with the rise of the regulatory state has come increasing special interest politicking for favors, privileges, and protections that carry with them the sickening odor of corruption, whether the resulting influence peddling is within or outside of the legal rules of attempting to "nudge" government policies in desired directions.

Big Bucks for Political Influence, and the Burden of Government

Everyone is tempted or incentivized to drink at the government trough to gain favors and privileges or to resist any that may go to others that might negatively affect one's own corner of the market. That is why, according to the Center for Responsive Politics, in 2018, Washington lobbyists spent nearly $3.5 billion trying to move legislation and federal regulations in their preferred respective directions.

And together Democrats and Republicans raised more than $2.7 billion during the 2018 Congressional primary and general election campaign season. So, in 2018, a total of at least $6.2 billion was spent attempting to influence government policy or to elect the "right" people for special interest groups to successfully get what they wanted during the congressional session that began in January 2019.

The welfare state redistributes vast sums of taxpayer money into politically determined directions. For instance, in the 2018 federal fiscal year that ended on September 30, 2018, Uncle Sam spent a total of more than $4.1 trillion, with 50 percent of it being spent just on Social Security programs and medical and health care costs. According to the Competitive Enterprise Institute, in its 2018 report on federal regulatory compliance costs imposed on private enterprise, businesses incurred $1.9 trillion in expenses in meeting the regulations and accompanying paperwork required by Uncle Sam's interventionist policies.

In 2018, U.S. Gross Domestic Product (GDP) was about $19.4 trillion. Total federal government spending of $4.1 trillion came to more than 21 percent of 2018 GDP. State and local spending combined came to an additional $3.6 trillion, for an extra 18.5 percent of GDP. This meant that all levels of government consumed nearly 40 percent of Gross Domestic Product in 2018. And private enterprise compliance costs of $1.9 trillion represented 10.3 percent more of GDP.

For a benchmark of comparison, in 1913, the year before the start of the First World War in Europe, the combined levels of government in the United States siphoned off less than 8 percent of national income. Or, in other words, 92 percent of everything produced and earned remaining in private hands to use as those people found most advantageous and profitable. In 2018, that came to less than 50 percent, free and clear, of all that government took for its expenditures and the costs of fulfilling regulatory rules and requirements. But according to the critics of "capitalism," we are living in a liberal free market society in which "business" does anything it wants and government is "starving" for the needed money to do good things!

Alas, No Apologies for Defending Socialist Tyrannies

In spite of all that has happened over the last century, the advocates and apologists for socialism and interventionist big government shrug it all off. They repeat the same tired rhetoric about greedy businessmen, selfish individualism, shortchanged social needs, selfless political office holders only desiring to do good for others – with other people's money! – and only wanting power to regulate and plan everyone's life for the betterment of humankind. Yogi Berra knew what he was talking about when he said, "It's déjà vu all over again."

Where are the confessions of guilt and the apologies from all those on "the left" who are old enough to have dreamed of a Soviet America, or who rationalized away the betrayal by all those who were Stalin's spies, agents and fellow travelers, not for money, but because for them socialism in Russia was the model society of the future that needed to be protected from capitalist Amerika? Or what about those who asserted that those who somehow had succeeded in escaping from the Soviet paradise were all liars with anti-socialist axes to grind or apologists for "business" when they told about the prison house that the Soviet Union really was?

And what about all of those on the political left not old enough to remember those "happy days" when Stalin lived and was the "best friend of every Soviet child," whose mass murders and imprisonments turned many of those children into orphans branded with the label, "children of the enemies of the people"? What about those, in other words, who looked for socialist utopia in other places: Mao's China, Castro's Cuba, Ho Chi Minh's Vietnam, the Sandinista's Nicaragua, or Hugo Chavez's Venezuela?

Have they owned up to the flowery rhetoric, the poetic prose, and the euphoric exclamations with which they heaped praise and ideological love on the tyrants of these socialist regimes? Or the cruel policies those governments implemented with all their human costs? Or have they admitted the disasters of the socialist central planning practices in these countries, or the systems of privilege and power that those who ruled and ran these socialist regimes unhesitatingly bestowed on themselves?

There have been a few honest souls who have confessed their ideological sins and attempted to atone for them by talking and writing truth about the nightmare socialist experiments. But for the vast majority it has all gone down an Orwellian memory hole. Never said, never endorsed, never fawned over, never rationalized and never justified. In other words, all these collectivists have been experiencing a collective amnesia. What was that other line of Yogi Berra's? Oh, yes, "I really didn't say everything I said."

New Dreams for the Democratic Socialists and Progressives

Instead, it's as if it's all just a clean slate. It's the cruel and unjust reality of evil free market liberalism versus a beautiful, virgin-like dream of hope and possibility that if we only implement "our" version of this freshly minted "democratic socialism" or if we enlarge "progressive" welfare statism with just that much more tax money and social and economic control, the new dawn will have arrived and a world of social justice will be in reach.

The political and economic system under which we live is not free market liberalism. It is a twisted and corrupted system of privilege, favors, plunder, and power-lusting through special interest politicking for economic or ideological purposes. It is what is sometimes called crony capitalism, but should be better called political cronyism, which is the essence of the interventionist-welfare state.

What we need, and I would say even desperately, is a reawakened understanding and desire for the free and prosperous society that, in fact, can only come with free market liberalism, and grounded in a social philosophy of individualism and voluntarism. Otherwise, history in a slightly different form of the same collectivist theme, will repeat itself here in America and many other places around the world, as whatever remains of degrees of individual freedom and free enterprise is swallowed up in a new Leviathan State.

That is, if the new democratic socialists and the collectivist race and gender warriors have their way. But they need not. Various political and ideological trends have often seemed inevitable and irreversible – until they have changed! And it can happen again. If only friends of freedom at least try.

CHAPTER 29

THE CASE FOR LIBERTY, THROUGH THICK AND THIN

One of the most important issues before those who care about the advancement of liberty is how the case for freedom can best be made, and what it should include. A controversy arose not that long ago among some friends of freedom about whether the case for liberty should be "thick" or "thin." This may seem esoteric or removed from everyday political issues. But, in fact, it is very important for the long-run success of free market liberalism and a free society.

"Thin" Liberalism and Non-Aggression

The advocates of the "thin" version of a defense of liberty argue that the primary and essential issue concerns the principle and logic of "non-aggression." That is, the classical liberal or libertarian basically should be concerned with one, and only one, issue: the moral and practical case for the abolition of coercion from all interpersonal relationships to the greatest extent possible in human affairs.

The "thin" libertarian should not be concerned, per se, with how and on what basis individuals act and behave in their personal life and in their private and voluntary relations with others.

It does not matter, it is argued, whether that private individual is a racist who thinks some ethic groups are "inferior," or who views the proper place for women to be in the home "bare foot and pregnant," or who expresses negative views about any sexual orientation that is not heterosexual and that does not involve the "missionary" position.

All that classical liberals or libertarians should be concerned with and focused on is the abolition of all political and governmental intervention, control, and regulation over the peaceful and voluntary affairs of the citizenry.

On all other issues concerning human actions and associations the classical liberal or libertarian may have his own "subjective" values and preferences about how people should act in their private lives and in their social interactions, but these are outside the domain of the case for freedom and the free society.

A Presumed Slippery Slope Toward Paternalism

On all such matters the advocates of liberty must be "agnostic" in viewing and judging the actions of others. Who are we to praise or condemn the beliefs, conduct and choices of others, because to do so threatens to put the camel's nose of government intervention into the tent of political discourse?

First you challenge the racist or anti-feminist, or sexual views of others, and before you know it, the classical liberal or libertarian has entered upon the "slippery slope" of opening the door to others who argue for government intervention, regulation and control to coercively impose the preferred values and human relationships through the power of the State.

Is this not how the older classical liberalism became transformed into the more modern version of liberalism under which the government takes on the role of political paternalist attempting to "engineer" the social and economic arrangements under which people are to act and interact?

First you condemn racist ideas and before you know it you have compulsory affirmative action and coerced integration. You challenge the traditional view of women in the household and soon you see regulations banning "men's only" clubs and insistences on so many women being appointed to positions on corporate boards of directors. You question the exclusivity of heterosexual relationships and in no time "straight" professional photographers are mandated to take the pictures at "gay" marriages.

It is argued that limited government liberalism is step-by-step transformed into big government liberalism with its compulsory arms enveloping every nook and cranny of human existence. Is this not how political individualism becomes mutated into social collectivism?

"Thick" Liberalism and Respectful Individualism

The "thick" classical liberal or libertarian also argues that the principle of non-aggression in all human relationships is the core political value for all advocates and defenders of freedom. But they ask whether that principle alone would be able to establish and sustain a society of free people.

How likely is it that equal rights before the law will be respected and maintained in a society in which many take it for granted that some human beings are racially "superior" while others are "inferior"? Will women be sufficiently respected and free from the aggressive actions of predatory men in a world in which women are viewed by a large number of males as mere sexual objects to serve the "stronger" sex?

And can a free society be sufficiently free of intolerance and aggressive behavior when a large number of "straights" take the attitude that "queers" and "homos" are fair game for ridicule and even physical abuse?

In other words, the political principle of non-violence in all human affairs does not and cannot exist in a social vacuum. The case for freedom from political power and control requires it to be situated in a wider philosophical and ideological setting of the nature, sanctity, and even sacredness of the individual human being,

Many advances in freeing people from political control and the establishment of a recognition of their possessing individual rights to their life, liberty and honestly acquired property first arose out of changing attitudes about human beings and what was right and just in the conduct of people towards each other.

The End to Slavery Began with Changed Views of Man

For all of recorded history one of the oldest and most enduring of human institutions was slavery. The presumption of the right of one human being to own, use and even abuse another person was taken for granted in practically every culture and civilization around the world. That only began to change in the 18th century in Great Britain when men deeply conscious of their Christian faith formed an anti-slavery movement to abolish this institution, a social and political effort that finally triumphed with the abolition of slavery throughout the British Empire in 1834 by an act of Parliament.

They argued that all men are creations of God, made in His image, and all equal in His eyes. Surely it was a sin, an abomination in the eyes of God for mere mortal men to presume to lord over other human beings and play God in the form of slavery when there is only one Lord in heaven, and only He owns us all and has jurisdiction over our fates.

This, in turn, had grown out of the early philosophical explanations and defenses of the idea that every individual human being has a "natural right" to his own life and liberty, given to man by God and also demonstrable by reason if man was to have the ability to sustain his life and prosper. Every human being as a unique and distinct individual, therefore, should be treated with respect and dignity, and not regarded as a mere "object" to be coercively used as the "means" to some slave owner's ends.

It is difficult to imagine how our especially American tradition of individualism and political ideal of individual rights, which is the foundation of the principle of non-aggression in human relationships, could have ever emerged if this wider conception of man, his nature, and his requirements to survive and prosper had not first begun to take hold over the minds of people concerning their fellow human beings.

Racism is Inconsistent with the Spirit of Freedom

Racist attitudes and beliefs are anathema to any philosophy of individual freedom. It is to claim that the individual does not exist separate from the biological and genetic traits of a collective group to which he belongs. That he has no meaning or identity distinct from these tribal characteristics, and any "rights" or "privileges" he may possess are based on this collective or group position and status in society.

In a free society, are individuals at liberty to believe in and hold any views about human beings they choose, without political oppression or mistreatment? Of course, they are, including racist ones. But the friend of individualism and classical liberalism should neither condone nor acquiesce in such views. A classical liberal or libertarian is not true to his own principles and their defense, if he remains silent in the face, for instance, of a Nazi arguing the inferiority of Jews, blacks or Slavs, and that as "sub-humans" they should be enslaved or eradicated for the good of some "master race."

Equal Rights for Women Began with Commercial Freedom

Again, for most of human history women across many civilizations and societies were viewed as the property of their fathers to be transferred to a husband through arranged marriages to serve some presume benefit for the family as a collective unit.

A women often could not own or inherit property; she could not enter into contracts or undertake an employment outside the household without the father's or husband's consent and permission; and all that was her's was really owned by the male authority.

Only the emergence of commercial capitalism in the late 18th and early decades of the 19th centuries began to change this. Employment opportunities in developing manufacturing centers gave women the first real chance to break free from this legal male domination. The new industrialists and enterprisers were only interested in finding willing employees to man the machines and production processes in the growing number of factories and market-oriented places of business.

Like many men, women left the rural areas of society and flocked to the cities and expanding urban communities to find better paying work in more attractive conditions than outdoor farming from dawn to dusk in the harsh physical elements. Over time, women were found, as a practical everyday matter, to be as hardworking, reliable and industrious as men in many avenues of employment. Earning their own way, they had income to spend, save or invest. Regardless of legal niceties they began to enter into contracts, acquire property and leave money and other wealth to their loved ones.

This changing practical circumstance of women in modern commercial and industrial society slowly began to transform people's attitudes toward them. In an increasing number of ways women were seen to be equal to men, and this led to reflections on the reasonableness and logic of extending equal individual legal and political rights to women, as well. Thus, for example, the great 19th century British classical liberal, Herbert Spencer, in his 1851 book defending liberty, *Social Statics*, devoted a chapter to "The Rights of Women." He pointed out that given their nature, qualities, characteristics, and potentials as human beings it was only reasonable and just that society formally recognize this by extending the same individual rights to women as increasingly men were enjoying.

Changing social attitudes and views concerning women in society and in relation to men, led to the more equal status of women before the law. With this came the accompanying attitudes over time that women should no more be abused or molested than a man should be. Why? Because having "natural rights," a woman, just as a man, "owned" herself and had a private property in her own mind and body, and had an accompanying right to the fruits of her own labor.

Disrespect for Women is Inconsistent with Individualism

Now, even in enlightened Western countries it has taken a long time for this to be fully recognized, respected and enforced. But the legal and political extension of equal individual rights to women would have been far more difficult or impossible if commercial and market-oriented societies had not emerged giving opportunities to women to escape from the traditional order of things in which they were the property of their fathers and husbands.

In a free society, men, of course, may personally hold any attitudes towards the "fairer sex" they may choose, and they may have any voluntary and consensual relationship they desire with a member of the opposite sex. But a friend of freedom, I would suggest, shows a disrespect and disregard for the dignity of the female half of the human population, a disrespect and disregard for them as individual human beings, if they pass in silence when another refers to them in degrading and vulgar and near animalistic sexual terms.

How can the idea of non-aggression toward other human beings be maintained when some men voice and express their view of a woman in a dog or cow-like conception of their use and abuse for another's pleasure, without dissent or outspoken disagreement?

Up until this point, I would hope that many if not most readers will have either agreed or at least been sympathetic with the idea that a politically free society in which non-aggression is a paramount principle relies upon the complementary and wider philosophical and social individualism that sees that liberty cannot be sustained in a cultural collectivist setting of widely-held racist and vulgar sexist conceptions of some members of society.

Sexual Orientation in Society

The issue of sexual orientation and its legal recognition is likely to be seen by some in a less sympathetic light. It is too new of a social and political issue to be thought about in the same dispassionate and reasonable way as slavery or a denial of equal individual rights for women.

It is an undeniable biological fact that the human species, like virtually all other developed life forms on earth, are divided into two sexes, the intimate association between which is necessary for procreation. The heterosexual relationship, therefore, has logically seemed to be the "natural" one for human existence.

But it is also the fact that for some percentage of the human species, for all of recorded history, there have been homosexual attractions. Whether due to "nature" or "nurture" or some quantitatively immeasurable combination of the two, it has been as present in the human circumstance as the male-female relationship.

The deeply religious person may be certain that God has made man and woman for a distinct purpose that makes the homosexual relationship "unnatural," or a secularist may be firmly convinced that cultural stability and continuity requires the predominately heterosexual family structure in society.

But as a friend of freedom, the classical liberal and libertarian, true to philosophical individualism upon which his principle of non-aggression is based, should be politely respectful and tolerant of the free choices that others make concerning their choice of intimate partners.

This does not require "acceptance" or "agreement" with another's choice in this matter. We take it for granted that the strong Christian believer may be absolutely certain that the Buddhist or the Jew, by not accepting Jesus as his Lord and Savior, may be facing damnation or separation from God in another life. But in the free society we expect that that Christian will respect the peaceful and non-coerced decision of that other person to find his own other way. Any Christian friend of freedom should expect from himself the courage and determination to speak out against any attempt to forcibly deny an individual the liberty to choose his own way in this fundamental matter, even if the choice made is not the Christian one.

In the same manner, the friend of freedom may personally believe strongly on religious or societal-cultural grounds the value and importance of the heterosexual relationship. But if he is an advocate of liberty he should respect and defend the right of any individual to make his or her sexual choice without an environment of rudeness, cruelty or physical aggressiveness.

In a free society, anyone is at liberty to be rude, crude, and cruel in his words and demeanor, as long as he does not violate the right of any other person to his or her life, liberty and property. But the friend of freedom should be no more tolerant or silent in the face such behavior when it is expressed about a person's chosen sexual orientation than when spoken by a racist to humiliate and belittle a member of some ethic or racial group.

The Spirit of Individualism for Preservation of Freedom

The "thick" classical liberal or libertarian understands, let me suggest, that the preservation of individual rights and the principle of non-aggression in human affairs rests on and can only succeed and be sustained in the long run in a social setting in which people believe in, respect, and practice the culture and spirit of individualism in all walks and aspects of life.

Unlike some "thin" classical liberals or libertarians, the "thick" classical liberal or libertarian does not fear that expressing "value judgments" about the type of conduct and attitudes we have been discussing will lead to the feared "slippery slope" of paternalistic modern liberalism.

This happened in the 19th and 20th centuries due to the peculiar turn from the idea of "natural rights" to a particular utilitarianism under which some asserted that certain desirable "social" outcomes were to take precedence for the good of "the society as a whole" over the rights of the individual. And as such, it was considered acceptable to abridge various individual freedoms in the name of this "higher" collective good.

Any friend of freedom who remains anchored and true to the idea of inalienable rights that belong to the individual, as the American Founding Father reasoned, need not fear that he will fall into the trap of a presumed "social good" coming before the good and rights of the individual human being.

Natural Rights and Natural Liberty

This idea and spirit of individual liberty and rights was expressed clearly and succinctly by the eighteenth century Scottish philosopher, Francis Hutcheson (1694-1746), who taught at the University of Glasgow and was the teacher of Adam Smith.

In his *System of Moral Philosophy* (1737), Hutcheson explained the concept and meaning of a "natural rights," when he said,

> "he following natural rights of each individual seem of the perfect sort: A right to life, and to that perfection of the body which nature has given, belongs to every man ... This right is violated by unjust assaults, maiming, and murder.

As nature has implanted in each man a desire of his own happiness ... tis plain that each one has a natural right to exert his powers, according to his own judgment and inclination, for these purposes, in all such industry, labor, or amusements, as are not hurtful to others in their persons or goods ...

This right we call natural liberty. Every man has a sense of this right, and a sense of the evil or cruelty in interrupting this joyful liberty of others ...

But do not other men sometimes follow courses of action and ways of living that may be considered unwise, wrongheaded and possibly harmful to them? Hutcheson readily admits this.

But if each person is to be secure in his natural rights in this social system of natural liberty, then what avenue is open to those who wish to assist such misguided individuals to redirect themselves into more enlightened and betters ways?

Hutcheson states that the only course open that is consistent with respect of other people's individual rights is reason and persuasion. Said Hutcheson:

Let men instruct, teach, and convince their fellows as far as they can about the proper use of their natural powers, or persuade them to submit voluntarily to some wise plans of civil power where their important interests shall be secure. But till this is done, men must enjoy their natural liberty as long as they are not injurious [by violating the individual rights of others].

> This right of natural liberty is not only suggested by the selfish
> parts of our own constitution but by many generous affections
> ... as the grand dignity and perfection of our nature.

The pinnacle of social morality, therefore, in Hutcheson's view, is to respect each individual to live his life as he peacefully chooses, without private or political molestation as long as he respects the equal rights of all others. And the proper ethical principle in advancing conceptions of a better life to others is the use of reason, persuasion, and the example of one's own life.

Hutcheson concluded that, "The natural equality of men consists chiefly in this, that these natural rights belong equally to all ... The laws of God and nature ... prohibit the greatest and wisest of mankind to inflict any misery on the meanest, or to deprive them of any of their natural rights, or innocent acquisitions, when no public interest requires it [due to the violation of another's rights]."

A "Thicker" Foundation for Liberty

The world and America has been drifting away from the political principle of non-aggression in all aspects of human affairs, because we have been losing our understanding, appreciation and practice of that wider philosophically grounded classical liberal individualism in our thinking, attitudes and actions in everyday life as well as in politics.

Without this "thicker" foundation to our arguments and defenses for freedom, a merely "thin" libertarianism may not be enough to resist and prevent the continuing creeping spread of political and social collectivism.

A philosophically reasoned defense of individual rights and an accompanying culture and spirit of individualism in our attitudes and actions in all our doings in society are, perhaps, the best basis and hope for the restoring and bettering of the free market liberal social order that gave us whatever liberty that was hard won in the past.

CHAPTER 30

LEARNING LIBERTY AND THE POWER OF PRINCIPLES

In *The Constitution of Liberty* (1960), free market economist and social philosopher, F. A. Hayek, quotes in a footnote the famous 19th century scientist, Louis Pasteur, that, "In research, chance only helps those whose minds are well prepared for it." What Pasteur was, no doubt, getting at is that unless the researcher already has been trained in the principles and methods of his own scientific field, and unless he is fairly knowledgeable about previous experiments and their outcomes in his area of study, he will not be able to see possibilities or opportunities for discovery that come his way that otherwise would just pass by the untrained mind.

I want to argue that the same applies in taking advantage of opportunities to advance liberty. Unless an individual is willing to take the time to make himself fairly well informed about the principles, applications, and some of the history of liberty, chances for advancing the cause of freedom may pass him by; opportunities that might have made a difference can be missed.

I should confess that my guide for emphasizing this are ideas developed by Leonard E. Read (1898-1983), the founder and long-time first president of the Foundation for Economic Education (FEE). In the June 1974, I attended a weeklong FEE seminar at the Foundation's original headquarters in a grand old mansion building located in Irvington-on-Hudson, about 20 miles north of New York City. There were many excellent lectures during that week. Some of them were by FEE staff members, including Ed Opitz (FEE's resident classical liberal theologian), Paul Poirot (editor of FEE's monthly magazine, *The Freeman*), and Bettina Bien Greaves (publications editor and expert on all things relating to Ludwig von Mises).

There were also a number of outstanding talks by outside speakers, including by Hans Sennholz (the head of the economics department at Grove City College in Pennsylvania) and Henry Hazlitt (the internationally renowned free market journalist, and the author of *Economics in One Lesson*). Sennholz was a real showman, using his native German accent to great affect to make his points in defense of economic freedom and highlighting the contradictions and errors in all forms of socialism. Henry Hazlitt was clear, calm and compelling in his emphasis on always looking beyond "what is seen" in government policies so as to not miss the secondary or "unseen" effects of government interventions that usually lead to disastrous consequences.

Being a Light of Liberty Through Self-Improvement

But I must admit, reflecting back on that week now more than 45 years ago, that I can picture in my mind and remember most of the content of only one lecture. It was a talk delivered by Leonard Read. The presentations were given in a lecture hall off the great library room of the mansion. At one point in his talk, Leonard Read asked that the lights be turned off. He held a small electric candle in his hand, and slightly turning its dimmer dial, there emerged a small flicker of light.

"Notice," Read said, "that though the candle gives off only a wee bit of light, how all of our eyes are drawn to it in the dark." He slowly turned the dimmer dial again, and remarked, "Now notice how as I add just a little more to the candle's illumination, we can now see more of me and some of those sitting in the front of the room." He continued to turn the dial until the candle was at its maximum. As he was doing so, Leonard Read pointed out how much more of the room was becoming visible to our eyes, until finally the darkness had been pushed back into the small corners of the room.

He said, "That is what each of us can be – lights of liberty. The more we are informed, knowledgeable, and articulate about the ideas of freedom the more intellectual light we give off in exchanges with others, and the more we may attract some of those others to also become illuminations of liberty. Finally, there will be enough of us that the ideas of collectivism and statism will have been pushed back to a few small, dark corners of society."

Changing the World Begins with Yourself

Leonard Read noted that many of us would like to change society for the better. But the question is, where and how to start? He asked us, out of all the people in the world, over whom do you have, personally, the most influence? The answer is, yourself! Making over the world, therefore, should and must start with improving your own understanding and dedication to freedom. In this case, it means being willing to take the time, attention, and courage to learn the meaning of liberty, and improving your ability to share what you know with others.

Leonard Read did not say that each of us has to dedicate ourselves to learning and sharing what he called the 'freedom philosophy" all day, everyday. We all have different circumstances, obligations, and willingness to do things. Some may only have the time and ability to become generally familiar with the ideas of liberty, and just try to live by them to the best that we can while doing all the other things of life.

Others might have the chance to read and think more about what freedom means, and the arguments for and against. If moved to do so, these people will have the knowledge and interest to more actively participate in conversations and other forums to advance the cause of freedom. And still others may have the interest and desire to become spokesmen and developers of arguments for freedom and the free society.

However bright we try to make ourselves as such lights of liberty, we have to accept the fact that change always comes one person at a time, one mind at a time. If freedom seems something important to you and for the world in which you live, then a little bit of the burden of learning about it and passing it on to others falls upon each of us, in our own ways and personal circumstances.

The other important point that Leonard Read made is that you cannot force the ideas of freedom on anyone, nor do people like to be "talked down to" in arrogant and know-it-all ways. Whether in comments during a conversation over a meal, or answers you may give when someone asks your opinion on some political or economic issue, Leonard Read reminded us to always treat others with courtesy and respect, and never with hubris or anger.

You Never Know Who You Have Touched About Freedom

Another takeaway from Leonard Read is to never allow disappointment to get the better of you. You never know how what you might have said may end up rolling around inside some person's head long after your exchange of views with them, or in others who may have said nothing themselves but overheard the conversation.

Many years ago, I found this out when I was first teaching while still in graduate school. One day I was waiting on line at the checkout counter in a small grocery store in New York City. The woman behind me on the line had been staring at me and said, "Aren't you Richard Ebeling? Don't you teach an evening course at Rutgers University?" Hesitatingly, I said, "Yes." The woman looked right at me and said, "You have ruined my marriage!" Everyone around just looked at me. "You've ruined my marriage," she repeated. "My husband took your economics class, and now all he does is come home from work, watch the evening news, and complain about government all night. You have ruined my marriage."

I had no idea who her husband was, or where he sat in the classroom, or whether he had ever asked questions or simply sat back and listened. But, clearly, some of the things I discussed and explained in that introductory economics class had clicked inside of him, and made a difference about how he thought about freedom, markets, and the role of government in society. None of us knows whom, how, or when something we say or do will impact and influence another, in one way or another, for good or ill.

The lesson that I learned from this was that whether students in any class of mine seemed wide awake or half a sleep, fully taking everything in I am saying or showing body language indicating that some of them wished they could be someplace else, I am always, to the best of my teaching ability, partly talking and explaining to that "anonymous" one that may be there, like that unknown student in that Rutgers class of mine very long ago.

Ideas Influence Events: the Free Trade Movement

Two of the momentous victories for liberty in the nineteenth century were the end to British trade protectionism and the abolition of slavery in the United States. Both of these advances for human freedom were during times of economic or political crisis. The British Corn Laws imposed high tariff barriers against the importation of foreign agricultural goods into the British Isles, especially, though not exclusively, on wheat, as a means of securing higher prices for the landed aristocracy. In the autumn and winter of 1845-1846 some of the worst rains in living memory destroyed much of the wheat and related crops throughout Great Britain. High bread and other food prices resulted in many facing starvation, particularly among the "lower classes." Social unrest threatened the country.

The issue of protectionism versus freedom of trade in food had been hotly debated for a long time in the British Parliament. But, finally, in June of 1846, both Houses of Parliament passed legislation repealing the Corn Laws, allowing unilateral free trade in virtually all food items. Cheap food from abroad could enter the land and feed the desperately hungry. But this "radical" answer of unilateral free trade, did not appear out of nowhere.

For decades the friends of freedom in Great Britain, a generation of thinkers influenced by the ideas of Adam Smith and others, had been arguing for freedom of enterprise and trade, at home and abroad. Individuals such as Richard Cobden and John Bright in the Anti-Corn Law League led them. They talked, they lectured, they published books, monographs and pamphlets, and they elected free trade advocates to Parliament.

An historical accident, a season of terrible weather, became the catalyst for the economic reform of ending government interference with international trade in Great Britain, but only because before that moment of crisis there had been more and more people who had come to see economic freedom as the answer to poverty and starvation. The idea of free trade had become so much a part of the climate of opinion by the middle of the 1840s, that children in poor parts of London would write graffiti on the walls of buildings with slogans such as, "I be protected, and I be starved."

Large segments of the British population among the poor and the "ruling classes" had been won over, one mind at a time, over a good number of years, in spite of many policy frustrations and disappoints along the way; until, finally, an economic crisis of failed food crops could open the door to the chance of changing the course of economic events in a dramatic way. But it would not have been possible if people who had came to see the importance of liberty had not been willing to learn, advocate, and speak out for free trade as a matter of moral as well as practical principle. Ideas, it was demonstrated, do have consequences, even if changes do not happen over night.

Human Slavery and the American South

Another instance is the end to slavery in the United States. Slavery was formally ended in all the Northern states of the, then, United States by 1802. And the importation of any more slaves into the United States was legally prohibited in 1807.

However, the institution of black slavery was embedded into

the very fabric of the Southern states. There were 31.2 million people in the United States in 1860, out of which almost 4 million were slaves, or about 13 percent of the country's total population. The overall population of the slave states before the Civil War was less than 9.5 million, so 42 percent of the South's population was made up of black slaves. Indeed, the 1860 census showed that the slave populations were in the majority in some of these Southern states (53 percent in Mississippi and 57 percent in South Carolina). Those 4 million slaves were held as human property by a total of 294,000 Southern slave owners, or by only seven percent of the South's population.

Yet, nonetheless, the vast majority of white slave owners and white non-slave owners in those Southern states considered this "peculiar institution" essential to the livelihood and culture of the South. It was said that white labor could not work in the southern climate; only blacks, originally made for the heat of Africa, were biologically fit to pick cotton, harvest tobacco, and wade into the rice fields in that part of the country. Besides, if slavery was ended not only would slave owners lose the market value of their investment, it would be impossible to get "free labor" to work for wages that would still make these crops profitable, so the Southern economy would be destroyed without low-cost slave labor. Finally, Africans, it was said, were inherently inferior to whites, and they needed masters to take care of them in beneficial ways that they could never do for themselves if they were free. Slavery, in other words, was a benevolent socialism, and so said some of the slavery proselytizers publicly arguing on behalf of the institution.

Northern Bigotry and the Abolitionist Movement

In the Northern states, slavery may have been ended, but the free blacks in these parts of the country were shunned, discriminated against, sometimes violently attacked, and generally considered an undesirable element in American society. Slavery may be wrong in the eyes of God and man, but most whites in the North did not want one of "them" living next door, marrying their daughter, or competing for their jobs. It was for this reason that the eloquent runaway slave, Frederick Douglass, delivered his 5th of July address in 1852 on why the Declaration of Independence was a mockery with its talk of inalienable rights belonging to all men, while millions languished in chains and slave labor south of the Mason-Dixon Line, and too many white Northerners considered Africans to be less than fully and equal human beings.

But like the enemies of slavery before them in Great Britain, where that institution was ended throughout the British Empire in 1834, the American abolitionist movement, led by people such as William Lloyd Garrison, spoke out against slavery as a matter of moral principle. Most were motivated by their deeply held Christian conscience, that human slavery was an abomination in the eyes of God. They insisted that we are all equally God's children regardless of where we were born and how we looked.

The cruelty of the slave traders and the harshness of the slave masters in the South called for one and only one answer: the end to slavery now and completely. And our African brethren in the United States, the abolitionists said, should be considered Americans with all the same rights and protections as all other citizens. Abolitionists were often scorned, physically attacked, sometimes murdered by racists and slavery sympathizers in the North. They were considered unreasonable and dangerous radicals threatening the unity of the country and the tranquility of society.

Lincoln, Slavery and the Civil War

But the abolitionists persisted, and their numbers slowly but surely grew. And then a national crisis emerged with the election of Abraham Lincoln as president in 1860. Lincoln was against the extension of slavery to any of the Western territories that would, over time, have populations large enough to apply for statehood within the Union. Lincoln was emphatic, however, that he did not intend and did not consider that he had the authority as president to abolish slavery in the Southern states where it already existed.

However, for the Southern states, attempts to stop the spread of slavery to any future new states in the Union threatened to bring the death knell to their peculiar institution. New states meant more Senators and additional Congressmen increasingly out numbering the Congressional representatives from the slave states. The free states, at some point, would try to overthrow their slave system.

(As an aside, it is true that there were disputes over protectionist tariffs and use of federal tax revenues for "internal improvements" – canals, railways, and roads – more for the benefit of the Northern and Western states than those of the South. But any reading of the declarations of secession issued by the Southern states following Lincoln's election makes it very clear that the only issue that mattered enough to explicitly refer to and defend in their secession justifications was slavery.)

For the first two years, the Civil War went badly for Lincoln and the Union side. Southern resistance had been stronger than expected, the Confederate Armies had routed Union forces an embarrassingly number of times, and the war was getting to be costly in terms of money and men. Draft riots ensued in New York City following Lincoln's imposing of military conscription. Members of his own Republican Party were hesitant to vote sufficient funds to continue prosecution of the war.

He needed the support of the abolitionists in Congress to vote his way. But they would not, if ending slavery was not made central to the Union cause. Finally, to win that support, Lincoln issued the Emancipation Proclamation in 1863, ending slavery in those parts of the South still in a state of rebellion against the U.S. government. It was an important, if only partial, victory for those who demanded the complete end to this immoral institution. Following the end to the Civil War, it set the stage for the 13th Amendment to the Constitution being passed and ratified by the end of 1865 for the formal end to slavery and any other form of involuntary servitude throughout the United States.

If the abolitionists had not been hard at work for decades earlier in the United States; if they had not made the moral argument for a complete end to slavery as an abomination in the eyes of God and man; and if they had not grown in influence and support enough to sway votes in Congress, there is no certainty that either the Emancipation Proclamation or the 13th Amendment to the Constitution would have been issued and passed when and how they were.

Here was another accident of the circumstances of history, with its outcome partly dependent upon ideas of principle concerning liberty being believed in and argued for even in a political setting in which all the cultural and social attitudes and forces seemed to suggest an unwinnable battle during all the years before the actual victory.

The Only Chance is to Fight for Liberty

It is never possible to know before hand or with full certainty whether right ideas will win out in a particular place and at any particular time. But what is far more certain is that if those ideas are not known, believed in, and argued and fought for, they have no chance of ever prevailing.

This is why it is so important to make the principled and uncompromising case for individual rights and economic liberty, however daunting the task seems, no matter how unwinnable the triumph of those ideas appear. It is why each of us must, to the best our ability and to the extent our time and circumstances permit, become one of Leonard Read's lights of liberty; intellectual candles of illumination offering the vision and vista of a free society.

In 1949, when the possibility of the triumph of Soviet-style socialism seemed possible around the world, Austrian economist, F. A. Hayek, penned an article on, "The Intellectuals and Socialism." The heart of his argument is that socialism appeared to be winning because it had captured the imagination of far too many intellectuals as a vision of a new, good, and more just society; and through them, a growing number of people in society in general were believing the same, due to the persuasiveness of their writings.

But, Hayek insisted, it did not have to end with a collectivist future for mankind. Friends of freedom had to restate and remake the case for human liberty in a way that aroused the excitement and moral attractiveness of a truly free society. He said:

> "Unless we can make the philosophic foundations of a free society once more an living intellectual issue, and its implementation a task which challenges the ingenuity and

imagination of our liveliest minds, the prospects of freedom are indeed dark. But if we can regain that belief in the power of ideas which was the hallmark of [classical] liberalism at its best, the battle is not lost."

That is our task, our duty; and if we but try, all of us combined as individual lights of liberty can and will bring about a liberal world of freedom and free enterprise.

SUGGESTED READING LIST ON LIBERALISM AND FREEDOM

Prefatory Note:

Over the last two hundred years, hundreds of books and thousands of articles have been written about liberalism in its various political, social, and economic facets. It is impossible for any one person to be fully informed about all of these writings. It is also an impossible task to decide what are the really important or essential writings on liberalism, especially since there are differences of opinion about the philosophical foundations and public policy implications of liberal ideas, even among liberalism's staunched advocates.

The following brief reading list on the themes of political, social, and economic liberalism is, inescapably, therefore, a highly subjective choice. It merely represents the works by a variety of authors that the present writer considers especially useful for highlighting some one or more aspects of the case for liberalism and liberty in general, and which may assist the interested reader for widening their own understanding and appreciation of liberalism in its various aspects.

The authors chosen offer no commonly agreed conception of the philosophical foundations of liberalism or the policy implications in terms of the size and scope of government in society. One common thread is their belief in the freedom of the individual in various sides of life, and the need to restrain government within relatively narrow bounds for the preservation of human liberty.

Finally, there will be, no doubt, any number of readers who will wonder why some particular author or book was not included, while another one was. I can only say that these are some of the writings that I, personally, have read and that had an impact on me, in some way or another, concerning my own thinking about liberalism and liberty, and consider of value for understanding the meaning and importance of liberal ideas for a free and just society.

Acton, Harry B. (1993). *The Morals of Markets and Related Essays*, ed. by David Gordon and Jeremy Shearmur. Indianapolis, IN: Liberty Fund

Acton, (Lord) John Emerich Edward Dalberg- (1985). *Essays in the History of Liberty, in Selected Writings of Lord Acton*, Vol. 1. Indianapolis, IN: Liberty Fund.

Barnett, Randy E. (1998). *The Structure of Liberty: Justice and The Rule of Law*. Oxford: Clarendon Press.

------------------(2004). *Restoring the Lost Constitution: The Presumption of Liberty*. Princeton, NJ: Princeton University Press.

------------------(2016). *Our Republican Constitution: Securing the Liberty and Sovereignty of the People*. New York: Broadside Books.

Barry, Norman. (1987). *On Classical Liberalism and Libertarianism*. New York: Palgrave MacMillan

-------------- (1996). *Classical Liberalism in the Age of Post-Communism*. Brookfield, MA: Edward Elgar.

Bastiat, Frederic. ([1850] 2012). "The Law" reprinted in Jacques de Guenin, ed., *The Collected Works of Frederic Bastiat*, Vol. 2. Indianapolis, IN: Liberty Fund, pp. 107-146.

----------------- ([1850] 2016). "What is Seen and What is Not Seen," in Jacques de Guenin, ed., *The Collected Works of Frederic Bastiat*, Vol. 3. Indianapolis, IN: Liberty Fund

Beaulieu, Paul Leroy. ([1885] 1908). *Collectivism: A Study of the Leading Social Questions of the Day*. London: John Murray.

Bethell, Tom. (1998). *The Noblest Triumph: Property and Prosperity Through the Ages*. New York: St. Martin's Press.

Blumenfeld, Samuel L. (1974). Editor, *Property in a Humane Society*. LaSalle, Ill.: Open Court.

Booth, Philip, ed. (2005). *Towards a Liberal Utopia?* London: Institute of Economic Affairs.

Bransted, E. K and Melhuish, K. J. (1978). Eds., *Western Liberalism: A History in Documents from Locke to Croce*. London: Longman.

Brennan, Geoffrey and Buchanan, James M. ([1985] 2000). *The Reason of Rules: Constitutional Political Economy* reprinted in *The Collected Works of James M. Buchanan*, Vol. 10. Indianapolis, IN: Liberty Fund.

Buchanan, James M. ([1975] 2000). *The Limits of Liberty: Between Anarchy and Leviathan* reprinted in *The Collected Works of James M. Buchanan*, Vol. 7. Indianapolis, IN: Liberty Fund.
-------------------- (1993). *Property as a Guarantor of Liberty*. Northampton, MA: Edward Elgar.
--------------------- (1999). *The Logical Foundations of Constitutional Liberty* in *The Collected Works of James M. Buchanan*, Vol. 1. Indianapolis, IN: Liberty Fund.
--------------------- (2001). *Moral Science and Moral Order* in *The Collected Works of James M. Buchanan*, Vol. 17. Indianapolis, IN: Liberty Fund.

Chodorov, Frank. (1959). *The Rise and Fall of Society*. New York: Devin-Adair.

Constant, Benjamin. ([1810] 2003). *Principles of Politics Applicable to All Governments*. Indianapolis, IN: Liberty Fund
-------------------([1819] 1988). "Liberty of the Ancients Compared with That of the Moderns," reprinted in, Biancamaria Fontana, ed., *Political Writings of Benjamin Constant*. Cambridge, Mass: Cambridge University Press, pp. 307-328.

Conway, David. (1995). *Classical Liberalism: The Unvanquished Ideal*. New York, New York: St. Martin's Press.

Cox, Harold. (1920). *Economic Liberty*. London: Longmans, Green

Dietze, Gottfried. (1985). *Liberalism Proper and Proper Liberalism*. Baltimore, MD: Johns Hopkins University Press.

Ebeling, Richard M. (2003). *Austrian Economics and the Political Economy of Freedom*. Northampton, MA: Edward Elgar.

--------------------- (2010). *Political Economy, Public Policy and Monetary Economics: Ludwig von Mises and the Austrian Tradition*. New York: Routledge.

--------------------- (2016). *Austrian Economics and Public Policy: Restoring Freedom and Prosperity*. Fairfax, VA: Future of Freedom Foundation.

Ebeling, Richard M. & Hornberger, Jacob G. (1995). Editors, *The Case for Free Trade and Open Immigration*. Fairfax, VA: Future of Freedom Foundation.

Epstein, Richard A. (1995). *Simple Rules for a Complex World*. Cambridge, MA: Harvard University Press.

-------------------- (2002). *Principles for a Free Society: Reconciling Individual Liberty with the Common Good*. New York: Basic Books.

-------------------- (2003). *Skepticism and Freedom: A Modern Case for Classical Liberalism*. Chicago: University of Chicago Press.

-------------------- (2014). *The Classical Liberal Constitution: The Uncertain Quest for Limited Government*. Cambridge, MA: Harvard University Press.

Flew, Antony. (1981). *The Politics of Procrustes: Contradictions of Enforced Equality*. Buffalo, NY: Prometheus Books.

------------ (2001). *Equality in Liberty and Justice*. New Brunswick, NJ: Transactions Books.

Friedman, Milton. ([1951] 2012). "Neo-Liberalism and Its Prospects," reprinted in Lanny Ebenstein, ed., *The Indispensible Milton Friedman: Essays on Politics and Economics*. Washington, D.C.: Regnary, pp. 3-10.

-------------------- ([1955] 2012). "Liberalism, Old Style," reprinted in, Lanny Ebenstein, ed., *The Indispensible Milton Friedman: Essays on Politics and Economics*. Washington, D.C.: Regnary, pp. 11-24.

---------------- (1962). *Capitalism and Freedom*. Chicago: University of Chicago Press.

---------------- ([1970] 1987). "The Social Responsibility of Business," reprinted in, Kurt R. Laube, ed., *The Essence of Friedman*. Stanford, CA: Hoover Institution Press, pp. 36-42.

------------------ (1980). *Free to Choose*. New York: Harcourt, Brace.

Greenleaf, W. H. (1983). *The British Political Tradition*, 3 vols. London: Methuen.

Halevy, Elie. ([1928] 1949). *The Growth of Philosophical Radicalism*. New York: Augustus M. Kelley.

Harper, F. A. (1949). *Liberty: A Path to Its Recovery*. Irvington-on-Hudson, NY: Foundation for Economic Education.

Hayek, Friedrich A. ([1944] 2007). *The Road to Serfdom: Text and Documents* reprinted in Bruce Caldwell, ed., *The Collected Writings of F. A. Hayek*, Vol. 2. Chicago: University of Chicago Press.

-------------------- (1948). *Individualism and Economic Order.* Chicago: University of Chicago Press.

-------------------- ([1960] 2011). *The Constitution of Liberty*, reprinted in, Ronald Hamowy, ed., *The Collected Writings of F. A. Hayek*, vol. 17 Chicago: University of Chicago Press.

-------------------- ([1973] 1978). "Liberalism" reprinted in *New Essays in Philosophy, Politics, Economics and the History of Ideas.* Chicago: University of Chicago Press, pp. 119-151.

-------------------- ([1973; 1976; 1979] 1982). *Law, Legislation, and Liberty: A New Statement of the Liberal Principles of Justice and Political Economy*, 3 Vols.. London: Routledge.

Hazlitt, Henry. (1946). *Economics in One Lesson.* New York: Harper & Row.

------------- ([1964] 1998). *The Foundations of Morality.* Irvington-on-Hudson, NY: Foundation for Economic Education.

Herbert, Auberon. (1978). *The Right and Wrong of Compulsion by the State, and Other Essays*, ed. Eric Mack. Indianapolis, IN: Liberty Fund.

Heyne, Paul. (2008). *Are Economists Basically Immoral? and Other Essays on Economics, Ethics, and Religion*, ed. by Geoffrey Brennan and A. M.C. Waterman. Indianapolis, IN: Liberty Fund.

Hirst, Francis. (1935). *Liberty and Tyranny.* London: Duckworth.

\------------- (1935). *Economic Freedom and Private Property.* London: Duckworth.

Holcombe, Randall G. (2002). *From Liberty to Democracy: The Transformation of American Government.* Ann Arbor: University of Michigan Press.

Jasay, Anthony de. (1991). *Choice, Contract, Consent: A Restatement of Liberalism.* London: Institute of Economic Affairs.

Kirzner, Israel M. (1989). *Discovery, Capitalism, and Distributive Justice.* New York: Basil Blackwell.

\------------------ (2018). *Reflections on Ethics, Freedom, Welfare Economics, and the Legacy of Austrian Economics*, ed. by Peter J. Boettke and Frederic Sautet. Indianapolis, IN: Liberty Fund.

Kohn, Hans. (1957). *American Nationalism: An Interpretive Essay.* New York: MacMillan.

\----------- (1957). *The Twentieth Century: The Challenge to the West and Its Response.* New York: MacMillan.

Lane, Rose Wilder. (1943). *The Rediscovery of Freedom.* New York: John Day.

Leoni, Bruno. ([1961] 1991). *Freedom and the Law.* Indianapolis, IN: Liberty Fund

Locke, John. ([1691] 1824). *Two Treatises on Government* reprinted in *The Works of John Locke*, Vol. 4. London: Revington.

Machlup, Fritz. ([1969] 1976). "Liberalism and the Choice of Freedoms," reprinted in, George Bitros, ed., *Selected Writings of Fritz Machlup*. New York: New York University Press, 1976, pp. 505-534.

MacKay, Thomas. ([1891] 1981) Editor, *A Plea for Liberty: An Argument Against Socialism and Socialistic Legislation*. Indianapolis, IN. Liberty Fund.

Madison, G. B. (1986). *The Logic of Liberty.* New York: Greenwood Press.

Meadowcroft, John. (2005). *The Ethics of the Market*. New York: Palgrave MacMillian.

McCloskey, Deirdre N. (2006). *The Bourgeois Virtues: Ethics for an Age of Commerce*. Chicago: University of Chicago Press.
    -------------------------(2010). *Bourgeois Dignity: Why Economics Can't Explain the Modern World.* Chicago: University of Chicago Press.
    ------------------------(2016). *Bourgeois Equality: How Ideas, Not Capital or Institutions, Enriched the World*. Chicago: University of Chicago Press.

Mill, John Stuart. ([1859] 1977). *On Liberty*, reprinted in John M. Robson, ed. *The Collected Works of John Stuart Mill*, Vol. 18. Toronto: University of Toronto Press, pp. 213-310.

Mises, Ludwig von. ([1927] 2005). *Liberalism: The Classical Tradition*. Indianapolis, IN: Liberty Fund.

-------------------- ([1953] 1981). S*ocialism: An Economic and Sociological Analysis.* Indianapolis, IN: Liberty Fund

-------------------- ([1956] 2006). *The Anti-Capitalistic Mentality.* Indianapolis, IN: Liberty Fund

-------------------- ([1958] 1991). "Liberty and Property," reprinted in *Two Essays by Ludwig von Mises*. Auburn, Al. Ludwig von Mises Institute.

------------------- -(1966). *Human Action: A Treatise on Economics*, 3rd ed. Chicago: Henry Regnary.

Morley, Felix. ([1949]1972). *The Power in the People*. Los Angeles: Nash Publishing.

Muir, Ramsey. (1940). *Civilization and Liberty*. London: Jonathan Cape.

Nock, Albert Jay. (1935). *Our Enemy, the State*. New York: William Marrow.

Norberg, Johan, (2003). *In Defense of Global Capitalism.* Washington, D.C.: Cato Institute.

Nozick, Robert. (1974). *Anarchy, State and Utopia*. New York: Basic Books.

O'Keefe, Dennis. (2004). *Editor, Economy and Virtue: Essays on the Theme of Markets and Morality*. London: Institute of Economic Affairs.

Ostrom, Vincent. (1997). *The Meaning of Democracy and the Vulnerability of Democracies: A Response to Tocqueville's Challenge.* Ann Arbor: University of Michigan Press.

Palmer, Tom G. (2009). *Realizing Freedom: Libertarian Theory, History and Practice.* Washington, D.C.: Cato Institute.

Paterson, Isabel. ([1943] 1964). *The God in the Machine.* Caldwell, ID: Caxton Printers.

Pipes, Richard. (1999). *Property and Freedom.* New York: Random House.

Polanyi, Michael. (1951). *The Logic of Liberty: Reflections and Rejoinders.* London: Routledge & Kegan Paul.

Raico, Ralph. (2012). *Classical Liberalism and the Austrian School.* Auburn, Al. Ludwig von Mises Institute.

Rand, Ayn. (1964). *The Virtue of Selfishness.* New York: New American Library
-------------- (1967) *Capitalism: The Unknown Ideal.* New York: New American Library.
-------------- (1971). *The New Left: The Anti-Industrial Revolution.* New York: New American Library.

Rasmussen, Douglas and Den Uyl, Douglas J. (1997). *Liberalism Defended: The Challenge of Post-Modernity.* Northampton, MA: Edward Elgar.

Read, Leonard E. (1958). *I, Pencil.* Irvington-on-Hudson, NY: Foundation for Economic Education.

--------------- (1964). *Anything That's Peaceful.* Irvington-on-Hudson, NY:

Röpke, Wilhelm. (1951). *The Problem of Economic Order.* Cairo: National Bank of Egypt.

---------------- (1955). *Economic Order and International Law.* Leyden: A. W. Sijthoff.

--------------- (1963). *Economics of the Free Society.* Chicago: Henry Regnary.

Ruggiero, Guido de. (1927). *The History of European Liberalism.* London: Oxford University Press.

Rothbard, Murray N. (1962). *Man, Economy, and State: A Treatise on Economics*, Princeton, NJ: D. Van Nostrand.

--------------------- (1974). *Egalitarianism as a Revolt Against Nature, and Other Essays.* Washington, D.C.: Libertarian Review Press.

--------------------- (1978). *For a New Liberty.* New York: Collier Books.

-------------------- (1982). *The Ethics of Liberty.* Atlantic Highlands, NJ: Humanities Press.

Rougier, Louis. (1971). *The Genius of the West.* Los Angeles: Nash Publishing.

Sanderfur, Timothy and Christina. (2016). *Cornerstone of Liberty: Property Rights in 21st Century America.* Washington, D. C.: The

Cato Institute.

Schneider, Louis. (1967). Editor, *The Scottish Moralists on Human Nature and Society.* Chicago: University of Chicago Press.

Schoeck, Helmut. ([1969]1987). *Envy: A Theory of Social Behavior.* Indianapolis, IN: Liberty Fund.

Shah, Parth J. (2004). *Editor, Morality and Markets An Anthology.* New Delhi: Academic Foundations.

Smith, Bruce. (1887). *Liberty and Liberalism: A Protest Against the Growing Tendency of Undue Interference by the State, with Individual Liberty, Private Enterprise, and the Rights to Property.* London: Longmans, Green

Smith, George. (2013). *The System of Liberty: Themes in the History of Classical Liberalism.* Cambridge, Mass: Cambridge University Press.

Sowell, Thomas. (1980). *Knowledge and Decisions.* New York: Basic Books.
          ----------------- (2014). *Basic Economics*, 5th ed. New York: Basic Books.

Spencer, Herbert. ([1851] 1970). *Social Statics.* New York: Robert Schalkenbach Foundation.
          ----------------- ([1884] 1981). *The Man versus the State, with Six Essays on Government, Society and Freedom.* Indianapolis, IN: Liberty Fund.

Sumner, William Graham. (1992). *On Liberty, Society, and Politics: The Essential Essays of William Graham Sumner,* ed. by Robert C. Bannister. Indianapolis, IN: Liberty Fund.

Tocqueville, Alexis de. ([1836; 1840] 2019). *Democracy in America.* Indianapolis, IN: Liberty Fund.

Williams, Walter E. (1982). *The State Against Blacks.* New York: McGraw-Hill.
--------------------- (1999). *More Liberty Means Less Government.* Stanford, CA: Hoover Institution.

Withers, Hartley. (1920). *The Case for Capitalism.* New York: E. P. Dutton.

Humboldt, Wilhelm von. ([1792] 1969). *The Limits of State Action.* Indianapolis, IN: Liberty Fund.

INDEX

A

academia, 165–66, 270–71

academic freedom, 166

accountability, 143

advice, 342, 350

Africans, 291–92

ancient societies

dreams of, 16–17

Greece, 67, 250–51, 338

labor's indignity in, 66–67

liberty in, 250–51, 259–60

slavery in, 291

anonymity, 197–98

anti-capitalism, 353–65

anti-Semitism, 56–58

aristocratic nobility, 94

asymmetric information, 135–37, 142–43

Austrian economics, 151, 231, 357

autonomy, 364

B

Berlin, 278

Berlin Wall, 58–59, 278

Berra, Yogi, 367, 376–77

Big Government

development of, in New Deal, 7–8

liberalism as meaning, 78

bigotry. *See also* racism; sexism

anti-immigrant, 56–58

in private affairs, 13–14, 41, 61–62, 380–88

religious, 41

state-sanctioned, 61, 62

Bill of Rights, 21, 82, 295, 297

Bismarck, Otto von, 314

Buchanan, James, 45–46

bureaucratic self-interest, 153–54, 320

business experience, 303

business failures, 32–33

businessmen, 360

busybodies. *See* meddlers

C

campaign finance, 374–75

capitalism, 219, 268, 279–80, 359–65

Cassidy, John, 217, 224–25

censorship, 271, 284

central bank independence, 174–75

central banking, 173, 179–85

central planning, 372

central banking as, 173, 179–85

in democratic socialism, 12

failure of, 176, 178, 230–31, 372–73

in Green New Deal, 304–11

individuals under, 6–7

local knowledge *vs.*, 133, 213

in public-goods provision, 151–52

via industrial policy, 347–48

chance, 393, 399, 403

charitable giving, 257

cheap talk, 149–50

Chevalier, Michel, 33–35

child abuse, 220

China, 276, 287, 289

Christianity, 41, 68

church attendance, 40–41

civil liberties, 20–21

civil society, 4–5

19th-century, 38–39, 42, 210–11

free choice in, 255–56

vs. government, 244, 247

non-market, 199–200, 222–23, 225–26

Civil War, 402–3

class consciousness, 188–89, 281

classical economists, 22, 314–15

classical liberalism

democracy in, 245, 253

historical accomplishments of, 11, 15–16, 19–26, 88–89, 214–15

individuals in, 4–5, 96–97, 190–93, 207, 220, 252–53

minorities in, 81–82

misplaced blaming of, 10, 91–92

non-interference in, 85–88

pluralism in, 200–201, 214

property in, 83–84

self-ownership in, 69

as spirit of the age, 24–25

system of natural liberty, 84–85, 335, 338

class struggle, 267, 280, 289

coercion

in democratic socialism, 246

historical prevalence of, 84

in industrial policy, 347–48

prohibition on, 97, 207, 379

collectivism, 6–7

20th-century, 277

civil society vs., 241, 247

gender-based, 281–85

of identity politics, 296

race-based, 268–69, 271–73, 281–85, 290

as threat to immigration, 64

tribal, 332–34, 339

colleges and universities, 165–66, 170–72, 261, 270–71, 315

command economy, 9

commerce, 71–72, 252

commodity moneys, 181–82

communication technologies, 30–31

Communist Party, 231–32, 276

community, 159–60, 225. *See also*

civil society

competition

decrying of, 93

as discovery procedure, 103–4, 137

dynamic, 109, 112–15

entrepreneurs', 95–96

in free markets, 96–99, 168, 172, 368

in labor markets, 74, 95

perfect, 106–9, 136

political, 94–95

Competitive Enterprise Institute, 322, 375

compromise, 47, 205–6, 209, 214

condominiums, 163

Congress, 300–303

Congressional Budget Office, 321–22

con men, 141

conservatism, 79, 92

Constant, Benjamin, 249–53, 259–60

Constitution, 21, 47, 193, 273, 403

constitutional limits, 6

consumers, 8, 102, 253–54

cooperation, 97–99

Corn Laws, 398–99

Cowper, William, 20

creative destruction, 112–13

crony capitalism, 91, 259, 338, 378

crowding out, 223–24

D

decency, 327–39

decision-making

entrepreneurial, 102

shifting locus of, 8–9, 78, 200–201,
233, 235, 374

Declaration of Independence, 18–19,
193, 273, 295, 401

defense contractors, 154

de Jouvenel, Bertrand, 360

democracy

demise of, 310

liberty vs., 245

in the marketplace, 152, 196,
199–200, 256

participatory, 219, 233–35,
300–301

scope of, 252–53, 257–58

support for, 22–23, 40

tyranny via, 82, 246–47, 250–51

democratic socialism

agenda of, 12, 232–34, 236,
242–44

coerciveness of, 246

favoritism in, 259, 306

group plans in, 7, 10, 235, 259,
306

vs. other socialisms, 242

political focus of, 201

return of, 92, 232–33, 377–78

Democratic Socialists of America (DSA), 232–34

demonstrated preference, 150

Demsetz, Harold, 211

de Tocqueville, Alexis, 29, 37–39

de Tracy, Destutt, 206

dignity, 13, 66–74, 76

discourse, 81, 89–90, 271, 358, 388, 396

discovery process, 103, 137, 194

discrimination (word), 285

disorder, 360

dissent, 229

diversity, 152, 187, 194–95, 208–10

division of labor, 85–86

Douglass, Frederick, 401

downtowns, 163

Dracula, 227–28

E

economic calculation, 176–78, 231, 305–7

economic freedom
    in classical liberalism, 83–86, 90–91
    crusade for, 21–22
    immigration due to, 59–60
    principle of, 60

economic growth, 22, 65–66

    via individualism, 354
    via property protection, 83–84, 145–46

economics, 355–58

The Economist, 175

economists, 22, 314–15

education, 165–72, 211, 242–43
    in economics, 357–58
    as path to success, 57
    prevalence of, 32
    of women, 35

Emancipation Proclamation, 403

Emerson, Ralph Waldo, 55

entitlement spending, 322

entrepreneurs, 95–96, 98–102, 130–31, 343

environmental externalities, 211–13

envy, 4, 362–65

equal rights, 384–86, 391

ethics, 197–99

etiquette, 271–72

Europe, 53–56, 276

exit, 221

expectations, 124–25, 129–33

experience goods, 138–39

experts, 153–54, 175, 324, 342, 349

exploitation, 188–89, 267

externalities, 211–12

extremism, 203, 208–9, 215

F

factors of production, 98–99

failure, 349–50

false advertising, 138

false consciousness, 281–82

families, 218–26

fascism, 189

Federal Reserve, 173–75, 184

feedback mechanisms, 142–43

feudalism, 68–69, 94–95, 364

fireworks displays, 148

Fitzhugh, George, 292

foreign relations, 43, 153–54

foreign visitors, 29–48, 61

foresight, 108

Fortune 500 firms, 114–15

Founding Fathers, 18–19

franchise businesses, 139–41

free association, 238–39, 285–86

free choice, 9, 179–80, 254–55

freedom of the press, 258

free exchange, 70, 75, 86, 194–95, 207

freeing of minds, 5

free market

    as community, 225

    competition in, 97–99, 168, 172, 368

    individuals' rights in, 96–97, 258

        moderation via, 12

    workings of, 11, 368–69

free migration, 25–26

free rider problem, 148–50, 158, 162

free society, 381–82

free stuff, 233, 242–43, 300

free trade, 195, 315, 398–99

G

Garrison, William Lloyd, 401

German Historical School, 314–15

Germans, 56, 189, 191–92

Germany, 221, 262–64, 313–14, 316–17

global warming, 204, 213

God, 192, 383, 401

gold, 181–82

good works, 36, 339

Gorbachev, Mikhail, 230

government

    19th-century, 40, 44–46, 89

    financing the, 304–5

    funding via, 166, 170–71, 242–43

    limited, 89, 100, 163–64, 226, 240, 260, 294–95, 335, 369

    scope of, 244, 322

    size of, 321–22, 375

government employees, 74–75

government failure, 142–43

government schools, 167–70

Great Britain, 19–20, 292, 315, 398–99

great experiment, 287–88, 297

Greeks, 67, 250–51, 338

Green New Deal, 323

central planning in, 304–11

childlike support for, 299–301, 305

criticism of, 301–2

groups, 6, 10, 188–90. *See also* identity politics

Grund, Francis J., 31

guilds, 95

Gurowski, Adam, 41–43

H

happiness, pursuit of, 260

Haque, Umair, 328–39

Hardin, Garrett, 211–12

Hayek, Friedrich A.

central planning, 231, 307

competition, 103, 109

intellectuals, 358, 404–5

knowledge, 119–23, 213, 307, 350

monetary choice, 180

Hazlitt, Henry, 394

health care system, 217, 224, 243

Heller, Mikhail, 264–65

higher laws, 17

Hobbes, Thomas, 353

homeowner associations, 163

homophobia, 281

Houghton, Walter Raleigh, 50–51

housing decisions, 257–58

Howe, Frederic, 316–17

hubris, 349–50, 358–59

human nature, 5–6

humility, 73–74

Hutcheson, Francis, 389–91

I

ideal types, 126–33

ideas, 190–93

identity politics, 10, 13, 243–44, 288–90, 296–98

ideology, 203, 205–8, 302

ignorance, 355–58

illiberalism, 10

immigrants, 46, 55–60, 63–64

immigration restrictions, 54

incentives, 343

inclusiveness, 194–95

income inequality, 196–97

individualism, 37–38, 286, 334–35, 337–38, 354–55, 386–89

individuals

knowledge of, 86

in liberal outlook, 4–5, 96–97, 190–92, 251–53, 295–96

in race/gender collectivism, 283–84

self-governing, 41–44

superseding of, 8–9, 188–90,
        264

industrial policy, 346–51

industriousness, 33–34

inflation targeting, 183–84

injustice, 198–99, 243–44

institutions, interpersonal, 222–23,
        239–41

integration, 46, 56, 64

intellectuals, 359–60

interest rates, 184

intersectionality, 282–83

interventionism, 373–74

    foreign, 153–54

    as halfway house, 374

    history of, 314–19

    monopoly via, 115–17

    postwar, 278, 320–22

    as privilege granting, 86–88,
        198–99, 374–75

invisible hand, 22, 160

Irish immigrants, 56

Islamic State, 287–88

J

Jacobs, Jane, 159–60

Jefferson, Thomas, 273

Jews, 41, 55–57, 190, 269

jobs, 36–37, 346–47, 385

K

Klemperer, Victor, 262–64

Knight, Frank H., 107

knowledge

    centralization of, 122–23, 307

    division of, 5, 120, 123

    localized, 120–21, 213, 342–43

    perfect, 107–8, 136

    pretense of, 350

    scientific, 120

    of self, 86, 370

    tacit, 121–22, 129

L

labor, 67–69, 72–74, 76, 99, 254–55

Lachman, Desmond, 175

laggards, 32

laissez-faire, 370–71

Lakier, Aleksandr Borisovich, 48–49

language

    manipulation of, 262–74, 285, 321

    policing of, 296–97

    role of, 261–62

Lee, Harper, 258

liberalism. See also classical liberalism;
        new liberalism

    ambiguity of, 3–4

contemporary, 78, 266

free market, 367–70, 378

meaning of, 4–5

outlook of, 4–6

revolt against, 10, 79–80

thick vs. thin, 379–92

as tolerance, 80–81

transformation of, 7–8, 80, 266–67

libertarianism, 205–6

liberty advocates, 13–14, 393–405

Liberty Dollar, 178

Lieber, Francis, 30–31

life expectancy, 28

lights of liberty, 395–96, 404–5

Lincoln, Abraham, 402–3

literacy, 32

Locke, John, 18, 294, 334–35

M

Macaulay, Thomas Babington, 89

Mackay, Charles, 44–46, 48

macroeconomic instability, 185

Madison, James, 273

magic, 281–82

majorities, 81–82, 259, 273

Mandeville, Bernard, 334

manufacturing mills, 36–37

Mao Zedong, Chairman, 270, 289

Marco Polo, 94–95

marketplace, 152, 196–97, 256–57

market process, 100, 110

market societies, 68–69, 152, 241, 354–55

Martineau, Harriet, 35, 37, 47, 61

Marxism, 188–89, 267, 280–81, 289–90

McCloskey, Deirdre, 68

McCulloch, John R., 83–84, 146

meanings, intersubjective, 126–28

meat eating, 257

meddlers, 234–35

political, 345–51

private, 341–45

melting pot, 64

migration, 25–26, 54, 58–59

Mill, John Stuart, 23, 81–82, 89–90

minding one's own business, 350–51

minimum wage laws, 356

minorities, 58, 81–82, 152, 196, 258–59, 371

Mises, Ludwig von

anti-capitalistic mentality, 363–64

central planning, 176, 178, 231, 305, 308

cooperative competition, 97

market process, 99–100

thymology, 129–31

mixed economy, 8–9, 278

moderation, 205–6, 208–9, 215

money, 179–82

monopoly

    criticism of, 105

    government-caused, 115–17

    as single seller, 110–12

    static, 109–10

moral worth, 197

Morgenstern, Oskar, 108

Mussolini, Benito, 189

N

national defense, 154–55

    irrationality of, 152–54

    as public good, 43, 147–52, 158

nationalism, 189, 247

natural rights, 17–19, 192–93, 206–7, 220, 238, 294, 334, 383, 385, 389–91

Nazism, 189–91, 262–64, 269, 289–90, 384

neoliberalism

    label of, 9–10, 79–80, 313, 319–21

    origins of, 314–18

    progressivism and, 16, 318, 323

Newcomb, Simon, 370–71

New Deal, 7–8, 218

new liberalism, 10–11, 13, 92, 378

newspeak, 237–38, 272

non-interference, 84–86, 195, 370–71

NotHaus, Bernard von, 178–79

O

Obama, Barack, 365

Ocasio-Cortez, Alexandria, 232

Old South, 62

opportunity, 55, 57, 62–64

oppression (word), 285

optimism, 5

Orwell, George, 271–72

P

Palmer, R. R., 54

parents, 218–20

parking areas, 162–63

Pasteur, Louis, 393

paternalism, 317, 344–45

    extensive, 78

    false premise of, 12

    psychology of, 13

    slippery slope toward, 380–81

patronage, 45–46

peace, international, 23–24

Perry, Mark, 114

persuasion, 396–99, 403

planned chaos, 178–79, 231, 307–9

plunder, 310–11

pluralism, 200–201, 210, 239–40, 246–48, 256–57

Polanyi, Michael, 121

political correctness, 171–72

political freedom, 22–23

politicians, 302

Poltergeist, 237

population growth, 65–66, 332–33

positive-sum games, 146–47

poverty, 28, 65–66, 354

Powell, Jerome, 174

power, 6, 235–36

prediction, 131

presidency, 45–46

pressure groups
  in crony capitalism, 91, 374–75
  plans developed via, 7, 10, 306

price system, 98, 119, 123–24, 177–78, 306

principle, 214–15

private enterprise, 42–43, 50–51, 157–64

private property, 83–84, 146, 211–12

private sector, 8

privatization, 169–72, 361–62

privileges
  granting of, 87–88, 115, 374–75
  in progressives' view, 244, 267–68, 282–83

removal of, 85–86

producers, 255

production, 87, 100

profit-and-loss mechanism, 101–2

progress, 332–34, 337

progressivism, 15, 79–80, 201, 219, 266–67

propaganda, 373

public choice, 319–20

public goods, 147–52, 157–58

R

racism
  as collectivism, 189–92, 289–90, 383–84
  discussion of, 90
  in progressive view, 258, 268, 281, 283

railways, 30

Rand, Ayn, 363, 365

Rappard, William E., 247

Read, Leonard E., 358, 394–97

reason, 192–93, 294

redistribution, 78, 310–11, 375

regulations, 322–23, 347, 375

religious tolerance, 40–41

repeat dealings, 72

reputation, 51, 72

resentment, 360, 365

residential choice, 254

respect, 384, 386, 388, 396

responsibility, 337–38, 364

riverboats, 31

roads, 160–62

Rodrik, Dani, 346–51

Roosevelt, Franklin, 217

Röpke, Wilhelm, 60

Rougier, Louis, 67

Rule of Law, 21

rules of war, 24

S

Sabel, Charles, 346–51

Say, Jean-Baptiste, 87–88

Schoeck, Helmut, 362–63, 365

schooling, 165–72, 211, 242–43, 361–62

Schumpeter, Joseph A., 112–13, 358

Schutz, Alfred, 126, 128–29

search costs, 342–43

search goods, 138

secret police, 229, 372–73

self-censorship, 271

self-determination, 364

self-government, 40

self-improvement, 358

self-interest, 70–72, 334–36

self-made men, 50–51

Senior, Nassau W., 85–86

Sennholz, Hans, 394

sexism, 61, 281, 384–86

sexual orientation, 387–88

Shils, Edward, 239–42

shopping malls, 162–63

short-sightedness, 302

slave auctions, 48

slavery, 400

   in ancient societies, 67, 291

   crusade against, 20, 214–15, 292–95, 382–83, 401–2

   justifying, 291–92, 400

   lie of, 295, 401

   revulsion toward, 47–49

slippery slopes, 344, 380–81

Smith, Adam

   commercial virtues, 71–72

   division of labor, 85–86

   impact of, 355

   invisible hand, 22, 335

   public goods, 147

   trade, 70, 335–36

social (word), 238–39

social classes, 188–89, 267

social contract, 207

social engineering, 302, 307

socialism

   appeal of, 228

connotation of, 238, 266, 321

in education, 167–68

human cost of, 229–30, 373

in practice, 279, 372–73, 376–77

presumptions of, 7

in roads, 160–61

slavery as, 292

small-band, 330–33

Stiglitz's, 320–25

transition from, 232

social status, 44, 49–50

society, 334, 339

Soviet Union

group identity in, 289–90

human cost of, 230, 373, 376–77

left's view of, 278–79

thought control in, 264–65, 269–70, 273

speaking out, 384, 386, 388

Spencer, Herbert, 385

spending, 8–9

spontaneous order, 132, 159–60, 207–8

Stalin, Josef, 265, 273, 279

Statue of Liberty, 53

Sterling, James, 30

Stiglitz, Joseph, 135, 320–25

students, 167

subjugation, 17

Sumner, William Graham, 235

supply and demand

in dynamic competition, 109, 130, 137, 231, 306

in mainstream view, 106–7, 109–10

in market community, 225

of money, 181

suspicion, 229

T

Talmon, Jacob L., 251, 253

tariffs, 356, 402

tax cuts, 169–71

Taylor, Jerry, 203–6, 209–15

teachers, 170, 361, 397–98

technologies, 304

Ten Commandments, 201

thymology, 129–31

time, 100, 112–15

tolerance, 40–41, 80–81

totalitarianism, 208, 229, 251, 373, 376–77

town hall meetings, 234

tragedy of the commons, 211–12

transportation, 30–31

travel, 35

treaties, 24

tribes, 330–33

Trump, Donald, 58, 174

tyranny, 81, 194, 229–30, 246–47, 250–51, 287, 376–77

U

uncertainty, 101, 139–41

urban planning, 158–60

V

valuations, 149–50

values, 204, 209, 360

virtues, 51, 71–72, 75

voluntary associations, 347. *See also* civil society

von Raumer, Frederick, 31

voters, 22–23, 82, 152–54

voting, in marketplace, 152, 196, 256–57

W

warfare, 23–24

warranties, 139

Weber, Max, 125–26

welfare state, 316–17, 323, 373–75

whites, 268, 292–93

women, 35–37, 61, 281, 384–86

words, meanings of, 77. *See also* language

work, 34

workers, 91, 254–55

Z

zero-sum games, 84

About the Author

Richard M. Ebeling, an AIER Senior Fellow, is the BB&T Distinguished Professor of Ethics and Free Enterprise Leadership at The Citadel, in Charleston, South Carolina. Ebeling lived on AIER's campus from 2008 to 2009.

About AIER

The American Institute for Economic Research in Great Barrington, Massachusetts, was founded in 1933 as the first independent voice for sound economics in the United States. Today it publishes ongoing research, hosts educational programs, publishes books, sponsors interns and scholars, and is home to the world-renowned Bastiat Society and the highly respected Sound Money Project. The American Institute for Economic Research is a 501c3 public charity.